The High Design

South Atlantic Modern Language
Association Award Study

The University Press of Kentucky

Lexington   *1970*

The High Design

George C. Herndl

English Renaissance Tragedy and the Natural Law

Standard Book Number: 8131–1217–6

Library of Congress Catalog Card Number 78–111511

Copyright © 1970 by The University Press of Kentucky

A statewide cooperative scholarly publishing agency
serving Berea College, Centre College of Kentucky,
Eastern Kentucky University, Kentucky State College,
Morehead State University, Murray State University,
University of Kentucky, University of Louisville,
and Western Kentucky University.

Editorial and Sales Offices: Lexington, Kentucky 40506

to Ralph Baldwin

Contents

Acknowledgments

I would like to express my gratitude to The Cooperative Program in the Humanities; the generous assistance of that institution, chiefly in the form of a Humanities Fellowship during the academic year 1966–1967, has made this study possible. I am also indebted to Professor Robert B. Sharpe and to the Reverend David Kessinger, o.s.b.

Introduction

MUCH OF THE world's great tragedy was written in Renaissance England, but some elements of the genre changed radically in the first years of the seventeenth century, and the conditions for achieving a certain kind of tragic power, peculiar to the earlier Renaissance, were not continued or repeated. The achievement had medieval roots, and the weakening of Renaissance tragic art began in the final displacement of certain medieval attitudes toward the world.

It is no longer necessary to argue the continuity which this implies between Middle Ages and Renaissance. The scholarship of several recent decades shows the break with the past more superficial than the self-consciously innovating humanists of the sixteenth century (who invented the "Middle" Ages and the Renaissance, and the myth of their polarity) wanted anyone to suppose.[1] Very close connections between medieval and Renaissance ideas of world-order and the achievement of Elizabethan tragedy have been minutely charted by the historical critics.[2] What we think of the characteristic Renaissance spirit now in fact appears as the last form of a cosmic vision fundamentally medieval and

Scholastic. The central and summary expression of this world-view was the medieval idea of the natural law, which long remained as an intellectual substratum, solid and continuous beneath the widening network of sixteenth-century ideological divisions. It was expounded by the Jesuit Francisco Suarez, the Lutheran Philip Melancthon, the moderate Calvinist William Perkins, the Anglican Richard Hooker, the Christian Stoic Justus Lipsius. It was the nucleus of that "Christian Humanism" which was almost as deeply ingrained in the "Puritan" poets Spenser and Milton as in Davies, Daniel, or Shakespeare. It was, in the mind of a Shakespeare, not altered by its confrontation with the alternatives emerging from the classical revivals of the humanists or the Augustinianism and Ockhamism of the Reformers; it was rather made conscious of itself and helped to its fullest imaginative realization.

In the Scholastic tradition, moral law was conceived as a body of norms discoverable in the elementary demands of human nature, itself regarded as primarily rational and free. The universal system of natural law of which it was the human and most important part (so that "natural law" or "the law of nature" ordinarily referred to morality) appeared in man as reason's perception of those things required by the essential human constitution, in the physical world as a regular and purposive ordering, in society as duties morally incumbent on men because innately a part of the civil life for which man's nature ordains him. Man, God, and the physical world were joined in a unity of reason.

Henry Medwall's secularized morality play *Nature*, written at the end of the fifteenth century, sketches this Scholastic cosmos very plainly. The character Nature commands that Reason direct World to accommodate Man. Both Reason and World obey Nature as God's regent, and Man in turn is subject to the authority of

Reason. He is able to "discern and find / Sufficient difference betwixt good and bad:. . . . And of all this," says Reason, "the chief doer am I." Receiving man's profession of allegiance, Reason replies, "Christ grant you therein good continuance." Man pledges to World that he will demean himself "As may be most unto Thy pleasure, / And unto nature not disconvenient," and Reason (whose "philosopher electe" is Aristotle) heartily approves of this. Sensuality, whom Reason recognizes as "necessary to [Man's] being," but who is of course rebellious, protests against "the sentence / That Nature gave unto me by Reason's advice." The essential harmony of God, reason, nature, the world, and sensual appetite is, in short, expressed in virtually every possible way. Even the relations of nature and grace, of natural reason and supernatural religion, are here suggested.[3]

In the philosophical tradition to which Medwall's play belongs, morality, conceived as natural law, is not primarily an obedience to external legislation but a fidelity to one's own being. Its ultimate premise lies in the conviction that "man and human society have their particular functions and proper operations discoverable by a rational examination of their natures. This conception presupposes a meaningful universe with a hierarchy of values: the right behaviour of each part of the universe can be read from the end and purpose for which it is destined in the harmony of the whole."[4]

This faith in the intelligibility of the world as an order commensurate with the human mind declined in the late Renaissance, as Elizabethan optimism faded. Bredvold, Harbage, Baker, Haydn, and others have documented the rise of skepticism, mechanism, and a Calvinist voluntarism common to the most important Protestant thought of the period, and thoroughly subversive of the natural-law view of the world.[5] At the same time, "tragedy, the form of drama responsible for interpreting to man the conditions of his own being, becomes satanic, revealing a world-order of evil power, or if it attempt excursions beyond man's immediate experience, bewildered and confused."[6] Whatever the specific features of this Jacobean "decadence" in tragedy, there is clearly a general loss of the Elizabethan feeling that man's ordained role is "to go with sway of all the world together,"[7] a loss of confidence that the innate principles of the universe are in harmony with human nature and human aspirations; there is a failure of power to reconcile us to the tragic outcome, and an abdication of the task of seriously "interpreting to man the conditions of his own being."

These years saw, too, the rise of a particular kind of tragicomedy (different in spirit from the Shakespearean romances), which by 1642 had virtually replaced tragedy. Even more than the late Jacobean tragedies, these tragicomedies and their inheritance of the tragic mantle attest the failure of that integrated moral vision which had been a condition of the peculiar achievement of Shakespeare's genius. The moral emptiness, the loss of tragic power represented by later Jacobean tragicomedy, despite its superb theatrical virtuosity, have eluded real explanation. Studies by Ristine, Waith, and Herrick[8] have furnished a history of tragicomedy from classical times, traced the sources of Renaissance tragicomic plot, and identified the forms of drama (chiefly pastoral and satyr-play) merged in English tragicomedy. They have considered the Renaissance theoretical controversies over the genre, examined its rhetoric, described its conventions of characterization and structure. Their recovery of literary, theatrical, and critical background is genuinely enlightening. But none has been concerned adequately to distinguish the sort of tragicomedy that came to dominate the Jacobean stage from other and earlier varieties: the implications of the fact that these plays were essentially a form of tragedy, or a substitute for tragedy, have remained obscure. There had in fact been a major shift in philosophical premises. An altered world-view underlies the choice and the manner of employment of the tragicomic sources and conventions; it enters into the form of Jacobean tragicomedies as Shakespeare's world-view had entered the form of his tragedies. For there assuredly is, in the conception of the universe where Shakespeare's dramas are set, an element which makes the great tragedies not merely dramatic examinations of evil, but moral interpretations; tragedy, that is, has a "theoretic" as well as an "executive" form, the first transcending litrary genre.[9] A critic or playwright of the sixteenth century would almost certainly have defined tragedy simply as drama showing noble persons brought to an unhappy end;[10] yet there is something always implied by Shakespeare about the meaning of tragic experience, quite different from what is implied by Beaumont and Fletcher, by Chapman, or by Ford—a difference apart from changing rhetorical style and theatrical convention, deeper than the influence of the newly distinct Stoicism or Platonism or skepticism. What, we may still ask, is this quality that enables the Shakespearean tragedies to continue as unique and current cultural facts and to provide their distinctive experience, with its almost universally attested effect of "relief" or "exaltation," its assurance of a world not inscrutable, but conformable to reason and habitable by the human spirit? What change explains the absence of this element from widely varying later tragedies and tragicomedies?

Some satisfying answers, I find, emerge from a study of the total transformation of the idea of natural law which occurred during the Jacobean period. Tragedy is concerned with the origins of evil and suffering; the degree of the tragedian's confidence in a certain kind of natural law enters, as much as his assumptions about human freedom, into the theoretic and perhaps the executive form of his plays; it is radical to his interpretation of experience—it structures the world he will imitate. Tragic literature always discovers whether the highest human axiologies are conceived as inherent in nature or alien to it, conformable or violent to the constitution of things. The question is never irrelevant.

In arguing a common thematic element in the great tragedies, I have not meant to reduce their polysemous wealth to a single meaning. It seems to me that no one myth or literary archetype is important to the kind of tragedy I am talking about. Criticism which prescinds from "detail" to seek such common patterns risks prescinding from the substance of the works it studies. Much has been heard recently of "redemptive" archetypes, so that there are few sacrificial acts in Renaissance drama, few selfless offers of love or help or even counsel, which have not by now been found to reveal another Christ-figure. The Redemption may in fact have been an absolutely central *point de repere* in the Renaissance, intellectually and emotionally; this does not justify our reducing different things to archetypal singleness by a generalizing process which leaves behind a significant part of their reality. There might be likenesses of pattern in Ojibway council meetings and conventions of the Modern Language Association, but there are significant differences in the discussions carried on. The mutual exclusion between extension and comprehension in classical logic is worth remembering.

To locate its thematic finality in a certain cosmic vision is not to seek in any play a paraphrasable "content" beneath or separate from its actual poetic reality, separable from the total dramatic form which *is* rather than *has* a presentational rather than propositional meaning. Everything depends on whether one begins with the play itself, and with due attention to the poetic medium, which may indeed create much of what it conveys. Conclusions about the cathartic or reconciling power of Shakespearean tragedy must accord with the principle that dramatic meaning is enacted, and not stated, is a function of whole plays, not of their separate parts. I do not mean to equate any play with a statement, like Hooker's *Laws of Ecclesiastical Polity*, of the beliefs which affect the structure of the Shakespearean tragic world. In analyzing the several versions of that world in the great tragedies, I am concerned with tracing the imprint of those beliefs, not in order to measure the plays by a hypothesized Renaissance ideological standard or an author's supposed prior intention, but to heighten the visibility, to a modern perception, of patterns which we may fail to bring into exact focus because of their unfamiliarity. I have tried to avoid the critical trap of explaining complex characters as exemplars of any single ideology.

The opposite critical error is the confusion of characters with real persons. The multifariousness of literary characters is not, like that of historical persons, practically inexhaustible; certain kinds of inferences can be made of persons, but not of characters, who, unlike persons, have no secrets from the writer who depicts them, nor from his audience. Qualities which the author does not reveal, or which, in performance, are not revealed by an actor, do not exist. All there can be of Hamlet is what Shakespeare created, and he is not likely to have created a psychic machinery unknown for centuries after, nor to have constructed plays around behavior inexplicable to him. This caveat against Freudian explanation of the nonexistent, although it does imply an a priori critical judgment (i.e., that sixteenth-century playwrights do not organize their materials by delineation of subconscious Oedipal drives), should raise no "intentional" specters. It involves only a negative postulate or principle of exclusion, and on grounds which if extrinsic to any literary work are also extrinsically verifiable, unlike an aesthetic "aim" or "intention." It erects no standard of evaluation, and it recalls us to the text from the pursuit of the uncreated, just as warnings against intentional fallacy recall us from the unknowable and the irrelevant.

Characters should not, then, be interpreted by appealing to psychic mechanisms of which their creator knew nothing (not to deny that Shakespeare saw motives unnamed by science until the modern period). If a sixteenth-century chronicler attributes an eclipse to magic, we rightly assume that he is mistaken and that it resulted from the operation of regular physical forces. But if a sixteenth-century play makes the same attribution, we must be equally sure of the magic: the projection of scientific astronomy into a fictional world where it does not exist is as much a falsification as is the projection of magical forces into the real world. (It is another matter to apply psychoanalytical method to the study of an author's personality.)

We must, finally, deal with *Hamlet* and *Macbeth*, *The White Devil* and *The Revenger's Tragedy* as poetry. There is nothing impossible in the idea of a propositional rendering which does justice to poetic drama, registering the historically substantiated meaning of parts as modified by their disposition in the whole and their interaction with other parts, and pursuing the associative values of metaphoric and other allusion. The analysis which results, a critical "translation" into directly referential discourse, must fragment the literary object and present its contents sequentially. But literature itself, even dramatic literature, is sequential: so is all language, as Marshall McLuhan, among others, has noted. The experiential (in which the preconscious, the sensuous and affective, bulk large) has already undergone in literature a translation to the analytically conceptual, in taking on the discrete forms of language. Revealed word by word—concept by concept—it has lost simultaneity, however much the literary work by nature aspires to become a *Gestalt* in which the interaction of parts conquers the temporal-sequential aspect of the medium—aspires, i.e., to the condition of a painting.

Yet the idea of complete critical analysis is as heretical as paraphrase. Literature retains, unlike directly referential discourse, enough experiential density and multiplicity so that any analytical statement of all that can accurately be predicted of its content would be much more lengthy than the literature itself. To exposit every complexity of the literary text, to transpose completely from the presentational to the propositional mode, would be to produce a monstrosity of size and an impassable maze of logical qualifications. Not only do I not pretend to exhaust the meaning of the plays treated here, I admit to isolating and emphasizing a single element of some. I believe I have done so without attempting to reduce any play to the aspect of it with which I am presently concerned.

More particularly with the plays of Heywood, Webster, Beaumont and Fletcher, and Ford, my aim is to illuminate in each one its own interrelational meanings, to describe the world created in the play, not the universe of Jacobean belief which may have served as its model. But it is also possible to discuss the philosophic meaning of the plays without locating their essence in prepoetic and predramatic ideas. Works of literature are referential not only in their medium (in that language is referential, and it is not the verbal sign but the signified which is the atom of literary form) but in their aesthetic totality. Obviously, these constructions assert something about human experience; i.e., they adumbrate a world-structure. Renaissance art generally bears a microcosmic relation to the intelligibly structured cosmos which it imitates, just as some modern art, avoiding Aristotelian articulation of parts, reflects the "dense, opaque, unintelligible" existentialist universe.[11]

My thesis regarding this kind of meaning in the drama of the English Renaissance is briefly this: A certain, originally medieval, conception of the natural law was vital in Elizabethan tragedy. It was violently altered by intellectual developments which achieved their fullest expression in John Calvin, Francis Bacon, and René Descartes, and which combined to redefine the "natural," destroying or transforming the old conviction of the natural law. This Calvin did by substituting will for reason and positing inscrutable divine fiat, unrelated to reason or nature, as the basis of morality; Bacon by conceiving natural law only descriptively and materially, accepting the Calvinistic divorce of nature and morality; Descartes by further and finally alienating the spiritual from the natural. Tragedy was in these same years transformed, giving way to a profoundly changed tragic drama and to tragicomedy. These facts of intellectual and of theatrical history are, as I hope to show, closely connected.

In surveying the literature informed by the older philosophical tradition, I have reviewed relevant aspects of some of the Shakespearean tragedies but have not found it necessary to examine all of them; nor do I claim that significant testimony to the medieval world-view is found throughout the mass of Elizabethan revenge plays, "domestic" tragedies, "conqueror" plays, or histories. It is sufficient that in the hands of Shakespeare and some others, tragedy did build its greatest achievements upon the foundation of the earlier idea of natural law. In the work of the Elizabethan dramatists, there is little contrary to the Scholastic doctrine; there may be plays innocent of cosmic implication, to which it is irrelevant, but there are few which reveal the crucial divorce of moral values from nature, or display the ethical voluntarism of the later drama.

My main concern in the Elizabethan period is naturally with Shakespeare. I hope that much of what I say about his tragedies is by now in substance commonplace. Although I propose to add to the understanding with which they can be philosophically "placed" (and have some specific readings to argue), I intend my treatment to be largely a review of what is already widely understood, a summary of the "before" without which the significance of the Jacobean "after" cannot be known. There are also critics who have found Shakespeare much less affirmative: the reader will judge for himself. The chief business of this book lies in the analysis of a number of the later plays set out in Chapters 6 and 7, where there is developed a new thesis, a reinterpretation of the history of Jacobean tragedy. Understanding of that drama, and of its differences from what it replaced, requires an awareness of its relations to the historical context. I have therefore found it useful not only to discuss Shakespearean plays, but to trace the medieval sources of the Shakespearean conception of natural law and to account for its decline in the seventeenth century, before turning to a detailed examination of the effects, in Jacobean tragedy, of its final disappearance.

The connection certainly can be shown between that philosophical shift and marked changes in the tragic drama. But in themselves these changes constitute a "decline" in one sense only: they are part of an increasing difficulty, and finally an impossibility, of achieving the "reconciling" or affirmative interpretation of life which is a vital aspect of Shakespearean tragedy. If there was also a decline in artistic powers (it would be hard to say this of Webster; I have no inclination to do so), I see no way to identify that with the "decline" of which I am writing. A modern reader or viewer might well find more relevance and power in the spirit of Webster or Tourneur, to the degree that their poetic and dramatic skill can sustain it. The "weakening" or decline of which I have spoken in my opening paragraph is specifically that of the earlier Renaissance tragic vision, the theoretic form of the kind of tragedy which Shakespeare wrote.

The concurrent decline of creative talent toward 1642 is an accident of history, or its cause is a question for which I have no answer. I will not conceal my belief that the one decline contributed to the other; but I do not preempt the title of tragedy for plays of one philosophical cast, thus demoting all others which are ideologically "wrong." I have described one kind of tragic achievement, explained how it became impossible to repeat, shown the different strategies to which following writers turned, and demonstrated the connection between their changed philosophical premises and the totally altered spirit which is analytically demonstrable in their plays. That this entailed a falling-off in affirmative potency, in the power to reconcile to life, is undeniable. Whether that in itself is to be considered artistic decline in some other sense, I leave to the reader.

Chapter One

The Law of Nature

SHAKESPEAREAN TRAGEDY is an imaginative testimony to the moral intelligibility of the world. Its universe constitutes an order in which human rationality accords with the good, evil is the perversion, rather than the course, of nature, and the highest moral aspirations are in harmony with nature's demands. Nowhere is it antinomian: nowhere in it is essential humanity fatally constricted, as in some later drama, by the confines of the moral law, nor human virtue destroyed by its incommensurability with the natural world.

Even in the darkest of the Shakespearean tragedies, the rack upon which Lear is stretched is not nature or its law. The evil in this play lies in the unnaturalness of his daughters and his son-in-law and the consequences of his own blindness to reality, his confounding of the accidental and the essential and his self-indulgent and willful flouting of fundamental order, a failure which flows from a culpable and vulnerable ignorance of the natures of things. Lear dies, finally, a man of genuine dignity. The drama has been one of unmerited suffering, of the terrible cost of his education. But Lear learns to see, distinguish, and value rightly. The "reconciliation" is Aeschylean; suffering is vindicated by its fruits in character.[1]

Although many critics agree in finding an affirmation of life in the old man's redemption,[2] some will always point to the final scene of *King Lear* as evidence of Shakespeare's dark conviction that "as flies to wanton boys, are we to th' gods, / They kill us for their sport"; men are the pawns of malevolent or indifferent fate. But the tragic reconciliation is meaningful only when it leads us to acquiesce in the conditions of life in full recognition of the worst possibilities. Unless the patterns of evil can be rendered comprehensible and conformable to a human and rational order in the face of the bitterest truths about the world, the tragic reassurance is ineffective.

Lear's first acceptance of life is meaningless; he has "but slenderly known himself." In consequence of his violations of nature, which invite catastrophe, he discovers evil, and through suffering he comes at last to understand both good and evil. The intelligibility of life is thus witnessed, and man is imagined as essentially neither meaningless, helpless, nor mean.

Macbeth finds life "a tale told by an idiot," but his own career and the dramatic universe of which he is a function reveal a legal order. Such characters as Lady Macduff and her son die innocently, and to her it seems a world in which "to do harm / Is often laudable, to do good sometime / Accounted dangerous folly." Yet where the moral structure of the world is manifested so largely as in *Macbeth*, we can bear not only the reality of particular evils, but even our nescient inability to relate some of them to that order. There is nothing here of the voluntarist world where nature really is hostile to virtue and "where it is danger to be good."[3] Equally in the other great tragedies, nature is seen not to work "at random" or by "frantic puffs of blind-born chance,"[4] but to suffer tragic disruption when violated, whether culpably or not.

It is not so much a specific hierarchical world order like that exposited by characters in some of the plays, and quite fully reconstructed for us by Tillyard and others, which gives the Shakespearean tragedies their still potent character of "vindication of inexorable moral law." It is rather an omnipresent shaping conception of a substantial nature in man and society which is never evil but to which some modes of feeling or thought or action, perhaps sympathetic to our own affections, are ruinously contrary. Shakespeare dramatizes particular ways in which one or another disposition of human powers may be repugnant to the deepest principles of the world's operation. This is not brought to easy or specific conclusions, but it excludes any impression of the innate futility of human actions. "Our souls, whose faculties can comprehend / The wondrous architecture of the world"[5] are quite at home in the order of nature. The world is rationally designed and man is rationally fitted to perceive what is natural to it and to restore the natural order where that is perverted. Hamlet curses what is for him the almost insupportable obligation to set right the time, but neither he nor Shakespeare doubts there is a "right" achievable within the order of nature: it is for this that Hamlet goads himself across the difficulties. The tragic hero such as Romeo surrenders freedom and control by allowing the natural roles of will and reason to be reversed within the microcosmic hierarchy at his inevitable peril. The realities of the human constitution itself are disregarded by a Richard II or a Romeo as he seeks goals which, though in Romeo's case sympathetic to our feelings, either are not those to which essential nature tends, or are sought by means not rational, therefore, in Renaissance terms, not natural.

Since Elizabethan tragedy, unlike most of the medieval tragedy *de casibus*, attempts to comprehend the fall of the great (or, in some of the homiletic or "domestic" tragedies, the ruin of ordinary people) as a result of visible and governable causes, its usual ethical premise is that men must struggle to guide themselves by reason, and so act in accord with an inherently moral natural world. This moral order is so universally assumed that there is little occasion to argue its existence, and it is not much alluded to,[6] as are its more debatable extensions into political and social principle. Shakespeare's Ulysses finds a definite social and political hierarchy to be a part of nature,[7] as did Tyndale, Erasmus, Elyot. The official Elizabethan homilies on civil obedience made a similar application of ideas of natural order to very specific political doctrine which suited Tudor purposes. The partisan theorists of the age could appeal to "the law of nature" in support of absolute royal power or of the limitation of royal power, to argue a "divine right" or to defend a contract theory of government. Its uses were innumerable, for it was a chief standard against which political and social ideas were measured. On one score, however, there was general agreement: universal natural law did underlie whatever more particular patterns of positive law could rightfully claim legitimacy. Only by demonstrating their congruence with it and their workable realization of its abstract axioms in the realm of historical contingency could they take on real authority. But this usually unspoken first principle of pre-Calvinistic and pre-Baconian thought did not long survive the Elizabethan age, and the thing most important to the spirit of Jacobean tragedy is not the changes in particular social or political beliefs, but the fact that the very bedrock—faith in the natural, rational intelligibility of moral law, the unity of morality as divine command with nature—was largely destroyed.

Even the most skilled modern analysis of the more specific Renaissance beliefs which assumed the aegis of "natural law" does not always lead toward the essential meaning of the Shakespearean tragedies. Ideological documents of the age like Sir John Hayward's or Robert Parsons' or John Ponet's controversial applications of the premises of natural law to such problems as the proper limits of a king's power, or the grounds of legitimate deposition, are certainly valuable in interpreting political and historical content, especially in the history plays.[8] But they are less relevant to the broad question of the Shakespearean tragic world-view, which derives more immediately from the universal assumption of a natural moral law in which virtually all of these conflicting particular interpretations sought their base.

Indeed, a difficulty in some attempts to apply it to Shakespearean drama has been the tendency to identify the concept of natural law, exactly as did many eager partisans during the Renaissance, with some one doctrinaire version of its specific applications, or to conclude that since it was represented by such partisans to be several differing things, it was never really any one thing which can be spoken of with confidence, in disregard of these differences. To be important to the drama, the belief in natural law, it is sometimes implied, must be present in plays as particular moral or political doctrine.

But while we labor to determine what the dramatists, encyclopedic hexameral writers, moral-political pamphleteers, and didactic poets—Shakespeare, Primaudaye, DuBartas, Bodin, Parsons, Davies, and Smith— meant by "natural law," what particular doctrines they deduced from it or referred to it, we may easily miss the more important point: the natural law is essentially rather a premise than a set of conclusions. Whatever they thought to be morally or politically or socially right and good, they thought was so because of, and not apart from or despite, the innate demands of a universal human nature. The enormity which has largely been overlooked is that a few years later almost no one believed this, and the change caused a revolution in sensibility that transformed the tragic drama.

Donne, like Montaigne, is disingenuous when he protests that "this terme the law of Nature, is so variously and unconstantly deliver'd, as I confesse I read it a hundred times before I understand it once, or can conclude it to signifie that which the author should at that time meane."[9] Siding here with the "counter-Renaissance" which undercut the doctrine, Donne points to the inconsistency and vagueness of its many versions. He knows perfectly well the central thesis which they share and from which they all begin. We, however, are liable actually to confuse the systems of the natural-law theorists with their common matrix, the natural law itself. Gregory Baum, a contemporary theologian, protests that this, "according to the metaphysical intuition of Saint Thomas," is "not a set of laws in the human heart . . . it is not conceptualized. . . . The knowledge of what the natural law in man's heart implies is not rationally derived from a definition of human nature; it is not extracted from premises by means of a syllogism; it is not the conclusion of an argument. We discover what the natural law demands of us in the various situations of life, not by rational knowledge, but by knowledge *per inclinationem.*"[10] Jacques Maritain speaks in a similar way of the Scholastic doctrine:

> The law and knowledge of the law are two different things. . . . knowing that there is a law does not necessarily mean knowing what that law is. It is because

this very simple distinction is forgotten that many perplexities have arisen concerning the unwritten law. It is written, they say, in the heart of man. True, but in the hidden depths, as hidden from us as our own heart. This metaphor itself has been responsible for a great deal of damage, causing natural law to be represented as a ready-made code rolled up within the conscience of each one of us, which each one of us has only to unroll, and of which all men should naturally have an equal knowledge.

Natural law is not a written law. Men know it with greater or less difficulty, and in different degrees, running the risk of error here as elsewhere.[11]

Richard Hooker spoke of "things which reason necessarily *doth* enforce but is not perceived that so it doth."[12] Aquinas had said of the natural law that "the truth is the same for all, but is not equally known to all." Indeed, "the precepts of the natural law in man stand in relation to practical matters, as the first principles to matters of demonstration."[13] Sir John Davies observed, in his preponderantly Scholastic verse-treatise *Nosce Teipsum* (1599), "We interpret *lawes*, which other men have made, / But reade not those which in our hearts are writ."[14] William Perkins, a preacher and writer of great popularity in Renaissance England (his works occupy three pages in the *Short Title Catalogue*) gave to Shakespeare's contemporaries a caution about the inherent difficulty of the human estate which is due to this obscurity of the natural law: "Morall law . . . is contained in the Decalogue or Ten Commandments: and it is the very law of nature written in all men's hearts (for substance though not for the manner of propounding it) in the creation of man: and therefore it binds the consciences of all men at all times, even of blind and ignorant persons that neither know the most of it nor care to know it."[15]

Natural law was believed, in the Scholastic tradition,

to give elementary directives, the applications of which to particular problems were derived and debatable, resting upon contingencies.[16] It was not conceived by its most authoritative expositors as fixed in its implications, as offering automatic solutions, nor as enabling one to predict the exact consequences of evil[17] (imaginatively to explore such consequences and their relation to character is one of the functions of tragedy). It was evidently the later work of men like Grotius and Pufendorf, rather than any authentically medieval belief, which was responsible for much of the overextension into particulars which contributed to the discrediting of the tradition.[18] Natural law was always understood, for instance, to prescribe the preservation of one's life by prudent means: but this, it was recognized, could imply one thing in one circumstance, another in another. It was held that moral evil, or the unnatural use of the faculties, does inner violence to the human constitution. For the Renaissance, this would mean a disruption of balance in the humors, but the humors theory was no essential part of the idea of natural law.

Still, Ulysses in the great speech on "degree"[19] may reasonably be accepted as a choric character, surrogate for Shakespeare: every age which accepts the doctrine tends to identify its own social order, or a certain conception of it, with the natural law. Inevitably, there develop systems even more vulnerable to time than Ulysses'; codifications of "natural law" which are "fancy masks for the prejudices of a single time or sect" and fall into a "strutting, self-anointed pseudoinfallibility."[20] Hence the tendency of confidence in the idea to be eclipsed by any great change in society. But to equate belief in the natural law with acceptance of particular specifications of it in social or political theory is misleading, like identifying the ideal of liberal education with the study of Greek and Latin letters: partisans have done so, and in fact one may be for its time a legitimate realization of the other, but the fate of the more universal proposition is not really involved with that of its logical subaltern.

Natural law has remained an option of Western ethical thought. Never wholly abandoned, it achieved in the twentieth century a recovery sufficient to be called, reasonably, a "natural law rebound."[21] Although its Renaissance political applications are now of interest only to historical scholarship, the underlying philosophy is still one which modern men can at least enter into imaginatively.

Similarly, much of the particular political and social theory reflected in Shakespeare is historically parochial and is lost on a modern audience, but the basic meaning of the tragedies is not. Their general subject remains: the fearful and splendid significance of the exercise of the free moral will in a world of intelligible order. This order is less definite and specific and more a matter of great underlying principles whose possibilities for realization are somewhat mysterious, than is sometimes seen by critics who seek in the drama a mirror of particular religious, social, and political doctrine.

The dramatic excitement latent in the Renaissance tragic view of man has been expressed in our own time by Leon Bloy. Freedom, says Bloy, is "that prodigious, incomprehensible, indescribable gift by means of which we are given the power to . . . excite at a single word all created spirits in the heavens and in hell . . . this inexpressible freedom is nothing but this: the respect God has for us."[22] When a conviction of such cosmically significant freedom joins with faith in a rational moral order whose violation risks natural consequences, the conditions of the highest tragic art exist.

Shakespeare, in his best tragedies, is Aristotelian to the extent that his plays do indeed take form from the impress of the tragic protagonists. Action flows from the morally determinate choices of the characters; heroes are shown to destroy themselves, or at least display those characteristics which invite their destruction by external forces, so that the fault, ultimately, lies not in their stars, but where the playwright can dissect its particular human workings more minutely, and the Elizabethan audience observe it to their greater profit. Shakespearean tragedy—most tragedy—is intrinsically a vision of law, a demonstration of effects produced by human (and other) causes;[23] it presumes an essential nature in man and in society. When these are violated, says Northrup Frye, the consequence is seen as "ethically and psychologically and even physically intelligible."[24] If we try the validity of this for Hamlet, Macbeth, Anthony, Romeo, or Othello, or for some, at least, of Marlowe's heroes, they will sustain it well.[25] A. C. Bradley, whatever the deficiency of his critical premises, arrived at this truth long ago, by inductive examination of Shakespeare's plays themselves.[26] He did not trace it to its roots in medieval thought, but the dramatic world which Bradley described in his general account of Shakespeare's plays is, as he observed, remarkably like the real world which Aquinas saw.

THE BEST GLOSS on this dramatic pattern is Richard Hooker's setting out of the underlying Elizabethan beliefs in his *Laws of Ecclesiastical Polity;* this summa of Renaissance Christian humanism was written in the 1590's as a defense of the Anglican system against the Marprelate tracts and the Calvinist treatise by Walter Travers which Thomas Cartwright had translated as *A Full and Plain Declaration of Ecclesiastical Discipline*—ultimately against Calvinism itself. In the first book of the *Laws*, Hooker treats of eternal and natural law, and their relation to all laws. "All things that are," he says, have some operation not violent or casual. Neither doth any thing ever begin to exercise the same, without some fore-conceived end for which it worketh. And the end which it worketh for is not obtained, unless the work be also fit to obtain it by. For unto every end every operation will not serve. That which doth assign unto each thing the kind, that which doth moderate the force and power, that which doth appoint the form and measure, of working, the same we term a Law. . . . All things therefore do work after a sort, according to law.

(I. ii. 1, 2)

This teleological ordering of means to ends in all things, as it exists "before all ages" in the mind of God, is the eternal law (I. iii. 2, 6). Most men, Hooker cautions, understand by "law eternal" the order which God "hath set down as expedient to be kept by all his creatures, according to the several condition wherewith he hath endued them." Those who speak in this way apply the name of law only to rules imposed by "superior authority," but Hooker understands a law to be "any kind of rule or canon, whereby actions are framed."

The sum of all such laws manifested in creation, Hooker calls the "second law eternal." This law "receiveth according unto the different kinds of things which are subject unto it different and sundry kinds of names." As it directs things lower than man it is "*Nature's* law"; as it is observed by angels it is "law *Celestial.*" And the law "which bindeth creatures reasonable in this world, and with which by reason they may most plainly perceive themselves bound," receives the name of "the law of *Reason*" (I. iii. 1). This last is in fact the natural law as it applies to man, who participates in it through reason. Although he thus treats it as a distinct species of the natural law (which in its broad sense is the sum of law governing all created things), it is to Hooker identical with and part of that natural law.

> Yet forasmuch as those things are termed most prop-
> erly natural agents, which keep the law of their kind
> unwittingly, as the heavens and elements of the world,
> which can do no otherwise than they do; and foras-
> much as we give unto intellectual natures the name of
> *Voluntary* agents, that so we may distinguish them
> from the other; expedient it will be, that we sever the
> law of nature observed by the one from that which
> the other is tied unto.

> (I. iii. 2)

Only the first of these subdivisions is today included
in the concept of "natural law": Hooker, in contrast,
finds it necessary to insist on a distinction between the
"law of nature observed by the one" (nonhuman things)
from "that [law of nature] which the other is tied unto"
—the moral law. Involuntary agents keep the law of
their natures "unwittingly"; men keep the law of their
nature only rationally or voluntarily. So then the law of
reason, the law proper to rational natures and discoverable by reason, is that part of the total natural law or
"second law eternal" which governs men:

> Law rational therefore, *which men commonly use to
> call the Law of Nature,* meaning thereby the Law
> which human Nature knoweth itself in reason uni-
> versally bound unto, which also for that cause may be
> termed most fitly the Law of Reason; this law, I say,
> comprehendeth all those things which men by the
> light of their natural understanding evidently know,
> or at leastwise may know, to be beseeming or un-
> beseeming, virtuous or vicous, good or evil for them
> to do.[27]

This then is what we would call moral law, what
Thomas Aquinas[28] primarily meant by "natural law,"
what Elizabethans commonly called "the Law of nature." It is the human portion of the total spectrum of

natural law. "All things therefore," says Hooker, "which are as they ought to be, are conformed unto this *second law eternal.*" And even those things which are in violation of it are yet "in some sort ordered by *the first eternal law*" (I. iii. 1). It is crucial that this does not imply either predestination or the incomprehensible willing by God of evil; it means only that the free violation of natural law which is possible to voluntary agents does not violate the order "which God hath eternally purposed himself in all his works to observe" (I. iii. 1), but occurs within that order. Such violations of the "second law eternal" or natural law are accounted for by the freedom of the human will, which is ordained by the "first eternal law."[29]

All things have, says Hooker, a teleological principle, "an appetite or desire, whereby they incline to something which they may be; and when they are it, they shall be perfecter than now they are. All which perfections are contained under the general name of Goodness" (I. v. 1). "As everything . . . doth desire the utmost good and greatest perfection whereof Nature hath made it capable, even so man" (I. viii. 1).

In the achievement of this desire, "The knowledge of that which man is in reference unto himself, and other things in relation unto man, I may justly term the mother of all those principles, which are as it were edicts, statutes, and decrees, in that Law of Nature, whereby human actions are framed" (I. viii. 6). This knowledge reveals, among other things, that the perfection toward which human nature aspires lies in the intellect; for "the best things, where they are not hindered, do still produce the best operations." And "where many things are to concur unto one effect," the best of them should guide the rest, so that, "it prevailing most, the work principally done by it may have greatest perfection." From this principle, by comparison of our intellectual with our other powers, it immediately follows that "the soul then ought to conduct the body, and the spirit of our minds the soul" (I. viii. 6). Natural law thus decrees the precedence of the rational power, and the ordering of life toward its rule.[30]

"A law therefore generally taken, is a directive rule unto goodness of operation," and "the rule of voluntary agents on earth is the sentence that Reason giveth concerning the goodness of those things which they are to do." Unfortunately for those who, like the Puritans, desire complete moral blueprints for life, this law is often difficult to discern, and "the sentences which Reason giveth are some more some less general, before it come to define in particular actions what is good" (I. viii. 4). Revelation gives particular commands, in effect further specifying the natural law. But the Bible is to Hooker a historical document, and he objects to a literal reading without regard to historical context.[31] Perkins, too, thought that the Old Testament must be interpreted in its particular commands with respect to the "particular estate and condition of the Jewes Commonwealth and to the circumstances thereof." There are some "judicial" or general biblical edicts which are binding to all times and places. But these are, in fact, nothing other than statements of the natural law: a "judiciall law" in revelation may be known as such if "Wise men . . . in other nations have by naturall reason and conscience judged the same to be equal, just and necessary" and "if it serve directly to explane and confirme any of the tenne precepts of the Decalogue: or, if it serve directly to maintaine and uphold any of the three estates of the family, the commonwealth, the Church" (I. viii. 5). Hooker believes that "there is not that good which concerneth us, but it hath evidence enough for itself, if Reason were diligent to search it out" (I. vii. 1), and he finds it necessary to give some account of "the cause why so many natural or rational Laws are set down in Holy Scripture."[32]

Of these dictates of natural reason, he names a few, some very basic and general, as "That the greater good is to be chosen before the less" (I. viii. 5), some more specific, as are those of self-preservation, propagation of kind (I. v. 2), "Proceeding in the knowledge of truth" (I. v. 3), prayer and worship of God, honoring of parents, treatment of others as we would be treated by them (I. viii. 5, 7), self-defense, and submission to just authority (I. x. 4).

The finest of Hooker's expressions of the natural law is one which contains the essence of the Shakespearean tragic view:

> As long as each thing performeth only that work which is natural unto it, it thereby preserveth both other things, and also itself. Contrariwise, let any principal thing, as the sun, the moon, any one of the heavens or elements, but once cease or fail, or swerve, and who doth not easily conceive that the sequel thereof would be ruin both to itself and whatsoever dependeth on it? And is it possible, that Man being not only the noblest creature in the world, but even a very world in himself, his transgressing the Law of his Nature should draw no manner of harm after it? Yes, "tribulation and anguish unto every soul that doeth evil." Good doth follow unto all things by observing the course of their nature, and on the contrary side evil by not observing it; but not unto natural agents that good which we call Reward, not that evil which we properly term Punishment. The reason whereof is, because amongst creatures in this world, only Man's observation of the Law of his Nature is Righteousness, only Man's transgression Sin. And the reason of this is the difference in his manner of observing or transgressing the Law of his Nature. He doth not otherwise than voluntarily the one or the other. What we do against our wills, or

constrainedly, we are not properly said to do it, because the motive cause of doing it is not in ourselves.
(I. ix. 1)

For its relevance to Elizabethan tragedy, two things in
this passage are notable: first, the natural law which
governs man is inherent in man; it is the law of his
nature. It is not the law governing sensitive or vegetable
natures or the inanimate world; it is that which tends to
the preservation and perfection—to the "virtue"—specifically of humanity. Since Hooker's tradition conceived man as a primarily rational and spiritual creature, it is different from, and almost opposite to, the
descriptive natural law of the physical world, which we
associate with science.

Second, although morally innocent transgressions of
that law, committed under constraint or in ignorance,
do not cause to their doers the evil "which we properly
term punishment," they do issue in evil consequences in
the natural order. The tragic dramatist need then not
moralize in any modern sense, need not blame his protagonist to attest this moral conception. Shakespeare's
Brutus is responsible for evil consequences through failures of discernment, weaknesses of judgment in which
the play is not much concerned to show him morally
culpable.

In the Scholastic mainstream of medieval thought
upon which Hooker drew, human rationality and ani-
mality were seen as complementary principles of one
substance.[33] Natural law was thus changed from its
earliest Stoic formulation, for it was no longer an utter
denial of the passions. Scholasticism emphatically made
man neither mechanism nor pure intellect, but a substantial compound in which cognitive and appetitive,
sensual and spiritual principles had virtuous place.
Never having heard of the unconscious nor considered
an Oedipus complex, the Schoolmen were in fact not

much less aware than we of the thrust of irrational forces into the psyche, for they recognized thought as an activity of a rational animal, conditioned by the organism. In Hamlet's encomium, man is, finally "the paragon of *animals.*"[34]

Aquinas and other writers might be cited at length, but an adequate proof of this unitive vision lies in the very existence, in medieval and Renaissance science, of the humors theory, once universally received as true. The educated man of the fourteenth century may have been wrong in thinking, as he did, that the balance of the body fluids—blood, phlegm, melancholy, and choler —regulated both his physical and mental life, but he was thoroughly Scholastic in the understanding upon which this "endocrine" theory was premised, that a man's thoughts and emotions and his processes of "concoction" were activities of the same subject, and that the health or disorder of no one of them could be separated from that of the others—an insight recovered at length in modern psychosomatic medicine. In the earlier Middle Ages (the Augustinian-Platonic period) and after the Renaissance, especially after Descartes, the animal was separated from the rational in man, producing eventually the "angelic" conception, both Platonic and Calvinist-Manichean, of a spirit "operating" a body distinct from and inferior to it, from whose materiality arises evil. The Scholastic conception could accommodate, as the angelic theory could not, the kind of knowledge of man which we think of as post-Freudian— knowledge of the ways in which the animal is present in the rational.[35]

According to medieval philosophy, says Etienne Gilson, man's earthly state is his natural state. The Fall "wounded" his nature but did not change it. Knowledge gathered through the senses is, contrary to Plato and the Augustinian tradition, the only knowledge natural to us, and the soul separated from the body is in an unnatural state.[36] "I should say," he concludes, "that the essential result of Christian philosophy is a deeply considered affirmation of a reality and goodness intrinsic to nature."[37]

Natural law was, then, neither disembodied reason, as it could be to a Cartesian-Platonic anthropology which made man an angel imprisoned in a machine, nor inexorable physical fact, as it could be to those, like Bacon, who identified nature with the machine rather than the angel. It was often enough referred to simply as the rule of reason,[38] but reason understood as dictating for man what it discerns as the demands of his whole nature, which, more than rational, is known to him in his rationality. It does not exclude the uncalculating love of a Cordelia, nor in fact the place of any natural passion.

Moral evil was, in Scholastic doctrine, the privation of those things demanded by nature and the perversion of natural function.[39] But as Hooker says, man in this medieval scheme differs from all other creatures in being subject to natural law in a way which permits its violation and requires the function of reason in recognizing truly human ends, and especially the particular means which will serve them. The idea that man is born to the hard necessity of achieving his nature is not exclusively an existential or modern one: it is quite conformable with the belief that *operari sequitur esse*, and it found eloquent expression not only in Pico's *Oration on the Dignity of Man* but in *The Laws of Ecclesiastical Polity*. To attain success in this permanent struggle, reason must overcome the impediments which lie in fallen human nature: the errors of the passions, which are blind; the humorous dispositions of the body; and the influence of the stars.[40] This contest and its consequences are the subject of Shakespearean tragedy.

There is a thoroughly orthodox Renaissance statement on the subject in the "complaint" of Jack Cade, from the 1559 edition of that oppressively orthodox Renaissance book *The Mirror for Magistrates:*

> Our lust and wils our evils chefely worke,
> It may be wel that planetes do doe enclyne,
> And our complexions move our myndes to yll,
> But such is Reason, that they brynge to fine
> No worke, unayded of our lust and wyl;
> For heaven and earth are subject both to skyl
> The skyl of God ruleth al, it is so strong.
> Man may be skyl gyde things that to him long.
> Though lust be sturdy and wyl inclined to nought
> This forst by mixture [i.e., of humors], that by heavens course
> Yet through the skyl God hath in Reason wrought
> And geven man, no lust nor wyl so course
> But may be stayed or swaged of the sourse,
> So that it shal in nothing force the mynde
> To worke our wo, or leave the proper kynde.

He adds that although every man has this "skyl," "for lacke of grace ful fewe use it can," for the flesh is weak. When the surrender of mind to "lust and wyl" is followed by disastrous consequence,

> For sure this hap if it be rightly knowen
> Cummeth of our selves, and so the blame our owne.[41]

The fault, that is to say, lies "not in our stars."

A constant hazard in the discussion of Elizabethan natural law is the way the term has shifted meaning. Since Newton's time, perhaps since Bacon's, it has referred to the description of unvarying relations between physical causes and effects, a description of things as they are, quite apart from the moral order. To Aquinas and Hooker it meant, at least in its human range, a set of norms, an account of things as they ought to be, but often are not. By the eighteenth century there had been such change that even in its application to man, natural law could be understood as "a description not only of things as they should be, but also of things as they are."[42] Hooker had thought of the terrestrial world as being like man, fallen away from a perfect observance of the law of its nature.[43] Sin and the radical contingency and imperfection of created things accounted for physical evils,[44] which did not extend to the stars. After Copernicus, Brahe, Kepler, and Galileo had demonstrated that celestial bodies moved irregularly and were geometrically "imperfect" and subject to change, even the heavens seemed cursed to disorder by sin. But as science progressed, the heavens and then the earth were revealed as perfectly regular in their operations. Finally it was possible to regard even man as unvaryingly subject to ordained laws. "Natural law," even in the moral sphere, became a picture of things as they are, and Pope could declare that "whatever is, is right." Moral evil—or what appears to our partial view as evil—was then a result of the operation of natural law, whereas to Aquinas and Hooker it had been always the violation of that law.

At the same time, a major Protestant version of the moral law, originating in the voluntarism of Luther and Calvin (the philosophical doctrine which made reason secondary to will), identified it as being nothing other than the absolutely arbitrary dictates of God, given in Scripture: it did not originate from and had no necessary connection with present human nature, nor could knowledge of it be obtained from study of that nature. It was purely prescriptive. Not only did it set forth what ought to be, rather than what is, it prescribed in fact what could not naturally be: it had no connection with any law of nature. The term *natural law* had taken on its modern sense, wholly descriptive, referring to the involuntary and unvarying, applying only to mechanism.

But the tradition which lived in Hooker and Shakespeare conceived natural law as both prescriptive and descriptive. It defined what was good or bad for man as man, i.e., as a free or spiritual creature: it was therefore normative and prescriptive. But it referred to morality not in the Calvinist-voluntarist sense of divine command, but in the Thomist sense of norms following from the constitution of man, the sum of things demanded according to his nature. It could be discovered through reasoning about human nature as known by introspection and observation. It was thus in a sense also descriptive and capable of limitless further illumination by the rational and imaginative exploring of human experience (as in tragic drama).

We encounter this traditional natural-law faith in any literature where there is the pattern of a moral-rational flaw or error as the seed of catastrophe. For when that which is seen as contrary to reason and virtue is seen also as having destructive practical effects, there is presumed an intrinsic natural order, to which a conformity of will or of action is synonymous with virtue, and a conformity of the intellect or of thought is synonymous with truth.

Some of Shakespeare's tragic heroes however, "seem to fall to the unforseen outcome of their good intentions" so that the tragic *peripeteia* is "the working in blindness to [their] own defeat."[45] This impression is compatible enough with the kind of tragic reconciliation which is here suggested, but has baffled attempts at an interpretation seeking some culpable hubris or hamartia. In cases like those of Hamlet, Brutus, Antony, or Romeo, there is difficulty in defining what the hero "did wrong." One answer is Lily B. Campbell's, that each failed to master a particular one of the passions, as those were known in Renaissance psychological theory.[46] Such interpretations, although Miss Campbell's development of this one has certainly been most valuable to Shakespeare study, have an intrinsic shortcoming, given the openness of complex things to many predications and classifications both true and compatible. Hamlet is perhaps a clear example of "melancholy of grief," but if an Elizabethan theory is illustrated by a dramatic character, it does not follow that the character is explainable by the theory. A character sufficiently complex may be assigned to many categories—biological, social, economic, psychological, political, religious —without exhausting his dramatic meaning.

There is, nevertheless, an extremely important fact about Renaissance tragedy to be learned through the many passages which Miss Campbell cites from Renaissance treatises on the passions and humors. These examine the impediments in human nature which may influence rational action and thus explain the folly, error, and crime from which tragedy arises in real life.[47] Willard Farnham also finds in much early Renaissance literature the tracing of catastrophe to the humors or to the influence upon mind and will of the power of the stars. This is exercised not mystically, but through man's physical nature, which in medieval philosophy and Elizabethan belief is, as noted above, substantially one with his spiritual nature.[48]

Farnham believes that the preoccupation of tragic speakers in *The Mirror for Magistrates* with "complexiouns" and "humours" is an early manifestation of "an Elizabethan compulsion to search for the springs of human action rationally, a compulsion which grew rapidly and lent of its force to the development of dramatic tragedy." "The internal impulse," he says, "chiefly the lust and the will . . . which man may choose to follow or not to follow has grown for them to be the more effective cause of tragedy."[49] The influence of humors was to take another direction in the emphasis of the

Jonsonian type-character upon the affected or "false" humor, a literary development quite separate from the gradual hardening of psychological thought into what became in some instances a thoroughgoing determinism. Timothy Bright, although antimaterialistic in his treatment of the humors, testifies to the presence of materialism in the Galenic tradition even in 1586 by chiding those who "have esteemed the vertues themselves, yea religion, no other thing but as the body hath ben tempered, and on the other side, vice, prophaneness, & neglect of religion and honestie, to have bene nought else but a fault of humour."[50]

It is evident that the Renaissance, in its differing way, was even more seriously concerned with the idea of tragic flaws in human nature than was classical Greece: in thinking of life, if not of drama, the Elizabethan habitually sought in deviations from the control of reason—from the human natural law—the explanation of tragedy. This conviction is also clear in much earlier literature. In the moral play *Mundus et Infans*, Conscience reveals to man (in man's final guise as Age) that Folly—the folly which has brought him to worldly ruin —is the seven deadly sins.[51] Like Medwall's *Nature* and Lydgate's *Reson and Sensuallyte*, the play teaches that nothing in creation is in itself evil, that even "sensuality" is good, but that anything within human control may be corrupted if reason fails to govern in accord with the demands of nature.[52] Calvinism was later to identify all sensual appetite with evil, making utter contraries of goodness and the flesh.[53]

Much of the medieval "fool" literature also identifies sin and worldly folly, or finds them different only in gravity. The two things, the evil or sinful and the foolish or impractical, are united in Scholastic thought by the idea of privation of that "which is natural and due to a thing"; they are deviations from the norm of reason.[54]

Vice is grotesque (therefore potentially comic, as the morality plays attest), and defect is the essence of both villainy and clownage. Perversion of rationality not only merits God's punishment, but of itself works inner and outer ruin.

The medieval poem *De Stulticiis* strikingly unites the spiritual and mundane—moral virtue and the rationally perceivable requirements of nature—in its recital of "sixty follies that are common in the world." The list includes not only atheism, avarice, and persistence in deadly sin, but also "that a man should give all and receive nothing, . . . tell his counsel to everyone, . . . put his own self to shame, . . . spend wildly what he wins, believe everything he is told, . . . not want to escape from prison." "This man," says the conclusion, "shall die in poverty, but he who learns this lesson shall have God's blessing."[55] Lydgate's *Order of Fools*, like *De Stulticiis*, puts the Atheist first and identifies folly and evil, ending each stanza with the refrain that the fool described "shale never the."[56] There could not be a more complete taking for granted of the implicit axiom that the natural order is moral, the moral order is nature, the whole proceeds from reason, and reason reveals it to man. This identification of the moral and the naturally expedient may suggest Weber's interpretation of Calvinism, but whereas the Puritan, at least as Weber and his school have seen him, was by worldly works in his "calling" displaying or proving a (predestined) election, the medieval Christian under the aegis of natural law strove to effect both his natural and eternal success, although he admitted the necessity of nature-perfecting grace as well for the latter.[57] In fact, despite its rationalism, the medieval philosophy did not grant to reason a complete autonomy. Reason without faith was inadequate. Nevertheless, it is the rationalistic aspect of the medieval world-view which needs to be highlighted: it was the removal of this keystone which rendered the natural-law synthesis impossible.

In *The Castle of Perseverance*, the hero, Humanum Genus, dies in possession of worldly wealth granted by Avaritia or Covetyse, but escapes damnation only through the outcome of the heavenly debate of Misericordia, Justitia, Veritas, and Pax. Worldly and spiritual "success" appear to operate on opposed principles. The play belongs to a medieval literature which had not yet assimilated to imaginative uses the Scholastic optimism and rationalism, and is perhaps the wrong place to look for natural-law thought. Focused exclusively on eternal salvation, it sets up a simple opposition between riches (the obvious form of the *bona temporalia*) and piety. The most subtle Schoolman would not have denied that these can be alternatives, nor demurred from a simple preachment which warned of the wrong choice between them. "World" is used here in its rather special theological sense[58] and is simply opposed to heaven. Structural embodiment of natural-law concepts had to wait other dramatic occasions. Yet even in *Perseverance*, the key ideas are emphatically present in the speech of Stulticia, who promises to work both temporal and spiritual mischief:

> And I, folye
> Schal hyen hym hye,
> Tyl sum enmye
> Hym over-goo.
> In worldes wyt,
> That in folye sit,
> I thynke yyt
> Hes sowle to sloo.[59]

Gorboduc, the first "regular" English tragedy, although co-authored by the translator of the definitive edition of Calvin's *Institutes*, is a foursquare dramatization of some of the political maxims of natural law:

> Onelie I meane to shewe, by certeine rules
> Whiche Kinde hath graft within the mind of man,
> That Nature hath her ordre and her course,
> Which being broken doth corrupt the state
> Of myndes and thinges, even in the best of all.[60]

In Skelton's *Magnyfycence*, the title-character follows his "owne wyll; / Be it Reason or none," and so is led by folly from felicity to adversity and poverty. Farnham has said of this play that it shows how "refusal on man's part to be virtuous, or reasonable, can lead to physical retribution according to the laws of cause and effect." It is "rational to the last degree."[61] The changing of the vice's names in productions like *Magnyfycence* and *Respublica* (their disguising as virtues) accords closely with the Scholastic account of the way the will is moved to evil.[62] Such disguising reflects, in its baldly schematic way, a belief which was to be assimilated to the uses of mature tragedy in Iago. *Othello* being a play whose symbolic elements are more controlling than those of most Shakespearean tragedy, Iago is much alike in dramatic function to the Skeltonic personifications. He is disguised, as evil is by nature; the doctrine of "reason" and sensuality which he urges on Roderigo (I. iii. 322–37) is evil by defect—a subtle distortion parading as truth. The bestial imagery with which he fills Othello's ear excites imaginations which overpower judgment; and this again is a Scholastic paradigm of sin. Like Edmund in *Lear*, he works by seeming other than he is and speaks for a "reason" and "nature" which are his perversions of the realities.

The theoretic form of Chaucer's *Troilus and Criseyde* is also substantially that of natural-law tragedy, despite the still-common tendency to accept at face value, and as adequately representing medieval tragic literature, the *De Casibus* formula of Chaucer's Monk, which reduces it to the narrative setting forth of

The harm of hem that stoode in heighe degree,
And fillen so that ther nas no remedie
To brynge hem out of hir adversitee.
For certein, whan that Fortune list to flee,
Ther may no man the cours of hire withholde.[63]

But Chaucer neither treats Troilus as a pawn of inscrutable "fortune" nor celebrates "courtly love" so simplemindedly as to make of Andreas Capellanus' code an enveloping ethical frame. What the hero suffers is his own surrender of liberty. He may indeed be helpless in the outcome, but he has delivered himself to fortune by an idolatrous pursuit of a worldly good (human love) as an ultimate end. This submission of reason to will (reproved in men as womanly, since it paralleled the equally unnatural usurpation of man's authority by woman) commits him to an order of things subject to uncontrollable fate. Troilus may well take the Boethian deterministic argument, without Philosophy's crucial reply in defense of freedom, which follows in *De Consolatione Philosophae*,[64] as a truth of his experience. He has abdicated his rational freedom, as medieval philosophy warned that one might easily do.[65] He has submitted to "the brief mockery of the goods that are committed unto Fortune."[66] The stars, says Aquinas, influence men through their physical organism, especially through the passions ("as both intellect and will receive something from the inferior powers which are affixed to corporeal organs"), so that men are much governed by the stars. Since man is by nature able to assert reason's freedom and control, "the wise man is stronger than the stars."[67] But like Troilus, "the majority of men follow their passions," so that "astrologers are able to foretell the truth in the majority of cases,"[68] i.e., he who subjects reason to the appetitive powers submits to the stars, or to "fate."[69]

Troilus is essentially a tragic figure of the tradition of

natural law, one in whom "reason panders will,"[70] who "would make his will Lord of his reason."[71] His earthly sufferings are no decree of fate or providence, but the working-out of a fundamental malaise which begins in a lack of that perspective provided by the epilogue.

WITH THE SCHOLASTIC development of natural-law thought, says M. D'Entreves, "The Christian religion is no longer a 'folly,' a flat contradiction of human nature and the abolition of the old Adam. Worldly and godly wisdom must be reconciled."[72] Eventually these were to separate again; the effects of the widening split are seen in the torment of Webster's Bosola or of Falmineo, who even at the moment of death, confesses that "while we looke up to Heaven we confound / Knowledge with knowledge."[73] But for most of the Elizabethans, the two wisdoms remained truly one.

Primauday instructed his many readers, in the very popular *French Academy* (1594), that "there is no sinne that can avoide punishment, and that findeth not a Judge even in him that committed it, to take vengence thereof by means of affections, which God hath placed in man to that ende."[74] This venerable and thoroughly orthodox conviction had been expressed by men of the natural-law tradition from Cicero to Hooker.[75] It is one of the central ideas which Shakespeare was to bring to life in Othello, Macbeth, and Lear, in the torments of Richard III on the eve of Bosworth field, and in the ironic inability of Claudius to escape the inner consequences of a brother's murder.

Chapter Two

The Role of Natural Law in Shakespearean Tragedy

IF WE COME to Shakespeare sufficiently familiar with this fundamental heritage of the Renaissance, his tragedies will be seen to reflect the cosmos of natural law. Generally, they interpret evil as defect and understand catastrophe to follow from the unnatural. Unfortunately, discussion of "tragic flaws" in Elizabethan drama is critically suspect. And in some cases, e.g., Hamlet's, the chief agent may have no particular flaw beyond the limits of common humanity. Yet there is still in *Hamlet* an intelligible cause in free human actions of the evil which surrounds the hero, and evil flows not from the nature of things in the universe of the play, but from the perversion of their natures. Our comfort here is found also in the hero's painful victory. Confronted by a world of evil, and so divided in his profoundest impulses that choice and action are almost insuperably hard, he is able finally to survive in integrity, to control what he becomes and govern at least his inner and ultimately significant fate. This achievement makes its affirmation most impressively in the face of outer and physical ruin—the worst that the world can do.

Hamlet is, in fact, a man who has succeeded or almost succeeded in acting "naturally," in a Scholastic rather than in a modern sense. "Nature" and "natural" assumed in the early seventeenth century something almost opposite to the medieval significations which they had possessed for Hooker and Shakespeare. Herschel Baker remarks that within this time "the educated man's conception of nature, and of man's place in nature, had undergone changes which to St. Thomas would be incredible, even to Hooker grossly improbable."[1]

We are, since the time of Rousseau or of his immediate predecessors, actually accustomed to seeing the natural identified with the instinctive and opposed to the rational or to restraint. But there remains a question of what one takes human nature to be. To the Scholastics, the human form, that which made man to be man, was the rational soul,[2] and the most natural human behavior was therefore intellectually regulated behavior; the more perfected as an intellect, the more human the man.[3] Given this picture of man and society (whose nature is a function of man's) it is, as Friar Lawrence says, the indulgence of "rude will," not its restraint, which is "unnatural."

Hamlet acts naturally, but not quite naturally enough. He is caught between the savage hatred and detestation of his uncle which urges him to a passionate and bloody revenge and, on the other hand, the obligations of the heir and true head of state, now left alone responsible for the restoration of a natural political and social order, to execute public justice in the public interest. The Prince of Denmark must kill the usurper Claudius and not become a murderer—for the son of Hamlet and Gertrude an almost impossible demand. The great soliloquy in act II, scene ii ("Oh, what a rogue and peasant slave am I") is, in part, a scene of temptation. His own motives are, in his deep emotional involvement, hard for him to know; he questions them continually. His position is one of inescapable responsibility, and the turbulence within him is so great that even the apparition of his father cannot be trusted, for passion makes his own motives suspect and the ghost may be an imposition of evil upon his agitated and precariously rational state (II. ii. 627–32). He wins this struggle and emerges Hamlet still: only once does he act in private passion, and "Heaven" as he immediately recognizes in a clear admission of guilt, "does punish [him] with this" (i.e., with Polonius, death, and Hamlet's loss of his temporary advantage over Claudius).[4]

To defend this requires lengthy discussion of the play; but about the general Shakespearean conception of what is natural to man there is less room for dispute. There are no noble savages in Shakespeare, and he holds firmly the ideal of human cultivation and the superiority of rational discipline over instinct and the emotions.[5] One of many examples is the long speech of the Duke of Burgundy in *Henry V*, a passage which contemplates the condition of France after the long wars with England:

> her hedges even-pleach'd
> Like prisoners wildly overgrown with hair,
> Put forth disorder'd twigs; her fallow leas
> The darnel, hemlock, and rank fumitory
> Doth root upon, while that the coulter rusts
> That should deracinate such savagery;
> The even mead, that erst brought sweetly forth
> The freckled cowslip, burnet, and green clover,

> Wanting the scythe, all uncorrected, rank,
> Conceives by idleness. . . .
>
> . . . .
>
> Even so our houses and ourselves and children
> Have lost, or do not learn for want of time,
> The sciences that should become our country,
> But grow like savages.
>
> (V. ii. 42–59)

Everything is left to physical processes "all uncorrected"—unregulated by reason. The children grow up according to instinct, or what we might incautiously call a "natural" mode of life; the hedges and fields are left in what we would surely think of as their "natural" state. Shakespeare's Duke sums this up as "everything that seems unnatural": it is the lack of imposed rational order in man's world which is unnatural. It is, in a purely modern paradox, artifice which is natural, in the human world.[6]

The objection which may spring to mind is that of the nature invoked by Edmund in *King Lear*. But this is the "nature" of Edmund's belief, not of Shakespeare's; nor is it a conception verified by the play-world of *Lear*, any more than the unfolding events of *Macbeth* show life "a tale told by an idiot." The play disproves, in fact, the thesis of identity between appetite and nature in man. In *King Lear* "there are those," says Robert Heilman, "who do what they want and call it 'nature'; there are those to whom right and justice, even though they are not apparent in the facts of the present, are 'Nature.' "[7]

Rival theories of nature are, in fact, central in *Lear*: the words "nature," "natural," and "unnatural" echo throughout the play, and opposed conceptions of nature underlie the conflict and distinguish character.[8] Edmund's invocation of nature reveals a belief which Shakespeare's audience would have found "heterodox and subversive," which is deliberately calculated to "shock and startle."[9] He is an "emancipated" Renaissance man like Webster's Bosola, who, seeing the contrast between the actual practices of men and the moral law to which the world gives lip service, scorns the antique belief in a moral universe. "Nature" means to him the laws of the animal world, the world of physical reality upon which he sees human codes ("the curiosity of nations") as artificially imposed. Edmund conceives nature and its relation to man as does Machiavelli, and Goneril and Regan concur. Lear, Albany, Gloucester, and Cordelia hold the traditional view: demanding a filial consideration by Regan, Lear speaks of "the offices of nature" due him (II. iv. 181). Albany warns Goneril

> That nature which contemns its origin
> Cannot be bordered certain in itself.
> She that herself will sliver and disbranch
> From her material sap, perforce must wither
> And come to deadly use.
>
> (IV. ii. 32–36)

Gloucester remarks, of Lear's unreasonable treatment of Cordelia, "the King falls from bias of nature" (I. ii. 120–21). When later, he comes to think "as flies to wanton boys, are we to th' gods, / They kill us for their sport," Edgar comments "Bad is the trade that must play fool to sorrow" (IV. i. 38–40). Cordelia upholds the order of nature in refusing to join that symbolic pageant of flattery where Lear requires of his daughters the allegiance which belongs to their husbands. "I love your Majesty," she says, "According to my bond, no more or less" (I. i. 94–95). But Lear, soon to begin his outraged appeals to the bond of nature, cannot now recognize its incarnation in Cordelia. Rash and knowing himself "but slenderly," he has not schooled the "natural faculty of reason . . . to judge rightly between truth and error, good and evil." In the sequel to his folly, it is Goneril's use of her unnatural power over him that first teaches Lear to distinguish the qualities of Cordelia (I. iv. 288–93), and it is to nature that Lear prays to "suspend [its] purpose" by rendering Goneril sterile.[10]

Edmund, accusing his brother of murderous plots against Gloucester, takes as his Machiavellian disguise the old-fashioned mentality which he has jeered at in his father; he piously decries Edgar's "unnatural purpose" (II. i. 52). The echo has special resonance in that his own real purpose is the vicious one he attributes to Edgar, and in support of it he has invoked that "Nature" in which *he* believes. The word works poetically like the Fool's reminders of "nothing."

Lear speaks to Regan of "the offices of nature, bond of childhood" (II. iv. 181)—the bond to which Cordelia (I. i. 95) stood—and is spurned. When he leaves in rage, she, Iago-like, declaims to Gloucester with perfect hypocrisy a truth which will be realized to her destruction: "O, Sir, to wilful men / The injuries that they themselves procure / Must be their schoolmasters" (II. iv. 305–307). Within a few brief scenes, this tutelage has in fact brought Lear from his blind egocentricity to a beginning of charity, humility, and justice (III. iv. 28ff).

From suffering he comes to such an awakening; from his discovery of evil he falls to a tormented madness in which he envisions men as bestial appetite (IV. vi. 109–34) and the order of society as a mockery (IV. vi. 153–75). From this trauma he emerges to a reconciliation, a return to the bias of nature. Lear's final acceptance of the world recognizes all its possibilities, and is meaningful, as his initial acceptance of it was not.

"Goneril and Regan," says Theodore Spencer, "not only violate natural law by their behaviour to their father, they also violate their proper functions as human beings by their lust for Edmund, a lust which ends in murder and suicide, and which makes the description of them as animals doubly appropriate."[11] Heilman, in a chapter on "The Nature of Nature," analyzes the opposed "natures" in *Lear*, and concludes that "in the metaphorical usage of this play, *nature* comes also to mean a normal, ordered functioning of the moral world, a final principle to which all moral phenomena are to be referred. If, on the surface, there is moral chaos, beneath there is a 'nature,' an eternal fitness of things, with which the chaos is inconsistent and to which it does violence."[12]

Edmund's role shows us only that Shakespeare can conceive nature in the later Jacobean and modern sense. But this nature is not the *human* nature and its law assumed everywhere in his tragedies. "In Shakespeare's world," according to H. B. Charleton, "the human being who departs from the natural law of humans to adopt the law of the beasts, has become less than a beast. He has proved himself a monster."[13]

The origins of catastrophe in *Lear* are traced clearly enough to the violation of recognizable demands of natural law: Lear's obligations inhering in the natural authority of fatherhood and rulership, Regan's and Goneril's filial and marital duty, the rational obligation to seek reality, i.e., truth. Lear first judges love by its rhetoric, then measures it by arithmetic, before he is schooled to understand it better. He is redeemed from willful blindness to the realities of good and evil by the suffering which follows from his failure to act according to the demands exacted by the nature of things. The outcome shows the terrible cost of the old man's education, but shows Lear and Gloucester to be right, and Edmund wrong, about what nature is. The ruin following Lear's ignorance of, and Edmund's, Goneril's, and Regan's rejection of, the demands of nature, attests the reality of what Edmund has derided as a myth.

In the final wanton chance that kills Cordelia and Lear, Shakespeare dares to surrender any claim to poetic justice or to happy endings, however merited. The play's testimony to human responsibility and significance and to a purposeful, intelligible, observable order in man and his world can be trusted even to such a test. It may be that for some readers, as the Tate revision suggests, this much honesty about human life is intolerable. But an evil, however pitiable its subject, which we can trace to the violation of law may witness at least to knowable order, and without diminishing freedom. An accidental electrocution, a death by freezing in Antarctica, do not move us to fear life or despise the world: the laws of electricity are understood; the lethal cold of the polar regions is known. We are thus not at their mercy. Confronting a maximum challenge, *King Lear* creates to this extent an acceptable world.

THE SAME PRINCIPLES of natural law undergird the powerful and densely polysemous dramatic poetry of *Macbeth*. To identify them briefly is at best to provide a reductive x-ray photograph of the tragedy: for assurance that a careful reading can verify their importance as a thematic understructure, we have the authority of Walter Clyde Curry's thorough study of the philosophical pattern[14] in *Macbeth*. It would be redundant here to do more than enlist that testimony and survey the main outlines of the Scholastic pattern which is discoverable in the play.

Macbeth explores minutely the paths along which the mind and will of the hero are drawn into ruin by fixation upon a temporal good chosen in explicit rejection of a higher good, and so in defiance of the demands of his nature. Macbeth is led to anticipate his rise to kingship, and this is brought before his imagination with such vividness and violence as to make its apprehension overpower rational judgment and determine this choice of the lesser good. Nature revolts in him at the murder (and his soliloquies in the earlier part of the play show him revolving that horror in imagination), but Macbeth defies nature.

The will, says Aquinas, is naturally inclined to follow reason, but can err when reason's knowledge of the ultimate good is defective, or when its judgment of the present good is perverted by a "vehement and inordinate apprehension of the imagination and judgment of the estimative power."[15] Demonic powers can influence the will only through man's physical nature (sense, imagination, and the passions), since the will itself is inviolate. *Macbeth* thus pictures, according to the Scholastic faculty psychology, a process in which expectation and phantasm or imagination excite a passion which usurps reason's determination of the will.[16]

The essential human nature of Macbeth by its own internal operation exacts terrible consequences which are the real subject of the play and beside which his outer ruin is relatively insignificant. He wishes for some force to "cancel and tear to pieces that great bond which keeps [him] pale." Curry's judgment on the play locates it exactly within the tradition of natural law.

> Macbeth's mind is in a state of great confusion regarding the processes taking place within him. The profound disturbance in the essential nature of the man expresses itself, psychologically speaking, in a horrible fear and torture of the mind assailing the individual and in the affliction of terrible dreams that shake him nightly. Wracking passions, frayed nerves and inordinate apprehension of the imagination have so impeded his reason that he conceives of Banquo's knowledge and possible suspicion as constituting the primary source of his distemper and the only threat to his peace.
> . . . He is somewhat aware also of the elemental

cause of his dismal experience. The natural good in him compels the acknowledgement that, in committing the unnatural act, he has filed his mind and has given his eternal jewel, the soul, into the possession of those demonic forces which are the enemy of mankind. He recognizes that the acts of conscience which torture him are really expressions of that outraged natural law, which inevitably reduces him as individual to the essentially human. This is the inescapable bond that keeps him pale, and this is the law of his own nature from whose exactions of devastating penalties he seeks release.[17]

OF 'HAMLET,' a great variety of critical positions on the play can be accommodated to the view that Hamlet's catastrophe follows upon a failure, or an incapacity to cope adequately with inner perturbation and outer evil, and that this incapacity is not due to the meaninglessness or chaotic or evil nature of the world, or to the unnaturalness of his own nobility and virtue. Bradley, it is true, maintained that the flaw and the greatness of each of Shakespeare's tragic heroes lay in the same excess,[18] and found therefore a large element of "painful mystery" in the plays, but the weaknesses of this position have long since been made apparent.[19] Hamlet, as E. E. Stoll demonstrated, is not intended by Shakespeare or seen by Shakespeare's contemporaries as having any particular flaw.[20] He is, however, a man set in circumstances where right action is unclear, yet where he must discover the right action, and where it is urgent that he act. (It is important that Renaissance conceptions of natural law imply an ultimate identity in the "moral" and "practical" senses of "right" action.)[21] He has powerful cause to act, great and ultimately fatal impediments, within himself, to wholly rational action.

In recent years it has been tempting, no doubt, to read

this as an existentialist play, for there is in it a continual dwelling on the necessity of decision and the guilt of decision; the necessity which presses on Hamlet to *become* a certain kind of thing, to create himself by a commitment, to define himself in some relation to the Denmark from which he shrinks. Hamlet yearns to escape the freedom of the existentialist "pour-soi" and longs for the existence of the "en-soi," that which substantively "is" something other than its choices, in a brute factual way. Hamlet wants to be a revenger like Laertes, at least to be something that will absolve him from further decisions, for he is intolerably aware of his independence and total responsibility, his onerous freedom to "decide the meaning of being." There are other deceptively existentialist aspects of *Hamlet;* the emphasis upon Hamlet's integrity, his consistency with himself, as the virtue which can redeem the outer ruin. Ophelia and others become enemies or mere "things" in Hamlet's world once he commits himself. Dread, death, the terror of freedom in the play, all might tempt us to such a reading of *Hamlet,* a reading which I think is mistaken.

In Shakespeare we should, I believe, find "essentialism," the extreme contrary of existentialism. A difficulty is perhaps that the Scholastic-medieval idea of essence underlying the natural law has so often been distorted by modern treatments. Aldous Huxley implies that Aristotle, in asserting men to be "essentially" the same and only "accidentally" different, asserts that they are potentially alike in all their faculties and powers and are different in these only because of the *chance* circumstances of their lives.[22] But this misrepresents Aristotle. A one-pound and a thousand-pound sphere are "essentially" the same, each a body with outer surface at all points equidistant from a central point: they share a single essence, for essence is that which constitutes a thing of its kind. If each, however, is to be carried away, their "accidental" and very real difference of quantity may take on an importance which no Aristotelian need deny in defense of their essential identity.

Scholasticism was essentialistic in relation to modern existentialism, with its final exalting of the unique, yet it was markedly existential in relation to the extreme essentialism of the Platonic tradition. Platonism equates being with essence; Scholasticism says (against existentialists) that being implies essence, but (against Platonists) that it also implies existence, the "act" of essence. The conception of essence lies, in fact, near the root of the entire classical tradition, a tradition of emphasis in art upon the "probable," the universal, the representative—upon whatever relates to or reveals the common nature. It is the universally human essence, with its intrinsic necessities or laws, obscurely seen in differing individuals, nowhere existing in its universal state, but everywhere embodied differently, which is, in a sense, the ultimate object of Shakespearean tragedy.

'Romeo and Juliet' is one of the first plays in which Shakespeare achieved something of what may be called the genuine tragic effect. Here he begins to explore the idea that "character is fate" (the phrase certainly oversimplifies the plays, but still is true to them). Interpretation must start by recognizing his insistence that the lover's destruction is "in the stars," that the incalculable figures decisively in their story. The imagery steadily tolls foreboding, doom, gathering darkness; the contributions to the tragic outcome of coincidence, of the feud, of the other characters, are evident to every reader and viewer.

Such is the world in which the lovers are placed, but what is their relation to it? What is the office of a human will in this particular Shakespearean world, where the limits of choice are so visible, the obstacles to moral navigation so impressively solid and numerous? Is Romeo agent or patient, victim or instigator?

A parallel may be helpful: Is Oedipus' character the sufficient (surely not the necessary) cause of his ruin and *therefore* of the oracle's foretelling? Or are the true relations of cause and effect the reverse? Widening the question to its fullest Augustinian scope, in which theological form it occupied the European mind for a millennium, it becomes the problem of divine free will and foreknowledge, of "necessity" and moral responsibility. It is partly a matter of which facet of the reality that Shakespeare gives us, we (rather than the play) find most significant. Most teachers of literature have discovered in the Sophoclean parallel a similar provocation to debate whose motion proves circular. The play presents to us, as did the world to the medieval theologian, evidence of both things and a need to reconcile them in our understanding.

Even here, where feeling is concentrated upon the balking of will by accidents, and the straitening limits of circumstance press cruelly upon human action, Shakespeare's conception of human nature and its moral ecology permit only the directing of imagination to fate, not the obliteration of freedom. He did not see these as alternatives, but (like most medieval and Renaissance thinkers) as rival influences both present in human life. The stars, fate, the humors, claim supremacy in man only as he abdicates rationality and surrenders inviolable reason to forces (subject to fate) which it should rule.

Shakespeare is often thought to have treated the principals *con amore* throughout, so that any critical attempt to discuss Romeo's "mistakes" must be futile.[23] Much of the play's power does indeed flow from its lyric evocation of the glamor of young love. Of the lovers we are made to wish that the force which asserts itself in them, rather than those forces which it must encounter to its peril, might move and rule the world. There is a transcendence of love in the play's poetry, as in that of *Antony and Cleopatra*. But a part of the theoretic form of the tragedy is the recognition that transcendent love has, among men, no pure world in which to exist, no other world but that of cities and families and human authority; it is here that love must be nurtured, and not in a romantic ether.

A proper reading of Friar Lawrence's role should suggest the enveloping frame of reference. There is much to make the audience conscious that however appealing Romeo's motives may be to its feelings, such a course of willful decision and action, under such circumstances, flouts the nature of things and surrenders all control. One need not deny the role of destiny, or of coincidence, or of the feud, to insist with Bradley that except for the weaknesses in Romeo's character, the fates would not have conducted the lovers to their doom.

In romantic tragedy, where the motives of hero and heroine are almost inevitably sympathetic to feeling, there is often a large choric element which keeps before the audience's consciousness the possibility of a more fully rational alternative course. The tragic poignancy of such drama arises from our perception that something attractive to the affections must be rejected by reason. Such is the role of Friar Lawrence in *Romeo and Juliet*, the philosophical soliloquies in Chaucer's *Troilus and Criseyde*, and Milton's own editorial and interpretive comment in Book IX of *Paradise Lost*, where Adam, for faithful love of Eve, consciously rebels against God and reason, and we are made at once to feel the action as affectively sympathetic, and to see that it is, within Milton's terms, irrational and unnatural, and ultimately disastrous. Here almost in its pure form is the essence of Christian-humanistic tragedy: the confrontation with the fact of our vulnerability to internal division, and the affirmation of our power and responsibility.

At the opening of act II, scene iii of *Romeo and Juliet,* immediately before the start of tragic complications, Friar Lawrence soliloquizes:

> Two such opposed kings encamp them still
> In man as well as herbs, grace and rude will;
> And where the worser is predominant,
> Full soon the canker death eats up that plant.
>   (II. iii. 27–30)

As the Friar, alone on stage, speaks these words, Romeo (who, we have been told by the Prologue, will shortly be dead) comes to him: surely in this moment what the audience sees and what it hears are intended as part of one meaning. Romeo's self-indulgent romanticism will have its way at all costs; it rejects reason and prudence. Government by such "rude will" is unnatural to man, as the Friar repeatedly insists, and it has dangers. Again and again, the Friar explicitly warns Romeo that his failure to control his emotions flouts his manhood (see especially II. iv. 108–58). The Friar's scolding is faithful to the idea that sin as a departure from reason reduces man to a perverse bestiality, being not reason's absence, but its usurpation.

As Eve's fall provided a trope of this rebellion of the lower powers, they were Eve-like and feminine, and a man given to their rule was, as the Friar says, an "unseemly woman in a seeming man." The comic reaction of the nurse to Friar Lawrence's longest lecture ("O Lord, I could have stay'd here all the night / To hear good counsel. O, what learning is!") (III. iii. 159–60) expresses, it may be, Shakespeare's awareness of the futility, perhaps the pomposity or fatuity, of addressing such counsels to a Romeo. But this does not discredit what the Friar says. Shakespeare is, in part, simply insulating Friar Lawrence's wisdom from the cynical reflex which it risks, just as he protects Romeo's highest lyricism by allowing a skeptical and jeering worldliness its voice within the play in the person of Mercutio (II. i).

He is almost heavyhandedly explicit about the dangerous (if sympathetic) failure of realistic rational discipline in Romeo's mooning over Rosaline in the first, second, and fourth scenes of act I. Of the extravagantly Petrarchan Romeo, the languishing sufferer who cannot be brought to smile at his own hyperbolical state, who abandons himself to transports of oxymoron (e.g., in I. i. 177–89), Friar Lawrence will exclaim

> Jesu Maria, what a deal of brine
> Hath washed thy sallow cheeks for Rosaline!
> . . . .
> And art thou chang'd? Pronounce this sentence then:
> Women may fall, when there's no strength in men.
>   (II. iii. 69–70, 79–80)

The Romeo who will not hesitate to set Juliet secretly against her father's natural authority, so that even Capulet's ignorant solicitude for his daughter (his regard is perfectly genuine, if a little testy and obtuse) can become deadly to her, is this same "young waverer," however more real his new love is than the old.

For the Elizabethans, no pattern within the human community was more genuinely felt to be an inevitable corollary of the nature of man than was the order of authority within the family. Parental rule and filial duty were believed immediately and connaturally derivable from right reason about the conduct of life.[24] In Sackville's *Gorboduc,* the counselor Philander warns the king against abdicating his throne to his sons in these words:

And oft it hath ben seene, where Natures course
Hath been perverted in disordered wise,
When fathers cease to know that they should rule,
The children cease to know they should obey.
(I. ii. 205–208)[25]

It is not only the natural pattern in the state which will be violated, but also the more elemental one of the family. The relation of parent to child is part of the great principle of order.

When *Romeo and Juliet* is seen in this light, the feeling it generates for the lovers is undiminished, but their tragic world is clearly not a place of intolerably random evil, nor are men mere grains of sand on the shore of the universe, at the mercy of indifferent forces beyond comprehension or control. We are, in fact, at the very farthest extreme from naturalistic pessimism, in a world where men receive not indeed what they deserve, but what they cause. Although Romeo's destruction, like that of a good man who has chosen to walk a mountain path blindfolded, may not be "just," it is neither mysterious nor menacing.

'JULIUS CAESAR' is a tragedy of delusion and deceit in which virtually everyone thinks he has meant well. Brutus is flawed by greed for honor and by a self-deceit which is the price of his self-solemnizing. His stern civic piety masks an insidious self-indulgence: he finds the sacred cause he requires in a coup d'etat, and a patriot band in a sordid cabal. Meaning to minister to the state, he joins with its scourges, for he can blind himself to the motives of his confederates when his self-image is touched. Thinking (although merely at the surface of consciousness) to sacrifice his private feelings and heed only the public weal, he acts to remove not so much a tyrant as the idea of one. He sees in Caesar a half-realized theoretical illustration of tyranny, rather than the man actually before him; he is an idealist almost in the technical sense that abstractions are more real to him than things. He takes the assassination in its theoretic character as an act of republican "honor," rather than its physical reality as a stabbing. His ritualizing of it in the bloody hand-washing over Caesar's corpse is a shocking dramatic confrontation of reality with this "ideal," repeated in the verbal juxtapositions in Brutus' speeches throughout this scene[26] ("Or else were this a savage spectacle") and in Antony's ironies: ("the honourable men / Whose daggers have stabb'd Caesar").

Giving explanations to Antony and to the Roman mob, Brutus wears his Stoic reason and honor like the emperor's new clothes, with such assured and sober dignity that we hardly credit our perception of the howling absurdity of such "reasons" and such "honor." Armored in his seamless self-righteousness, he is a dangerous innocent, one of the Shakespeare heroes who nourish a "domesticated monster"—an appalling reality invested by fear or desire with the appearances of reason and allowed the freedom of his daylight life, until its depredations force him (Othello, if not Brutus), intolerably too late, to admit to recognition what was too obvious and too horrible to be seen. Its half-glimpsed monstrousness keeps him desperately committed to the folly he has maintained at such a cost. Brutus perhaps never clearly realizes that he has wasted himself on a delusion. He dies convinced that "I found no man but he was true to me"; in fact many have been false to him; he has been surrounded by falsenesses, from Cassio's forged writings thrown in at his windows "As if they came from several citizens" to Antony's use of the pulpit which Brutus has granted him. Not that Brutus is crushed between a wicked world and a noble code of honor; his defeat and the ruin he visits upon the civil order are the price of his own failure rightly to discern good and evil.

Although the conspirators' cause would have had plausibility for an Elizabethan audience, in light of the qualities of the traditional tyrant of natural-law political theory by which Caesar's character is marked,[27] Brutus' undertaking is folly, and its tragic sequel is not an arbitrary or capricious evil.

THE TRAGEDY OF *Othello* begins in a slight and sympathetically motivated disturbance of the natural domestic order of the family and ends in a terrible rending of that same order.

When Iago makes his first, feignedly reluctant intimation of Desdemona's guilt, he takes up a weapon which Othello has shaped for him, using two potent arguments that underlie the plausibility of accusations against her. Iago in fact reveals unarguable a priori grounds for distrust; he exposes an original weakness in the union of mutual faith, which renders it vulnerable:

> *Iago* She did deceive her father, marrying you;
> And when she seemed to shake and fear your looks,
> She loved them most.
> *Othello* And so she did.
> *Iago* Why, go to then.
> That she, so young, could give out such a seeming,
> To seel her father's eyes up close as oak—
> He thought 'twas witchcraft.
> (III. iii. 206–11)

"Look to her, Moor," Brabantio has said, "if thou hast eyes to see; / She has deceiv'd her father, and may thee" (I. iii. 293–94). Othello is shaken. The deception of Brabantio has inescapable wider meanings than he has intended. Although Desdemona be virtue itself, the element of vulnerability in Othello's faith is real, and he is its author. Iago simply recognizes and uses this advantage, as he uses his perception of the Moor's heroic self-image and the strong hint in the marriage of the magnification of Othello's ego. This taint of self-aggrandizement is unmistakable: Othello insists on his own spartan and soldierly qualities; he solicits recognition even of his modesty; his descent is "From men of royal siege, and [his] demerits / May speak unbonneted to as proud a fortune / As this that [he has] reached" (I. ii. 20–24). The confidence that underlies his splendid power of effortless command ("Keep up your bright swords, for the dew will rust them") vanishes upon Iago's hint of a blemish in that conscious magnificence with which he has always compelled love or obedience. He laments the loss of the "pride, pomp, and circumstance" which belong to a generalship of which he is no longer capable, being no longer magnificent to himself, but liable like other men to betrayal (III. iii. 349–51). His characteristic language often approaches bombast: proposing to leave his bride in Venice, he is careful to specify "fit disposition . . . / Due reference of place and exhibition, / With such accommodation and besort / As levels with her breeding" (I. iii. 237–40).

His disavowal of sensual interest is betrayed as a complex illusion by the concentrated sensual emphasis in the imagery of his own speech. He is a fully seasoned military leader but a dangerously incomplete private man, whose professional virtues are not adequate to the human and personal crisis which is thrust upon him by the Vice-like Iago,[28] but is predicated upon the shallowness of his self-knowledge and upon his childishness in discerning moral reality from appearance. He is (*pace* Bradley) jealous to madness, and as he gives himself to that weak passion, he simply glances away from possibilities too terrible to see—even more terrible than Desdemona's treachery—the possibility of his own weakness and of Iago's deception, which directly violates the official soldier's code[29] and is therefore unimaginable. Othello himself recalls the other flaw in the marriage, and Iago elaborates skillfully:

> *Othello* And yet, how nature erring from itself—
> *Iago* Aye, there's the point; as—to be bold with
> you—
> Not to affect many proposed matches
> Of her own clime, complexion, and degree,
> Whereto we see in all things nature tends—
> Foh! one may smell in such, a will most rank,
> Foul disproportion, thoughts unnatural.
>
> (III. iii. 228–33)

Iago, who has filled Othello's ear and the air of the play with an animal imagery insinuating the wholly physical nature of love (and thus the aberrant quality of Desdemona's), means by "nature" what Edmund meant in *Lear*—animal impulse, appetite, instinct. He makes explicit his identification of nature with the mechanical and physical, with "rude will," and its opposition to all higher and rational rule—all "grace"—in his words to Roderigo: "her delicate tenderness will find itself abus'd, begin to heave the gorge, disrelish and abhor the Moor. Very nature will instruct her in it and compel her to some second choice" (II. i. 234–37).

Although his protests reveal that he too considers love a matter of the senses, Brabantio is a better chorus than Iago, a good father to Desdemona, and an eminently reasonable man. Discovering that his daughter "deceives me / Past thought," he describes her marriage as "against all rules of nature" (I. iii. 101), a thing "t' incur a general mock" (I. ii. 69). Confronted with the accomplished fact and assured of her wish, he surrenders her to Othello, whom he has loved, in these terms:

> Come hither, Moor,
> I here do give thee that with all my heart

Which, but thou hast already, with all my heart
I would keep from thee.

(I. iii. 192–95)

Although neither Iago's nor Brabantio's ideas about nature need be taken at face value, the point is significant. Not miscegenation specifically but simply disparity or alienness is the reality that impresses those who surround the elopement. Whatever the source of their feeling, to flout as Othello does both paternal and social authority—the "settled degrees, observances, customs, and laws" whose "confounding contraries" are mere confusion[30]—is, in the very nature of a structured world, to incur dangers. This consulting of his will alone is, in the Scholastic and Shakespearean sense, dubiously and imperfectly natural. Iago, allied with "all the tribes of hell" (I. iii. 362–63) and swearing, like evil itself, by Janus (I. ii. 33), can easily shift the light upon the flaw in the marriage contract, so that the insecure and self-glorifying Othello will see the threat as external to himself.

The degradation of an epic figure in a nightmare of irrational jealousy, the final horror he inflicts on himself in the murder of his innocent wife, the ruin and anguish of nature violated: these fit with the deception of Brabantio as variations upon the theme of domestic disruption. The catastrophe is undeserved by Othello; neither his imprudence nor his (more often recognized) promiscuity of belief merits his ruin. There is again the Aristotelian tragic disproportion between the initiating evil and its consequences, but the events of act I are not to be disregarded in any just interpretation. Like *Romeo and Juliet, Othello* has as one of its themes the revelation of how slight-seeming a failure of moral judgment may allow the power of evil an entrance to human affairs.[31]

In his final speech, Othello reviews the course of the

tragedy from the perspective which he has gained at such terrible cost (and which he need not articulate, since we have seen him learn the truth). In this last of the play's "trial" scenes, he justly convicts himself of loving "not wisely," and of rejecting the greatest good within his grasp;[32] in a faithful reflection of that violation of the law of reason which is the Scholastic image of sin and folly; he is one who "Like the base [Indian] threw a pearl away / Richer than all his tribe" (V. ii. 347–48).

'ANTONY AND CLEOPATRA,' more than the other tragedies, is an achievement of poetry whose unique and irreducible meaning resists discursive re-presentation; here especially the medium "creates what it conveys." In the poetic assimilation of "Nilus' slime," of the "dungy," "riggish," vitality of the animal world to the most exalted possibilities of human experience, it achieves much of its cathartic fruition, a transcendent affirmation of the natural condition. To extract "plot" or "character" from its realization in the imaginative multiplicity of the play's texture, with its weaving of evaluative allusion and connection, is to betray the poetic reality.

There is a strain of gypsy earthiness in Cleopatra, and it is seen from many points of view. She is imaged as a serpent, a "ribaldried hag," a mare, a cow, "a morsel cold upon / Dead Caesar's trencher," as the earth itself, for Caesar "plough'd her, and she cropped." The habitual word-play of Cleopatra and her court (Charmian, Iras, Alexis, and Mardian) is heavy with gross sexual punning. Her running fire of irony upon Antony as romantic lover, the voluptuous abandon of their "gaudy" carousing,—she recalls a session when

> Ere the ninth hour, I drunk him to his bed;
> Then put my tires and mantles on him, whilst

> I wore his sword Philippan
> (II. vi. 21–23)

—these give the play a wider vision than that of the
other tragedies. It encompasses more of our sense of all
that undercuts tragic and romantic elevation, while yet
sustaining the most exalted tragedy and romance, more
real and powerful for its basis in the earth, in a lust-love
imaged in terms of eating and drinking and the earth's
fruitfulness, and in a cool-eyed estimation of political
and martial glory.

Cleopatra's shrewish, unreasonable, intensely human
pettishness with the messenger who announces Antony's
marriage to Octavia (III. iii) is a folly which testifies to
her woman's love and is complemented by Antony's
vacillations and reversals, his bursts of temper and fits
of tenderness. Ventidius' telling revelation about the epic
soldiership of conquering generals (III. i) with its exposure of public greatness, serves, like the steady unmask-
ing of sordidness in the affairs and causes of empire, to
endorse by contrast the personal and human love-values
to which Antony is unwillingly drawn. It is in the presence of a mocking and satiric perception that the emer-
gence of what is genuine and splendid in the love stirs us
most powerfully.

It is understandable that critics within the Victorian
aura should have strained at the intense sensuality
which is of the essence of *Antony and Cleopatra*'s affirmation of life,[33] even more than at the tavern career of
Henry V, which has been explained and dismissed in
various and surprising ways. Hal and Antony share an
important quality in that each has a highly developed
private character and is able clearly to distinguish his
own reality as a man from the official categories he
occupies—from his rank and station and office. This
knowledge frees them from cant and from the delusions

of a Lear, an Othello, or a Brutus. Much of *King Lear* is occupied with the hero's discovery of what it means to be human; the office has devoured the man, as it has, quite differently, in Henry IV. Othello is destroyed partly by the blindness of his monumental conception of himself. With this inability to separate what is official and public from what is genuinely human, it is instructive to compare Prince Hal's sworn brotherhood in "a leash of drawers," his sounding of "the base string of humility," his command, like Antony, of his soldiers' hearts, and his skepticism toward social pieties and the reality of "pomp and circumstance."

Brutus, like Othello, lacks self-recognition; in their destructive innocence these two perpetrate enormities which a simple perception of reality would have exposed. Hal and Antony are freed by their realism to be capable of insights into greatness and rule which we do not find in the other two, or in a Bolinbroke or a Richard II. Both are journeyman soldiers, professionals. (Shakespeare makes Othello a lifelong and expert soldier, but in spirit he is at a polar extreme from the professional.) We hear from other characters of Hal's and of Antony's prowess at war and command; when they comment on their own martial qualities (in each case, while facing likely defeat and estimating their chances) it is with the pride of professionals ("Thou shouldst see / A workman in't"; "warriors for the working day"). They are worldly men, experienced in a sense in which many of the tragic heroes are not. *Antony and Cleopatra* is in fact a love-tragedy of experience, as *Romeo and Juliet* of innocence.

Yet Antony mismanages his life, failing until too late to realize essential truths of his situation; there are human realities to which he remains blind. He sees in Cleopatra both the royal queen and the gypsy harlot which the world sees, but not, until near the end, the real woman. To him she is mostly the temptress, and he reproaches himself, in his "Roman" times, for submitting to an enchantment. Whether we do or not, he accepts as chorus Enobarbus, who consistently voices a Roman view allowing some place to erotic diversion but none at all to sexual love as a commanding value, as a reality involving anything to be placed beside conquest and rule. Antony braces himself to cast off his "strong Egyptian fetters" (I. ii. 120), confesses that "the beds i' th' East are soft" (II. vi. 51), assures himself that "though I make this marriage for my peace, / I' th' East my pleasure lies" (II. iii. 39–40). But the effort to turn his back on dalliance and find again the "real" Roman world, is, as he discovers with slow comprehension, a denial of another reality less public and a set of values less readily definable.

The rhetoric of Antony's earlier protestations of love ("Let Rome in Tiber melt, and the wide arch / Of the rang'd empire fall! Here is my space") is correct to the occasion, *de rigeur* for the courtier and servant who understands what is due to "the love of Love and her soft hours"; Antony is hardly one who would count Rome well lost for anything so ephemeral. Cleopatra genuinely loves him, but understands him perfectly and chooses strategically to accept these terms:

> Excellent Falsehood!
> Why did he marry Fulvia, and not love her?
> [*aside*]
> I'll seem the fool I am not.
>
> (I. i. 40–42)

She is a seductress, and without scruple in the arts she uses on Antony. But they are used in the service of a quite unswerving love; she is never faithless to Antony, although he often thinks so. It is in fact Antony (turned "womanly," as Caesar says) who is false to Cleopatra as to Fulvia. Then in his cynical political union with the "holy, cold, and still" Octavia, he is false to this second wife, to Caesar, and to Cleopatra; false to his obligations toward both love and empire. The aim of Cleopatra's guile is made quite clear; when Charmian advises her "In each thing give him way, cross him in nothing," she replies, "Thou teachest like a fool: the way to lose him" (I. iii. 9–10). This is the legendary enchantress who "makes hungry / Where most she satisfies," so that "Age cannot wither her, nor custom stale / Her infinite variety." Her unhappiness is quite real at the sad paradox presented to her feelings by Antony's response to the death of Fulvia (I. iii. 62–78). She recognizes the irony suffered by those who receive love which betrays someone else: every evidence of passion is an evidence of its impermanence. In her very real grief at Antony's departure, her tongue stumbles and she cannot find words; her turncoat memory, deserting her at need, is "a very Antony" (I. iii. 90).

With Caesar's ambassador Thyreus (III. xiii) her manner ("Go on: right royal") is the one she has used with Antony in the early scenes, the mocking tone with which she entertains performances which it is strategic to hear out, but folly to believe. Her guile as she fences with Thyreus is, as ever, in Antony's service as much as her own. Antony's anger here wrongs her, and she bears it patiently. She has not, as he again believes after a final defeat, "Pack'd cards with Caesar," (IV. xiv. 19) nor sold her lover "to the young Roman boy." It is, in the full rigor of the term, *tragic* that Antony should still so misconceive the human purposes to which she is "cunning past man's thought." His rage drives her to the (typical) subterfuge of feigned suicide: when Antony hears false news of her death, he sees at once that if she is gone, "the torch is out" (IV. xiv. 46). He falls on his sword, and Cleopatra, resolved, as he dies, upon her own

death, pays to his flawed magnificence a peerless tribute
we are made to feel is just:

> Young boys and girls
> Are level now with men; the odds is gone,
> And there is nothing left remarkable
> Beneath the visiting moon.
>
> (IV. xv. 65–68)

The lovers have entered on this final passage of their
lives ripened by experience to a real but incomplete
wisdom, a deliberate and knowing acceptance of the
essential human corporeity, and of some at least of
the possibilities of sexual love. Their error—Antony's
really; Cleopatra knows " 'tis sweating labour / To bear
such idleness so near the heart" (I. iii. 93–94)—is to
think this sexual communion merely frivolous, to think
the realities expressed in the body are not those of the
person. Antony has little inkling that what he must
reckon with is the transcendent power of love. As the
play proceeds, imperial policy shows more and more
tawdry beside this unfolding reality, which is something
quite beyond Antony's confident expectations. He does
indeed "make his will / Lord of his reason." He over-
reaches himself in insult and defiance of Caesar, braves
his enemies with crass folly in his choice of the sea-fight,
and gives visible shape to the womanliness of usurped
judgment in his flight after Cleopatra at Actium: "Experience, manhood, honour, ne'er before / Did violate so
itself" (III. x. 23–24). Cleopatra asks "Is Antony or we in
fault for this?" and Enobarbus, no glosser of her offenses, soberly answers, "Antony only."

Perhaps the Roman world would be well lost for love,
but these are not really alternatives. Antony's self-willed
blindness risks the loss not of love for the sake of the
world or the world for the sake of love, but of essential
humanity by a willful misrule of his relation to both; he

has been false to the business of state partly because of the unforeseen reality of love, and false to love, whose value he learns too late, out of cold policy. Cleopatra claims him for that private, complete, and inviolable domain of personal love which is opposed to "the world," to what E. M. Forster has called in our time "the outer world of telegrams and anger." Her deepest hope is that he come to her "smiling from / The world's great snare uncaught." Antony has not known her or himself well enough to mediate the claims of these two worlds. In fact neither of them, not the grizzled veteran of political and military wars, nor the fabled priestess of Isis, have known fully the demands of their own natures. Against the gloom of his titanic ruin Antony at last perceives the reality of persons, realized in and inseparable from love, which rises free of policy in this twilight. The rhetoric of his earlier protestations assumes now a new ring, a real substance:

> Fall not a tear, I say; one of them rates
> All that is won and lost: Give me a kiss.
> Even this repays me.
> (III. xi. 69–71)

Enobarbus, reckoning that "When valour [preys on] reason, / It eats the sword it fights with," abandons Antony and dies of grief, learning, with Antony, of a reality which transcends the merely politic considerations that can preempt the name of reason. Antony's "huge spirit," deeply flawed and enmeshed in error, struggles free at last. He is possessed by what he thought to possess and use, but there is an enlightenment in the defeat. Cleopatra too, is in her love finally "no more but [e'en] a woman"; the full estate of persons is the noblest of all. She is, most tellingly, "A *lass* unparalleled."

By the compounded (hylomorphic) human essence, love, rooted in mortal flesh, is the act of spirit, timeless and immortal like Cleopatra's longings and the biting of the worm. This is the transcendent vision achieved in the poetry of the final scenes, a glimpse of a possible human greatness learned late and at tragic cost.

THE TRAGIC PATTERN appears in *Richard II* because Shakespeare identifies political order with natural law, as did the medieval tradition,[34] and because the play focuses on Richard as man almost as much as on *respublica* and Richard as ruler: his political failures are so identified with private, human ones that it may be considered in the aspect of tragedy as justly as in that of history.

There is a definite conception of political order throughout the history plays, and of national history as fundamentally a series of disturbances and restorations of that order. This design, says Tillyard, "which in its general outline consisted in the distortion of nature's course by a crime and its restoration through a long series of disasters and suffering and struggles, may indeed be like Shakespeare's scheme of tragedy, but it is genuinely political and has its own right to existence apart from tragedy."[35] Yet it shares with the tragedies a basis in natural law. "In his most violent representations of chaos Shakespeare never tries to persuade us that it is the norm: however long and violent is its sway, it is unnatural; and in the end order and natural law will reassert themselves."[36]

The histories are distinct, however, in that, as political plays,[37] they touch mostly upon a different part of the legal spectrum, an area in which the natural law passes into particular positive applications less immediately determined by the intrinsic constitution of human nature, more contingent on varying historical conditions,[38] and more closely identified with a particular body of beliefs about the hierarchies in nature and

among men. To the degree in which they depend thematically on such matter, these plays must lose effect for
the modern reader or audience.

The most famous sermon in the Elizabethan homily
books, *An Exhortation concerning Good Order, and
Obedience to Rulers, and Magistrates*[39] is echoed in
meaning by Ulysses' famous speech on the principle of
"degree"; it construes that principle as a part of the
natural law, attributing to angels, planets, physical elements, animals, plants, seasons, human faculties and
organs, and to rightly ordered society, the most rigid
hierarchy and subjection to a chief or head. Such rule
was a feature of the natural law in its inexorable government of involuntary agents. It seemed a universal feature of the communal life of men.[40] Christian, Stoic,
Neo-Platonic, and Aristotelian views converged in its
support. It was therefore enjoined in society as an axiomatic inferior of the natural law.[41] A king is not, to this
understanding, an executive enforcing static legal abstractions; as the continually reiterated analogy insists,
he is the head of which the people are the body. He
shares a corporate life, nourishes and is nourished by
and expresses the nature of the community. Like all of
the natural law, the order of the state proceeds from the
individuated nature of the creature it perfects; its universals are particularized in the living body they in-
form.[42] The logicism of a Henry IV, even when his logic
is right, is not enough; rule is not an external manipulation of the state as an object: it involves a communion,
a continual intuiting of the body's experience. Kingship,
as Henry V can learn and his father cannot, is not a
series of strategic problems, but an intimate participation in the nation's life; as he can learn and Richard
cannot, it is neither ceremony nor privilege, but sleep-
less responsibility.

  This is one meaning of the recurrent image of the

state as a human body. In regicide, pronounces Eubulus, the sage counselor of *Gorboduc*, we see "the hand cut off the head." "No parte's sound," says Du Bartas of the state, "if once the Head be sicke." "As the soule is the forme which to the body giveth being, and essence; and the body is the matter which desiringly affecteth his forme," so, says a Jacobean writer, is the ruler to his people, and they to him. And as diseased humors emanating from the head injure the body, unbalanced or unnatural humors secreted in the body will affect the head. In the state there is no "synew" or "vaine" not "replenished with this power," i.e., the king's.[43]

The "politicosm"—the state as organic system paralleling both the human constitution and the ordered universe—is one feature of a thoroughly sacramental world-view in which, as the same teleological principles penetrate creation, operating upon and organizing all the hierarchical levels of existence, lower things and their operations are emblematic of the higher. Every beehive and human body and family and state bears a microcosmic relation, one to the other, and all to the earth and the solar system, so that each lower level is an allegory of the higher ones, and every garden a moral paradigm. A man and a civic community, each a *microcosmus* or *minor mundus*, are morphologically and dynamically congruent.[44] Scholarship now uses the terms "microcosm," "geocosm," and "macrocosm," but could as well coin others to indicate the places in this system of state, family, and vegetable and animal orders. Thus with respect to rule: God in his creation, the sun in the planetary system, reason in each man, the king in the state, the father in the family, the lion among beasts, the eagle among birds, the dolphin among fishes, must exercise an appointed power and dominion if the economy of the whole is to be sustained.

Henry VII, we are told, commanded the execution of

some mastiffs for fighting a lion, and of a hawk for attacking an eagle.[45] "The lion," Falstaff triumphantly reminds us, "will not touch the true prince."[46] As the mind turns in on itself in affliction, so the spider, disturbed, retires to the inmost part of his web, bees fly in stormy weather to the hive, blood returns to the heart in time of danger, and men retire to towns in wartime.[47] The mutually destructive combat of the dragon and the elephant is an image of civil war.[48] From all the phenomena of nature, celestial and mundane, there are moral principles to be learned. In the "unnatural natural history" of *Euphues*, stylistic exploitation of this doctrine may have dwindled into mere rhetorical fantasy, which only the youthful Elizabethan passion for "fine invention"—a passion nourished on the long tradition of *Elocutio*, which reduced poetry to style and style to ornament—could have accepted as a virtuoso performance. But the profoundly thematic metaphor which gives cosmic dimension to Shakespeare's poetry springs from the same philosophic root.

Medieval theory acknowledged not only *allegoria in verbis* (what we would call allegory) but *allegoria in res*, the world and history as allegory, long a fundamental tenet of biblical exegesis,[49] reflected in such products as the *Bestiary*. To St. Augustine the world furnished a symbolic language of God: the moon is a symbol, not merely of fanciful or imputed meaning, of the Church, which reflects God as the moon the sun. The Virgin in medieval lyric is *anima* and *ecclesia*, for soul and church are God-bearers and must "give birth to Christ."[50]

The apprehension of real unity in disparate beings, which would be for Coleridge (on the other side of a mechanistic revolution in thought) the achievement of transcending imagination, lay for the Elizabethans ready-made in the facts of their universe.

This imagery of microcosm and macrocosm manifests a deep sense of the oneness of private and political morality (i.e., human natural law) with the rest of nature; the laws even of the physical world are moral, all things being linked, in a pyramid of subordinations, to the total purpose of creation. When Duncan is murdered, it is "natural" that the sympathetic hierarchies in nature deracinate: "a falcon, tow'ring in her pride of place, / Was by a mousing owl haw'k at and killed." Duncan's horses "eat each other."[51] The two domains are not only analogous, but continuous, parts of a larger order in which they are mutually accommodated and oriented to the same ultimate telos. Timothy Bright speaks, in his *Treatise on Melancholy* (1586), of how disorder in the humors generates "those domestic storms that arise more troublesome and boisterous to our nature than all the blustering winds in the ocean sea."[52] The tempest which rages about Cyprus before the breaking out of the domestic storm in *Othello*, observes Winney, is "no mere literary figure, but a statement of literal similarity: an instance of the sympathetic link which united man with the natural world."[53] Even more impressive are the disturbances in nature reverberating from the human to higher and lower planes in *Julius Caesar* (I. iii. 4–39, 63–68; II. ii. 16–31; V. i. 81–87), in *Hamlet* (I. i. 112–25), in *King Lear* (I. ii. 112–27), and in *Richard II* (II. iv. 8–24).

This teleological hierarchy of creation provided also an objective standard of worth and dignity, so that value was firmly conceived as intrinsic rather than imputed. In Sebonde, in Ralegh's *History*, throughout Elizabethan literature, water is "nobler" than earth, gold higher than brass, ruby more worthy than topaz. Jacobean doubt may assert in Shakespeare's plays that "there is nothing either good or bad but thinking makes it so" (*Hamlet*, II. ii. 255–57), but always in the face of a stronger belief that

... value dwells not in particular will;
It holds his estimate and dignity
As well wherein 'tis precious of itself
As in the prizer.
(*Troilus and Cressida*, II. ii. 53–56)

Yet all the political metaphors of the great chain draw upon the application of natural law to a domain where its tenets were recognized even in the Renaissance as of lesser certainty and universality than the principles of private conduct. Spencer's Aristotelian distinction of *Ethice* from *Politice* (in the letter to Ralegh introductory to the *Faerie Queene*)[54] conveniently separates two areas, in only one of which natural law was felt to be the innate and immediate principle of guidance and sanction. In the other, although natural law was the ultimate basis of all constitutive and regulatory principles in the state, it was not identified with any one system of polity, and it immediately dictated only certain elementary rules of justice and right. "The case of man's nature," says Hooker, "standing therefore as it doth, some kind of regiment the Law of Nature doth require; yet the kinds thereof being many, Nature tieth not to any one, but leaveth the choice as a thing arbitrary."[55] Sir Thomas Smith, prominent in Elizabethan state affairs (he belonged to Elizabeth's Privy Council), wrote in *The Common-Wealth of England* (first published in 1565 as *De Republica Anglorum*) of monarchy, aristocracy, and democracy, and of their possible mixtures, that "all these three kinds of Common-wealths are naturall," and that therefore the one is to be adopted which best suits the character of the people to be governed.[56]

Thus, Sir Robert Filmer was able to defend the doctrine of absolute divine right by an appeal to natural law, and Jean Bodin (cited by Gabriel Harvey as much read at Cambridge) to erect on it a theory of sovereignty which, though it declared a "droit gouvernment" to be one "suivant les lois de la nature" and held the king always bound by natural law, denied to subjects the right to resistance or rebellion under any conditions whatever,[57] whereas Sir Thomas Smith and his pupil John Ponet clearly, although prudently, appeal to it (as did Aquinas) as a basis for the legitimate deposition of a tyrant. According to Aquinas (and to other medieval writers, e.g., John of Salisbury and Manegold of Lautenbach), such a deposition is within the power of those whose delegation of sovereignty has made him king,[58] but must be done in the public interest by public authorities.[59] Smith devotes a chapter to the overthrow of tyrants, cautiously citing only classical instances. He sets down conditions on which deposition may be justified but warns that it is a "doubtful and hazardous matter to meddle with the changing of lawes and government." Ponet restricts himself to examples of regicide from Old Testament and classical sources, but is clear enough about right of deposition (such apostasy from the official Tudor view by an Anglican bishop being explainable by his purpose—to attack the Catholic government of Queen Mary). Robert Parsons, the Jesuit whose dedication of *A Conference about the Next Succession to the Crowne of Ingland* was so embarrassing to the Earl of Essex, could argue against royal succession by blood that it was not prescribed by natural law,[60] while Hooker insisted that "unless we will openly proclaim defiance unto all law, equity, and reason, we must (there is no remedy) acknowledge, that in kingdoms hereditary birth giveth right unto sovereign dominion."[61]

Until the time of Hobbes, virtually all political theory (Machiavelli being the most striking exception) based itself upon traditional natural law. Bacon was unorthodox in admiring Machiavelli because the Italian wrote of "what men do, and not what they ought to do"; because, that is, he had not grounded his study on the prescriptive or normative conception of the natural law, which was still generally admitted as the principle by virtue of which positive law took on its legitimate force.

This founding of social and political order in the natural law had been accepted from classical times. Cicero had written: "Nothing . . . is so completely in accordance with the principles of justice and the demands of Nature (and when I use these expressions I wish it understood that I mean Law) as is government, without which existence is impossible for a household, a city, a nation, the human race, physical nature and the universe itself. For the universe obeys God; seas and land obey the universe, and human life is subject to the decrees of the supreme Law."[62]

Aquinas in the thirteenth century and Hooker in the sixteenth share this judgment. It is of the essential nature of man that he live in society,[63] which is therefore not an arbitrary, but a natural association having, says Hooker, two bases: "The one, a natural inclination whereby all men desire sociable life and fellowship; the other, an order expressly or secretly agreed upon touching the manner of their union in living together."[64]

The natural end of society is to secure the common good.[65] Since this may be sought in different ways, a ruler is needed to direct and coordinate men in the choice of means for pursuing it. Without such rule there would be disorder, and the purpose of communal life could not be achieved.[66] Men therefore subject themselves to government so that "unto whom they granted authority to rule and govern, by them the pease tranquility and happy estate of the rest might be procured,"[67] or as Aquinas says, so that there may be preserved in society "its unity, which is called peace." For "if this is removed, the benefit of social life is lost. . . . The chief concern of the ruler of a multitude, therefore, is to procure the unity of peace."[68]

Sovereignty originates in "the body" of the state and is delegated to the ruler by a contract which has hereditary force.[69] In England, says Hooker, this compact puts the law above the king, so that it is the law which makes the king, rather than the reverse.[70] Thus, the ruler who treats his powers as originating in himself and absolutely his violates natural law, for he breaks a contract arising from the nature of society and binding upon him in reason and justice.

Since the natural principle of government is the common good, to seek one's private interest by rule is contrary to nature. One who rules in his own interest is, says Aquinas, a tyrant, as distinguished from a legitimate king, who is the executor of the law for the common welfare.[71] In medieval political doctrine, according to Gierke, "Rulers are instituted for the sake of peoples, not peoples for the sake of Rulers. Therefore the power of a Ruler is, not absolute, but limited by appointed bounds. His task is to further the common weal, peace and justice, the utmost freedom for all. In every breach of these duties and every transgression of the bounds that they set, legitimate lordship degenerates into tyranny. Therefore the doctrine of the unconditional duty of obedience was wholly foreign to the Middle Age."[72] The great medieval texts on jurisprudence gave "Rules of eternal validity flowing from the very nature of things."[73]

> However many disputes there might be touching the origin of Natural Law and the ground of its obligatory force, all were agreed that there was Natural Law, which, on the one hand, radiated from a principle transcending earthly power, and, on the other hand, was true and perfectly binding Law. . . . And men were also taught that the highest power on earth was

subject to the rules of Natural Law. They stood above the Pope and above the Kaiser, above the Ruler and above the Sovereign People, nay, above the whole community of mortals.[74]

Medieval doctrine was thus "filled with the thought of the inborn and indestructable rights of the individual."[75]

Smith, whose work Hooker probably used, also assumes the natural-law basis of all social and political order, although he does not discuss it explicitly. He refers to Aristotle's dictum on man's natural need for society[76] and warns, like Hooker, that absolute royal power is dangerous to both king and subjects, because of the constitution of human nature.[77] Like Aquinas and Hooker, he defines the natural society or commonwealth as a society of free men "collected together and united by common accord and covenants among themselves, for the conservation of themselves in Peace as in Warre."[78] Again and again, he asserts that only that is a legitimate state where men are freely subject to a power which seeks the common good. He defines a king as one who

> by succession or election cometh with the good will of the people to that Government, and doth administer the Common-wealth by the lawes of the same, and by equitie, and doth seek the profit of the people as much as his owne. A tyrant they name him who by force commeth to the Monarchie against the will of the people, breaketh Lawes alreadie made, at his pleasure, maketh other without the advice and consent of the people, and regardeth not the wealth of his Commons, but the advancement of himselfe, his Faction, his kindred.[79]

According to this refinement of the Scholastic definition of tyranny, one may be a tyrant by accession, rule, and purpose, *Richard II* aptly illustrating the latter two.

Since the existence and the basic functions of government were prescribed by the natural law—God's "second law eternal"—submission to legitimate political authority was an essential part of morality. This aspect of the doctrine was promulgated in Tudor propaganda and preached in the homilies on civil obedience which according to law were read several times a year in Elizabethan churches. The 1574 *Homily Against Disobedience and Wilful Rebellion* vehemently denies to subjects any right to resist even a tyrant; evil kings are God's punishment and must be endured, for it is a "perilous thing to commit unto the subjects the judgement which Prince is wise . . . and which is otherwise: as though the foote must judge of the head; an enterprise very hainous." And rebellion is "worse than the worst government of the worst Prince."[80] Even Hooker maintains that kings are, on earth, "not accountable to any."[81] This opinion is more cautious than consistent, since he has also maintained that no individual person is naturally a ruler, that kingship rests on a social "compact"[82] delegating sovereignty from the body of the state and requiring general consent, and that the king is bound by the Law of Nature.[83] Yet, in the case of a tyrant, so far as his subjects are concerned, "the quarrel is God's." This does not mean that the king's violation of the natural law of the state will "draw no manner of harm after it." The tragic potentiality of natural law remains unaffected by the political doctrine of the subject's nonresistance.

But if the connection of kingship with natural law stood behind the "divinity" of the king's authority, there was, as an almost inescapable corollary, a belief in the appeal which may be had from a tyrant to the higher natural law which is above kings, whose observance is the measure of legitimate kingship, and of which tyranny, or failure to rule in the common interest, is an open violation. The doctrine of lawful deposition of tyrants, found in Aquinas, in Sir Thomas Smith and John Ponet, in Huguenot, Catholic, Anglican, and Puritan political writings,[84] has always the clear implication of a law of natural justice in society, a law above the king and to which he is answerable, as he is to lawful obligations and hereditary covenants arising from it. There were the theorists of the divine right of kings, represented most prominently in the sixteenth century by Jean Bodin, who believed sovereignty to be by nature absolute and liable to no limitation; yet even Bodin held that the king was subject in his actions as ruler to the natural law, and that when he gave to any of his subjects commands which violated it, although they could not rebel, they must disobey and accept the consequences.[85] "A theory of sovereignty in which [positive] law and right became one and in which no right exists except that of the sovereign's creation was held by no one in the sixteenth century."[86]

It is, ultimately, the natural law against which Shakespeare's Richard II destroys himself, by culpable violence done upon the innate constitution of society. The catastrophic consequences witness the operation in political life, as in every human activity, of an intelligible law which is convenient to human nature and whose observance secures the good.

The audience is pointedly reminded of Richard's complicity in the death of Gloucester (I. ii. 1–36). The king unjustly banishes both Bolinbroke and Mowbray in a scene that shows clearly his vacillation and theatrical impulsiveness. In preventing the judicial combat at the last moment, in the arbitrariness of his sentences, in his peremptory shortening a moment later of Bolinbroke's term of exile, he displays the quality of a king to whom the royal imperium is a power to be wielded according to his private will, answerable to nothing beyond himself.

Richard confesses that he has wasted England's wealth in "too great a court," and is "enforc'd to farm [his] royal realm" (II. iv. 44–45). The dying Gaunt, mouthpiece of orthodox political wisdom, pronounces upon this abuse of the nature of rule that England "Is now leased out . . . / Like to a tenement or pelting farm" (II. i. 59–60); and to Richard, within whose crown "a thousand flatterers sit," he declares, "Landlord of England art thou now, not king, / Thy state of law is bond-slave to the law."

Richard rules, then, like Aquinas' tyrant, perverting the state from its natural form as a commonwealth of free men; its laws are administered not for his subjects' good, but to benefit himself. Treating the kingdom as a possession, he has sold those rights in it which are by the nature of society a public trust, and "The Earl of Wiltshire hath the realm in farm" (II. i. 256).

"Since a tyrant," says Aquinas, "despising the common good, seeks his private interest, it follows that he will oppress his subjects in different ways according as he is dominated by different passions to acquire certain goods. The one who is enthralled by the passion of cupidity seizes the goods of his subjects."[87] Upon Gaunt's death, Richard illegally seizes the patrimony of Bolinbroke. York protests:

> Take Hereford's rights away and take from time
> His charters and his customary rights;
> Let not tomorrow then ensue today;
> Be not thyself, for how art thou a king
> But by fair sequence and succession?
>   (II. i. 195–99)

Richard's willful course violates hereditary and contractual rights which rest upon the natural law of society.[88]

After further recital of the tyrannical injustices of the "most degenerate king," Richard's nobles turn to Bolinbroke, who comes home to defend his hereditary right. Hereford can justly claim "I am a subject, / And I challenge law" (II. iii. 133–34); "I come but for mine own" (III. iii. 196 and III. iii. 149), and "If that my cousin king be King of England, / It must be granted I am Duke of Lancaster" (II. iii. 123–24). Yet Gaunt—"time-honoured" exemplar of political rectitude—has earlier refused to punish the murder of his brother Gloucester, since it had been committed by Richard, "God's substitute, / His deputy annointed in His sight." Northumberland has, possibly before the seizure of the Lancastrian estates, heard news of Bolinbroke's armed return, for he speaks of it in the scene which sees Gaunt's death and the king's announcement of his intent. This is a bit more difficult to accept as a dramatic foreshortening, significant only to an overliteral reading, than, for instance, the merely convenient inconsistencies of *Othello's* double time-scheme.

There begins with Bolinbroke's return an inevitable shifting of sympathy away from him, as he faces the need and grasps the opportunity for usurpation, which, even when demanded by justice, is seen as a terrible necessity, usually done evily and with evil effect in the state. Such is the feeling for the sacredness of royalty (quite another thing from "divine right"). Once the office is submitted to any process of seizure, for however good a cause, it becomes an object of ambition, and this perverts the very nature of the civil body. Deposition produces unrest, strife, and deposition, the political order passing into the keeping of wolves rather than shepherds. Even the justly deposing king is driven to tyranny, like Henry, in order to escape domination by those whose power has advanced him, and in order to secure himself from partisans of the old regime.

York's horror at the attempt "to find out right with wrong," his insistence that "the quarrel is God's," his loyalty to his nephew the king, whom he has rebuked in the same terms Bolinbroke now uses to justify rebellion; the Bishop of Carlisle's denunciation of those who would give sentence on God's anointed deputy, his solemn prophecy of the horrors to follow; these cloud Bolinbroke's right and bespeak the terror of deposition.[89] Richard himself, as he assumes the character of victim and martyr, repeatedly paralleled with Christ, makes the play's fullest statements of the holiness of kingship (e.g., III. iii. 72–100) and foresees the civil discord to be unleashed when the crown is made the creature of power (V. i. 55–68).

It is about these political issues that the conflict turns, but Richard's role has also the tragic focus on character as the root of destiny. He has acted, like Romeo, from a feckless self-will which shakes off counsel and prudence and has its way at all costs. Connected with his domination by impulse and feeling is his gift, again like Romeo's, for amazing lyric flights. He is incapable of the considered and firm judiciousness which kingship demands.[90] He protects himself with dreams and words, and the play has scenes of tumultuous rhetoric accompanied by little action. Such is the deposition scene at Flint Castle, and the even more revealing one of Richard's return from Ireland to the Welsh coast (III. ii). Here the king veers wildly from an overweening assurance grounded upon his nonrational conception of kingship (4–26, 36–62), to dejection (79–81), again to an unreal exaltation, finally to the abandoned despair of "For God's sake, let us sit upon the ground / And tell sad stories of the death of kings" (III. ii. 155–56). Faced with the inescapable facts of "the sick hour that his surfeit made," Richard struggles to find reality. Does the "divinity" of a king make him magically impregnable, or is all royal pomp mockery? Neither is true, but Richard asks the question too late. He has lacked the rational discipline which lives with reality and truth. This unnaturalness has led him to a reckless flouting of fundamental justice and prudence, of his own nature and the nature of society.

The evils treated in the play are specifically political (the moral is stated by Marlowe in *Edward II:* "Mis-governed Kings are cause of all this wrack"),[91] but it is not merely their explanation by political doctrine through which we are led to acquiesce in the outcome. The political issues are instrumental to the moral ones. Richard's faults as king have to do with necessities of governing so fundamental that they are felt as part of the nature of things, not merely as positive laws. Justice is an intrinsic necessity, and it is the order of nature against which the partly sympathetic figure of the hero opposes itself.

Richard's luxuriant emotional self-indulgence gives us a potent impression of the will ordered to the self as its highest end, the very type of unnatural and dangerous action, to the medieval view. Aquinas' account of the origin of moral evil can serve as a description of Richard's career: Sin is "adherance to a mutable good," and evil originates in excessive desire for the temporal.[92] One desires a temporal good inordinately because "he loves himself inordinately." Self-love is therefore the ultimate principle of sin.[93] The object of the rational will is good,[94] and "evil, which consists in a certain privation, has a deficient cause," in that "the natural rule fails, which man, in accord with his nature, ought to observe."[95] The inordinate self-lover who prefers the lesser good may choose spiritual evil and may even sin through "certain malice."[96] But "evil cannot be intended by anyone for its own sake," although "it can be intended for the sake of avoiding another evil or obtaining another good."[97] The evildoer is usually moved by "sensible experience" which "doth oversway" reason.[98]

Richard's monstrous self-love and its consequences in the moral-political order, his fascination with his own image, fitly pointed by his demand for a looking-glass in the scene of his final deposition, his wanton clutching at the immediate good which excites his imagination—at pleasure, glory, power—are obvious. The emptiness in his character, the hollow absence of manhood and substance, perhaps merely regrettable in another station, visibly cause the political disasters which are the issue of evil or unnaturalness in the state.

THE SHAKESPEAREAN plays, then, manifest everywhere a faith in natural law, a faith too deep, usually, to be a subject of conscious or overt treatment. They present evils and suffering men, but never meaningless evils nor essentially insignificant nor morally helpless men; never men unfitted for survival in the natural world by their possession of a virtue and nobility alien to that world, as in the plays of Chapman, Marston, Webster, Fletcher, or Ford, where often "Nature against virtue cross doth fall, / Or virtue's self is oft unnatural."[99]

Shakespearean tragedy displays not a "poetic" justice, distributing mundane reward for virtue and punishment for wickedness, but a profound revelation that the nature of the world is good and that the moral laws to which men are subject are dictated by the constitution of things as we know them, are never contrary to that constitution or to men's own natures, as in the Calvinist and voluntarist world of much Jacobean drama, and are never intrinsically inexplicable. Evil is unnatural, and man's highest virtues profoundly natural to him. Suffering yields a reconciling assurance by the meaningful form into which it is set. This theoretic form is quite different from that of other and especially later Jacobean plays, and the difference is not one of degree only, but of kind, arising from the pattern of Scholastic belief in a unified cosmic moral order based on the reason of God, not on the arbitrary and incomprehensible will of God, as was the moral law of most later Jacobean belief.

Chapter Three　　　Medieval
Origins: The
Philosophical
Basis of the
Tragic Pattern

THE ELIZABETHAN concep-
tion of the natural law came from medieval Scholasticism. It is therefore worth demonstrating that Scholastic philosophy survived as a fundamental influence in
the Renaissance. This will mean, in part, attention to the
superficiality of Renaissance Platonism, whose role has
been unduly magnified. It may be useful, too, to notice
some persistent misconceptions of Scholastic thought
which can still impede historical criticism. Finally, and
most important, some outline is needed here of the
basic Scholastic tenets upon which rested the doctrine
of the natural law. If these foundations are brought into
view, the significance of later philosophical developments will easily be appreciated.

Walter C. Curry, although he does not make the connection here suggested between the medieval world-view and the reconciling power of the greatest Elizabethan tragedy, has demonstrated the thoroughgoing Scholasticism of *Macbeth*, a play which is, he believes, a mirror of the Aristotelian synthesis which had long dominated European thought.[1] He also finds Scholasticism in Hooker, in Davies and Shakespeare, in Walton, Pico, Bruno, Vives. Much of what we recognize as Scholastic doctrine, he reminds us, was simply fact, self-evident truth to Renaissance men hardly aware of alternatives. Humanist vilifiers of the medieval "hog-doctors," repudiating what they attributed to the schools, often stood on a platform which was itself, in our perspective, Scholastic, and fought with Scholastic weaponry.

Alfred Harbage agrees that the medieval tenets of Hooker (whose *Laws of Ecclesiastical Polity* he calls "the best of English explanations" of the traditional doctrines) were diffused in the Renaissance by the "very habits of speech of schoolmasters, local magistrates, and some of the preachers. A wealth of allusion in the later popular plays argues a general familiarity with the idea that man was the central figure in an orderly, beautiful, and divinely planned universe. The salient fact was that it was a universe of law, not of chance or brute force."[2]

The Aristotelian tradition, says Kristeller, "continued strongly and vigorously to the end of the sixteenth century and even later. . . . During the fifteenth and sixteenth centuries, university instruction in the philosophical disciplines continued everywhere to be based on the works of Aristotle."[3] Glanville's attack on "the modern *Aristotelianism*, which yet obtains in most of the schools of *Christendom*"[4] testifies to the persistence of Scholastic influence at the universities. Milton protests the "assinine feast of sowthistles and brambles,"[5] the "monkish and miserable sophistry" served up to students there, which has, he says, left "a scholastical bur in their throats," and "cracked their voices for ever with metaphysical gargarisms."[6] His famous reference to Spenser as "a better teacher than Scotus or Aquinas" implies, after all, the magisterial place still held by the latter two (although, in view of the self-perpetuating nature of academic disciplines, this survival as curriculum might by itself prove little).

Daniel, in his *Defense of Rhyme,* does nothing startling or original when he praises Aquinas as a profound theologian and Scotus as a logician of unrivaled acuteness. The Thomistic proofs of the existence of God "were used by Renaissance apologists of all creeds."[7] Of the original "Oxford Reformers," only Colet did not revere Aquinas, and Colet's hostility to Scholasticism was based largely on his opinion of the Scotists, insofar as it was not simply an antirationalistic hostility to philosophy itself.[8] Both More and Erasmus held St. Thomas in high esteem.[9] *Encomion Moriae* satirically roasts Scholastic niggling over, for example, the formal, material, efficient, and final causality of baptism; but Erasmus, too, is after the Scotists, the Scholastic decadence. There was no real abandonment of the basic medieval inheritance.

The Renaissance broadening of intellectual activity had carried the inherited philosophical ideas further than ever before into the general consciousness and toward artistic assimilation. At the same time, some of those ideas had gained in definition by being measured against opposing views.

There is still a temptation, however, to label as "Platonic" or "Neo-Platonic" many things in Renaissance literature which, as common property of European thought, are more reasonably referred to the eclectic, but basically Aristotelian, Scholasticism into which they had long been assimilated. A recent study points out in the *De Planctu Naturae* of Alanus de Insulis the "Platonic notion" that "Nature is herself responsible for man's moral nature, as well as for the stability and continuity of the created universe; in other words, that reason is *natural* to man, and that the demands of one part of his nature do not conflict with those of another."[10] The presence in Alanus' work of Boethian influence (and Boethius was an Aristotelian as well as a Platonist) and of a Plotinian element acquired through Proclus may be firmly established, but if this conception of nature must be considered Neo-Platonic, so must Scholasticism itself, permeated by the same belief. The doctrine is essentially more congenial to Scholastic hylomorphism than to any form of idealism.

In the degree that Platonic thought remains consistent with its own essential monism, a view of nature embracing harmoniously both the spiritual and the sensate or corporeal is intrinsically hostile to it. The body really is to Platonism the prison of human nature: the denigration of matter which accompanies the Platonic celebration of man as a spirit and of knowledge as a direct apprehension of intelligible forms, a reaching beyond the obscuring sensate world to a realm of pure and subsistent universal ideas, carries always a latent Manicheanism. Plotinus, it is true, protested the extreme *contemptus mundi* of the Christian gnostics, but like all Platonists he regarded the soul's "descent" into the body as a lessening of its power and freedom. Plato's hostility to art, that reflection of reflections which leads men to the earthly and from the real, expresses truly the idealistic repugnance for the mundane.[11] The latent Platonic affinity with Cathar world-hatred, obviously congenial to Calvinism, is made clear in such a figure as Origen, a Christian Platonist who saw human corporeity as the punishment for original sin. St. Augustine himself never lost a quasi-Manichean attitude toward corrupted nature, and his Platonism was serviceable in accommodating it, as it was in providing an epistemology of innate and intuitive truths which bypassed the senses.

Many ideas genealogically Platonic are more significantly Scholastic. Comprehending Platonic elements assimilated not only from its Augustinian inheritance but from such sources as the Neo-Platonized Arabian Aristotelianism upon which it drew so fruitfully, Thomistic Scholasticism is quite certainly the main philosophic force of the later Middle Ages and early Renaissance. The medieval definition of evil as privation is, for instance, originally Stoic and Platonic, but it is misleading to call it so in any implied distinction from Thomism. It is true that astonishingly heterogeneous things, variously derived from Plato's earlier or later dialogues, or from eclectic "middle" Platonism or Neo-Platonism, have been called Platonic.[12] To some Elizabethans, as to some of the quattrocento Florentines of the first Platonic Renaissance, Platonism was a system of demonology.[13] To some it was a syncretic esoteric wisdom gathering in from Pythagorean, Orphic, Cabalistic, Hermetic, and other occult sources a body of arcane myth, magic, and symbolism,[14] all of which certainly occupied the Renaissance literary imagination, but is hardly to be thought of as supplanting the systematic and interlocking structure of Scholasticism, which undergirded the very universe of European thought.

Lorenzo's words in *The Merchant of Venice,*

> There's not the smallest orb which thou behold'st
> But in his motion like an angel sings,
> Still quiring to the young-eyed cherubins,
>
> (V. i. 60–62)

once annotated by references to directly Platonic sources, now seem more probably an echo of the angel lore of Dionysius, transmitted by Thomas Aquinas.[15] C. S. Lewis even concludes that there is no "real" or philosophical Platonism in Renaissance love poetry.[16] It is a long time since historians were able to discover Platonism not only in those places in Donne, Drummond, Spenser, and Sidney where it really appears (although often as a Plotinian mythology rather than as the influence of systematic philosophy), but in the most centrally Scholastic ethical and psychological doctrines. Yet some of the tendency survives. Spenser's teaching that the rational soul ought properly to rule the irascible and concupiscible powers has quite recently been labeled a "Platonic doctrine"—taxonomically like calling the Anglican Church Eleusinian because the Greeks employed a ritual washing. Other Renaissance commonplaces (the union in knowledge of the knower and the known, goodness as a transcendental property of being and God as absolute goodness, the process of abstraction in ideogenesis) are still called Platonic, evidently in lingering reluctance to recognize the historic place of Scholasticism, into which they had long since been absorbed.

Some Renaissance Platonism is actually medieval realism (Augustinian and ultimately Platonic in its beginnings), the dominant pre-Thomistic philosophy in which universals were held to have extra-mental existence. Such a view prevailed at least through the time of Anselm, meeting its first nominalist attack in the (now lost) work of Roscelin of Compiegne and in the quasi-nominalist "conceptualism" of Abelard. This was Wycliff's position, Luther and Calvin turning to the opposite (nominalist) extreme. In the Renaissance, the realistic tradition merged again with Platonism, influencing both Descartes and the Cambridge Platonists.[17]

For instance, much of the Platonism in Donne's poems is merely grist to an analogy-mill, which uses equally Scholasticism, the new science, Petrarchan con-vention, and classic myth. Platonic thought is alluded to, revolved critically, analogized; rarely is the meaning of the whole poem Platonic. In the drama, too, Plato-nism is ordinarily the contained, a Scholastic universe the container. Hamlet's vow of love "while this machine is to him," Lorenzo's reference to "this muddy vesture of decay" whose relation to the soul is simply that it "doth grossly close it in" (*The Merchant of Venice*, V. i. 61–65), perhaps even Donne's declaration that our bod-ies "are ours, though they are not wee" ("The Extasie," 1. 51), are largely dramatic, and do not express a view which organizes whole plays or constitutes, in poems, any total philosophical statement. This Platonic-Mani-chean "spirituality" is mostly a convenient romantic hyperbole.

If we admit all the *Renaissance* meanings of the label, there is some justice in the tendency to find Platonism wherever there is a mythic, "poetic," or "spiritual"—in short, an imaginative rather than a rational—interpreta-tion of the world. But this sort of Platonism belongs to the history of sensibility and of confused terminology rather than of philosophic thought. Much of Renais-sance Platonism is superficial. Platonic tradition may illuminate themes and images in Renaissance poetry,[18] but the understanding thus gained of, for instance, the love theme in *Romeo and Juliet* should not be allowed to obscure the more obvious, more basic, Scholastic ortho-doxy of the play in its conception of natural law.

Renaissance Platonism has, then, surely been exagger-ated, but the false separation of medieval and Renais-sance thought has also included an underestimation of the Platonic strain in the enduring twelfth- and thir-teenth-century synthesis, into which it had found many avenues. The influence of such teachers as Origen, Clem-ent, Augustine, Dionysius, Bernard of Clairvaux, and

John Scotus Erigena was never wholly lost. Paul Kristeller points out that Platonism "remained a powerful
current even during the later middle ages."[19] Early Neo-
Platonism had adopted a great deal of systematic Aristotelian thought; Porphyry's treatise on Aristotle's *Categories* became "almost an integral part of the Aristotelian
corpus," and this chapter in Neo-Platonic history "left
profound traces in the later history of Aristotelianism."[20] Ficino, the editor of Plato and Plotinus, quotes
Aristotle more often than Plato,[21] and Aquinas more frequently than any other medieval writer.[22] Kristeller attributes the "strongly medieval, scholastic character
which we notice in [Ficino's] works" to his training at
the University of Florence, and observes that his use of
"Materia," "Forma," and "Privatio" comes from Aristotle's *Metaphysics*. What Ficino evidently dreaded was
the "hard" Averroistic Aristotelianism which threatened
to split faith from reason. Even Pico, despite his syncre-
tism and his fascination with the Plotinian emanation-
ism of the Cabala, was, inescapably, at bottom a Scholastic.[23]

Despite both the Platonic prejudice and the surviving
influence of the "Renaissance myth," a great deal has
been done in recent years to illuminate the medieval
elements in Elizabethan literature. Yet Scholasticism is
still not always justly treated by literary scholarship.
Between those who preserve the prejudices of Michelet
and those, like C. S. Lewis, whose medieval enthusiasms
lead them to see more of "new ignorance" than "new
learning" in the Renaissance,[24] there still reaches a wide
spectrum of opinion. Basil Willey's deservedly well-
known study of the seventeenth century gives a moderate view, finding both good and evil in the decline of
Scholasticism, yet calls the medieval belief that heavenly bodies are unalterable and incorruptible "metaphysically" true, but empirically false.[25] This relativism

is Michelet's deprecation in the disguise of tolerance. The medieval theory is metaphysically neither true nor false; it is not a metaphysical proposition but a physical and empirical one. Other much-cited examples of Scholastic thought have to do not with medieval philosophy, but with the opinions of medieval philosophers about matters of physical cosmology, an area where they lacked both data and method, and in which their staunchest defenders do not suggest that they achieved much of value.[26] Mistaken ideas about stars and planets are metaphysically indifferent—metaphysically *possible* if they involve no contradictions. To interpret differently the relation of astronomy to metaphysics is not only to discredit medieval metaphysics but to misconstrue the meaning of metaphysics itself.

Literary historians sometimes, as I have said, equate the metaphysical with the mythical, the religious, or even the imaginative. But Scholastic ontology was not like this. Aquinas' commentary on Aristotle's metaphysics assures us that the Schoolmen distinguished the study of "being as such," prescinding from all material conditions. Such was the definition of metaphysics from Andronicus of Rhodes to Suarez. Aquinas, says Father D'Arcy, "distinguished clearly in his own mind the provinces of physics and metaphysics, and of the possibly passing value of the former."[27] His errors regarding "heavenly bodies," following Aristotle's, were based on misinformation about stars, which led him to think that astronomy could be conducted on metaphysical principles. This makes nonsense of his astronomy but does not impugn the metaphysical principles.

Willey notes that the usual medieval comment upon the regular physical motions of bodies was simply to refer them to their final causes, that is, to the end to which each thing is ordained in the generally purposive economy of the universe.[28] The implication, however, that attributing final causes to all things contradicts or excludes any recognition of material, efficient, and formal causality is less than generous in dealing with the age which developed these Aristotelian concepts. Bacon levels such a charge repeatedly; coming from one who is immediately engaged in overturning the reiterative Scholastic decadence, it is reasonable enough. We, however, have the advantage of a longer perspective. It is rather hard that the Scholastics should be condescended to for this teleological naivete, while scholarship honors Emerson for realizing, six centuries later, that scientific knowledge of efficient, formal, and material causes provides, in Whitehead's words, "no reason in the nature of things why portions of material should have any physical relations to each other," and that some answer to the question Why?—some concept of the interrelated *purposes* of all motions—may be necessary to render reality intelligible.[29]

In our own time, the work of Teilhard de Chardin, whatever the validity of his conclusions, demonstrates the renewed possibility, for even the most scientifically sophisticated mind, of a world-view in some ways very like the medieval and pre-Cartesian one. Subatomic physics reveals that the contours of the world of ordinary perception disappear at the level of the electron, that "the stuff of which all stuff is made [is] reducible in the end to some simple and unique kind of substance."[30] There appears therefore more than ever an "essential difference between a natural whole and the elements into which it is analysed"[31] so that mechanistic explanations declare their inadequacy. Since "some natural function really does link the mega-molecular to the micro-organic,"[32] the continuity principle of the "great chain of being" is reborn. Teilhard's treatment of evolutionary processes restores to a degree of scientific respectability something very similar to the Schoolmen's conception of natural "virtues."[33] It certainly recovers teleology as an essential complement of science and goes behind Cartesian mind-body dualism to restore a Scholastic continuity of animal instinct and human thought, a thing impossible in the Augustinian-Platonic-Cartesian tradition and achievable in recent centuries only by a thoroughgoing materialism. The nub of Teilhard's thought, which has assimilated the relevant achievements of post-Cartesian science, is the restoration not only of a teleologically conceived earth, but of a quite literal, if scientifically complicated, hylozoism and animism.

The earlier idea of a *living* earth, of the breathing, semivolitional geocosm which was the world "of Aristotle, of Ptolemy, of Augustine and Dante, of Shakespeare,"[34] is closely related to that of a purposefully functioning earth, guided by an end, if not by its own conscious intent. This is the world whose destruction at the hands of Kepler, Brahe, Galileo, et al. seems after Teilhard not quite so irreversible.

"The Scholastic heritage," says Curry, survived in the Renaissance

> as the primary groundwork of traditional cognition. Here was a vital body of doctrines and ideas skillfully built into a complex intellectual system, which in the Middle Ages had served universally as the foundation of social institutions, political theories, and religious faith. It exerted such a unifying effect upon mediaeval life and activity that the attitudes which it created became, as it were, communal; its essential principles were axiomatic. Learned men and the masses alike, shared, according to capacity, in the common fund of knowledge, were actuated by the same modes of thought, and came to *assume* the validity of the scholastic *Weltanschauung*. For almost eleven centuries this knowledge, these modes of thought, this way of life had been in process of shaping the very character

and conscience of Western peoples. Thus cognition became so traditional that in a sense it may be said to have been congenital.

How then, should the humanistic period hope to escape the discipline of eleven medieval centuries?[35]

And Curry concludes that in fact "the scholastic deposit represented the stable point from which all excursions were made; it was the intimate standard by which values of the new learning were consciously or unconsciously measured. It was the foundation upon which were erected more outlandish super-structures—both pagan and Christian—but it was nevertheless still sound and ineradicable. It had become, in short, the primary groundwork of cognition."[36]

Some historians maintain that the medieval philosophy was intricate, artificial, and brittle—"a frail bridge of reason" across the universe—and that it could not outlive the Renaissance shift in emphasis. Farnham, although he has revealed many medieval strains in Elizabethan literature, thinks Scholasticism at best was a "precarious balance" between extremes, which could not survive changes in the institutional system in which it was created.[37] Yet, Aristotelian Scholasticism gave an interpretation of experience which, unlike Platonism, denied none of the normal, infraphilosophical, human assumptions about reality.

Near the heart of Scholasticism, central to the varying "Scholasticisms" of Siger of Brabant, of Albertus and Aquinas, of Abelard, Roscelin of Compiegne, and Scotus, and, in the Elizabethan years, of Suarez,[38] lay the hylomorphic theory of matter and form as the complementary principles of all physical beings. This was a theory which defended the objective validity of knowledge by defending the reality of substances, i.e., entities subsisting rather than inhering in a subject, as do accidents or properties,[39] and of their persisting identities, as really continuous despite and throughout material changes in them. That either idealism, which solved the problem by denying the material world, or materialism, which solved it by denying the truth of ordinary cognition, is more congenial than this hylomorphic realism seems doubtful. Farnham grants that Scholasticism is "heroic in its effort at justification of evil and pain" and alien to "thorough-going contempt of the world," that it insists "upon a meaning always lying behind the order of life" and is "very near indeed to the Aeschylean acceptance of that world as caught up into a universal scheme of justice." Yet he believes still that its basic hylomorphism is a

> precarious balance where spirit and matter, or good and evil, are always threatening to destroy each other and can be kept from doing so only by a philosophy which seems to the true idealist or the true materialist an utterly unsatisfactory patchwork. Thus, Thomistic Christianity in abandoning the ascetic integrity of Augustinian Neo-Platonism was deserting a secure fortress to fight in dangerous open country. It was exposing itself to, even using the methods of, a force which was fated to grow stronger, to cause desertion from the religious ranks, and eventually to find its own logical integrity in materialistic monism.[40]

Of the two principles into which hylomorphism holds that all substances can be analyzed, matter is potential, wholly indeterminate, not existing apart from substances, in which it is informed and determined by form. Form is that which makes a thing to be what it is, determines its quiddity or essence and constitutes it of its kind or species, but does not determine its individuality (unless one was a Scotist). The Scholastics in this way laid the basis for their solution of the problem of substantial change (of one kind of thing into another, as of a body after death) by postulating the persisting substratum of a "prime" matter, potential of successive forms,[41] thus avoiding the necessity of an appeal to continual annihilation and creation of really distinct substances.

More important here, on this hylomorphic basis the Scholastic solved for his time the central problem of knowledge, the problem of universals (although nominalism and realism divided the period as to exactly which hylomorphic solution was correct). All members of a species are constituted such by identical "form" or essential nature. The universal term and idea—"man," "dog," "stone"—is thus univocally true of every member of the species it names, by virtue of a formal and essential identity; true equally and in the same sense, although the singular things are not therefore identical, but only identical in essence.

So from the total reality of an individual, the "active intellect" through the senses abstracts and comprehends that which makes the individual to be of its kind, prescinding from its accidental qualities. The potency of the "possible intellect" is informed by the specific forms of things, as is the potency of matter (although of course immaterially).[42] Disengaging the intelligible forms from the data of the senses, the mind in its unchanging universal concepts thus truly knows the changing and particular things of the outer world.[43] "From their grosse *matter*," says Davies, "she abstracts the *formes*" or "universall / kinds" (*Nosce Teipsum*, Vol. I, p. 43). Plato, having discovered the universality of concepts, says Aquinas, postulated the world of Ideas to establish the possibility of knowledge by providing appropriate objects of cognition.[44]

To the Scholastics the rational soul was the human form, the body the informed material principle, and the person an irreducible compound of the two. Human nature was a fusion of the animal and spiritual, and the soul separated from the body not in a natural state.[45] St. Augustine had disseminated a Platonic conception of the person involving a very different hylomorphism of the soul, which was to the Augustinian school not the form of the person but the person itself, an independent spiritual entity open to direct "illumination," perceiving the divine "ideas" by an inner light, the relation of soul to body being hardly more than occasionalistic. Scholastic hylomorphism effectively cut off the possibility of any such "illumination" or direct apprehension of the intelligible by making the soul dependent on the body in the processes of knowledge, as, indeed, in all its operations.[46]

The "accidental qualities which constitute individuality—the *"haecceitas"* or "thisness" of the singular—were to the Scholastic no less real, but were not due to its specific form. Aquinas thus preserved essential identity in members of a species without the disregard of individual subsistence which the nominalists feared. Duns Scotus, on the other hand, in saving the reality of individual men, destroyed in effect any meaningful concept of "humanity."[47] Even to Aquinas, the problem of individual reality required a series of subtle distinctions. Without bodies there could be no human individuals, but "it does not at all follow that it is from the body that the dignity of the individual derives, or even that it is the body that defines his originality." Matter individualizes, but "once individualized, it is the form which is individual";[48] and it is "signate" matter which individualizes, "common" matter belonging to the species.[49] Briefly, for the Scholastic, the nature which is "universal" does exist in outer reality. But in its abstracted state, from which the individuating qualities which accompany it in things outside the mind are excluded, it is found only in the mind.

William of Ockham (1300–1349) and the nominalists held, on the contrary, that the universal is only a "name" and has absolutely no extra-mental reality; nothing exists but particulars. Universal terms refer solely to mental concepts and are no more than convenient substitutes, each one for a collection of radically differing individual realities. Universals are fictional labels which help us to catalog our apprehensions.[50] Both Luther and Calvin were to profess themselves ardent Ockhamists, and the consequences of their nominalism for English thought were to be momentous.

Indeed, the stand taken on this problem of universals is critical to the question of a natural law in anything like the Scholastic and Shakespearean sense, for if there is no "form" or nature common to all members of a species, there can be no such natural law. Ockham's teachings, says Rommen, "split the Scholastic doctrine of natural law to its very core. . . . the so-called Reformers had drawn the ultimate conclusion from Ockhamism with respect to theology . . . thereby the traditional natural law became speculatively impossible."[51]

Scholasticism, then, affirmed the truth of ideas and above all the reality of substances with definite natures, having definite functions and characteristic modes of perfection or of realizing the specific potentialities of their natures, and therefore having laws or innate necessities of activity. A man, as a true and distinct substance, whose form was the rational soul,[52] had such a substantial nature, and therefore had law governing his (free) activity.[53]

This essence or nature, determined by the substantial form which makes a thing to be what it is, controls internal structure and defines both needs and potentialities. In living things, it manifests itself as the directing principle of growth, development, and operation. It is expressed in connatural inclinations[54] directed toward that perfection of which the creature is naturally capable, and toward the necessary means of achieving this perfection. Thus, a tree preserves and perfects itself by turning its roots into the earth and its leaves to the sun and the air. To do so constitutes its "virtue."[55]

Goodness is to this system an analogous concept, referring to different qualities in each kind of substance to which it is applied. What is good in a thing is that which represents the perfection of its particular nature. Law, too, partakes of what the metaphysicians called the analogy of being, an analogy of proper proportion, according to which each thing embodies in a differing way a universal principle which is, abstractly considered, the same in all. In man the thrust toward perfection, which is identical with the desire for happiness, must be directed to some exercise or attainment of the intellectual and voluntary faculties which make him human. Some of these basic inclinations, from which may be derived the essential dictates of natural law, are the desires to exist or to preserve one's life, to be happy, to live in society (which leads to certain basic political laws), and to know truth and exercise the will in government of one's own actions.[56] These tendencies of nature are ordered, Aquinas concludes, not only to the perfection of the individual, but to that of the human community. Such ordering as it originally existed in the mind of God is the Divine Law. Its embodiment in human reason is the natural law.[57]

Man knows connaturally, then, that he should seek happiness, preserve his life, join in sexual union, live in community, and use his powers of reason and will in governing his acts. Certain conditions attach to these acts because without them the purposes of the natural inclinations cannot be realized; ungoverned sexual union and unreasonable (unjust) use of external possessions or of one's mental powers are unnatural and evil.[58]

Natural law also prescribes, generally, justice, truth, and good faith. It does not change, but the ultimate ends to which the inclinations of human nature are ordered may be differently secured under differing conditions: to refuse to restore goods to their owner may rightly follow from the inclination to exercise reason and judgment, if they would thus be restored to a "betrayer" for the purpose of "fighting against [his] country."[59]

"A law," says Aquinas, "is a dictate of practical reason." And as a law implies an order to an end, the Divine Reason, foreknowing all things, conceives their ordination to Himself as the end or purpose of all. This raises for Aquinas the objection that there may be little law in man, because he is governed sufficiently by the eternal law. He answers with an argument concluding "now among all others, the rational creature is subject to Divine providence in the most excellent way, in so far as it partakes of a share of providence, by being provident both for itself and for others. Wherefore it has a share of the Eternal Reason, whereby it has a natural inclination to its proper act and end. And this participation of the eternal law in the rational creature is called the natural law."[60] Subrational animals "partake in their own way of the Eternal Reason, but because the rational creature partakes thereof, in an intellectual and rational manner, therefore the participation of the eternal law in the rational creature is properly called a law since a law is something pertaining to reason. . . . Irrational creatures, however, do not partake thereof in a rational manner, wherefore there is no participation of the eternal law in them, except by similitude."[61] This semiexclusion of the merely instinctive or physical from natural law shows how profound is the difference of the pre- and post-Baconian, pre- and post-Calvinistic meanings of "nature" and "natural law." Aquinas' meanings are almost exactly the reverse of the modern ones; the scientific conception of natural law as a description of some regularity in the behavior of the physical world is only distantly related to this Thomistic conception.

The first precept of natural law, says Aquinas, flows from the "habit" or inclination of the practical intellect called "synderesis,"[62] and it dictates that "good is to be done and ensued, and evil is to be avoided. All other precepts of the natural law are based upon this: so that whatever the practical reason naturally apprehends as man's good (or evil) belongs to the precepts of the natural law as something to be done or avoided."[63] In general principles, then, the natural law is the same for all; in particular precepts, it varies with respect to individuals and to circumstances.[64] This belief implies what has been called an

> essential point in any discussion of natural law . . . the revolution which Aquinas worked in the entire conception. This revolution, it is true, was soon stifled by the advent of nominalism and a horribly decadent logicism, and was lost sight of in the narrowness of the Counter-Reformation. Its originality was precisely the rescuing of the focal point of natural law from the innate eternal laws of Plato, and the placing of the focus—with all the risk this entails—in the deep hunger of the individual, personal intelligence for full growth to free, interiorized consciousness.[65]

Hugo Grotius, whose *De Jure Belli et Pacis* is sometimes reputed to inaugurate an age of natural-law thinking, denies this Thomist flexibility to the natural law, conceiving it rather as a rigid pattern imposed from without, as it was conceived by some Renaissance Stoicism. With St. Thomas, says Rommen, "teleology, the doctrine of ends or final causes, enters the scene. The essences of things . . . constitute at the same time the end or goal of the things themselves. The perfection or fulfillment of the things is their essence."[66] Aquinas, by right reason, *recto ratio*, refers not only to an abstract logic, as do eighteenth-century appeals to "reason," but to a right way, a right disposition of the total nature. "The possibility of ethics, according to St. Thomas," says a modern Scholastic, "reverts ultimately to the possibility of man's grasping in his experience his basic tendency toward his ultimate end . . . any ethical judgment is demonstrably valid only insofar as it can be shown to be an expression of what man fundamentally desires."[67]

Intellect is a faculty of the soul corrupted in the Fall,[68] so that there can be no sharp division between the "erected wit" and the "infected will"; "wit" is affected in fallen man as a link in a fallen chain, or a sound produced by a damaged instrument. Yet, recognizing this frailty of reason, Scholasticism was powerfully rationalistic in a sense different from the one now usual. "Man derives his species from his rational soul: and consequently whatever is contrary to the order of reason is, properly speaking, contrary to the nature of man."[69] Reason was the guide not only to natural truth and conduct,[70] but even to supernatural and revealed religion.

The Renaissance was in part "a recoil from the inflexible rationality of medieval thought,"[71] and the Reformation violently repudiated this Scholastic union of faith and reason, which had approached in Anselm of Canterbury (1033–1109) to their virtual identification.[72] Luther's curse upon the "Devil's harlot"—"the whore, Reason"—signals a long and bitter hostility to which Hooker replies at length in his defense against the Puritan disparagement of reason and learning.[73]

Even St. Augustine had in some degree foreshadowed and shared in the later medieval rationalism and optimism. He considered the body to be good in itself, and he held that men should ask reasons for faith. It was, however, later Scholasticism which established as axiomatic the total compatibility of reason and faith, nature and grace, holding thus a middle ground between Pelagian denial of the causality of grace and Protestant denial of the freedom of the will. Grace, it is true, was understood by the Scholastics as a gratuitous divine clemency, necessary to salvation, which man could not merit by his unaided natural powers; the Molinist-Thomist controversy demonstrates the precision demanded by mutual accommodation of the ideas of grace and free will. Yet the supernatural was understood always as supplementing and perfecting the natural, grace as supplying powers lost to nature in the Fall and restoring the fullness of natural freedom.[74] To Hooker as to Aquinas, nature attested its need to be completed by a perfection above itself, and reason its need to be supported by what was beyond it but never opposed to it.[75] Vergil and Beatrice cooperate in guiding Dante toward the ultimate fulfillment of his nature. There was a sense, to medieval thought, in which nature was itself a grace.[76]

Evil is to Aquinas "the absence of the good, which is natural and due to a thing"; it is "a privation of form" or "a privation of order."[77] God orders all things to himself as ultimate end and is not the cause of sin[78] in the Calvinist sense, for evil is man's refusal of, rather than the incomprehensible working of, God's intention, a refusal possible in that Providence obliterates neither contingency and secondary causes, nor free will.[79]

Nor is man wholly corrupt. The entire privation of good is not possible unless the will inclines to evil as such for its object. Evil, however, is not capable of moving the will, which is the intellectual appetite for the good.[80] The intention of the doer of evil must end at some object in which there is a good, so that the privation of due order is never directly intended.[81] Man is not so fallen as to be incapable of ruling himself in accord with the demands of his and the world's nature, which are the source of morality and are inherently rational and comprehensible.

This in fact is the paradigmatic Scholastic form of the tragic vision which long survived, which shaped the Shakespearean universe, but which gave way in the early seventeenth century.

Chapter Four

The Decline of
Natural-Law
Beliefs [1]

THE ELIZABETHAN tragic
sensibility, with its medieval taproot, was blighted by
the increasingly pessimistic, mechanistic, and skeptical
Jacobean intellectual climate, and especially by the
growth of Calvinist voluntarism. Some of these forces,
too, had medieval beginnings, but it was through their
revival in the movements represented by Calvin and by
Bacon that they prevailed widely in the seventeenth
century. Not only voluntarism, but that abomination of
the natural world which had appeared before in Manichean, Albigensian, and certain aspects of Platonic
thought, grew powerful again in Calvinism.

The two world-views whose foci were Scholastic and
Calvinistic did not succeed one another in a neatly divided chronology. Elements of both were present over a
span of centuries. Some parts of Calvin's writings look
much like Aquinas' or Hooker's;[1] some of theirs like
Calvin's.[2] Scholastic theology had held divine grace to

be indispensable and infallible, and spiritual merit impossible without it. It had held faith to be above reason, and free will to be finally a mystery. Yet, without claiming a Socinian or Arminian sufficiency for natural man, it had maintained a harmony of nature and reason with grace and faith, and this concord prevailed until the opposed tradition of Ockham, Luther, and Calvin (and in the Catholic Church, of Jansen) achieved a hegemony. The Scholastic and Calvinist emphases were distant enough to make the men of the medieval tradition feel differently about the human situation than did those of the post-Calvinist milieu. The disentangling of these strands is work for specialists, but there was plainly more of Scholastic rationalism and world-acceptance in the Elizabethan years and of Calvinistic voluntarism and world-rejection in the seventeenth century.

To Aquinas, reason was the essence of God, the operative principle of the world, and the faculty which united man to both. "God," he had said, "cannot will affirmation and negation to be true at the same time."[3] Grotius, the proponent of natural-law theory in international politics, declared in 1625 that "measureless as is the power of God, nevertheless it can be said that there are certain things over which that power does not extend. . . . Just as even God cannot cause that two times two should not make four, so He cannot cause that that which is intrinsically evil be not evil."[4] The rational first principle of contradiction is transcendentally a property of the divine being; law is reason and God is intellect,[5] and even God, having created a nature, cannot make natural to it that which by its essence is not so.

Already in Aquinas' time, John Duns Scotus, the English Franciscan, *"Doctor Subtilis,"* who was for several years professor at Oxford, effectively denied this by making will superior to reason in both God and man. Only if the will is wholly autonomous and undetermined by knowledge, he insisted, can there be freedom ("The whole root of freedom," says Aquinas, "is located in reason").[6] Things are good or evil because God wills them so, not because of their relation to any nature or essence. The present human condition results from the fall of the *will*, which is not as to Aquinas the appetitive function of intellect, but the sovereign faculty, which can work independently of reason and contrary to it.[7]

Behind this voluntaristic exaltation of will (suggestive perhaps of some of the Machiavellian supermen in Jacobean drama) lies the more primary theory of nominalism, the belief that nothing in external reality corresponds to the universal concepts and terms of which general propositions are formed, and upon which thinking is based. It seems that Scotus' epistemology also approached in certain respects a kind of Platonistic "realism," in the place it gave to subsistent *divine* ideas. Its overall nominalism, however, was far more consequential: this reduced the "universal" to a convenient fiction by the doctrine that individual beings are formally and essentially individuated and thus immediately intelligible, so that there is no common specific form on which to found the universal concept. Reality is wholly particular, said Scotus; no two things have the same nature. Universal terms apply only to thought-objects, not to extra-mental ones. They, and the concepts to which they refer, are useful in arranging knowledge, but as group labels they bespeak a merely imputed unity of essence. But if there is no substantial nature common to things of a given "kind" (to men, for instance) there can be no regular expression of the demands of their specific essence—no law of nature.

The influential nominalist, William of Ockham, a Franciscan and a student of Scotus (and in some things his philosophical adversary), denied all necessary relation between the particular data of perception and the universal concepts which are the stuff of thought. In what might be roughly described as a return to Abelard's view of universals, Ockham allows them a purely logical status, so that the Aristotelian categories apply merely to concepts and to no outer world.[8] Logic becomes the study of significations arbitrarily given to words and propositions; it is purely semantic and relational. The connection between our universal ideas and the real objects of our cognition is not one of formal identity, but merely of arbitrary signification. Concepts are mental signs, "termini" based only on physiological responses to the data of sensation. Ratiocination, however useful, is incapable of general truth or of discovering any universal nature. The idea that universality can somehow be present in singular things Ockham calls "simply false and absurd," specifically denying a "humanity" which belongs to the essence of separate persons.[9]

Will, free of intellectual determination, is supreme in man as in God. Evil or sin is "an act of commission or omission when there is an obligation for man. . . . But God cannot be obligated to any act. With Him a thing becomes right solely for the reason that He wants it to be so."[10] Ockham conceived in fact "a God whose absolute power knew no limits, not even those of a stable nature endowed with a necessity and an intelligibility of its own."[11] Identifying the divine essence with the divine will, and morality with God's arbitrary decree,[12] he closed off the possibility of rational theology. "Right" became quite incomprehensible to reason and unrelated to the inner natures of men, upon whom it was merely externally imposed. To nominalism, says Rommen, "the natural moral law is positive law, divine will. An action is not good because of its suitableness to the essential nature of man, . . . but because God so wills. God's will could also have willed and decreed the precise opposite, which would then possess the same binding force as that which is now valid. Law is will, pure will, without any foundation in reality, without any foundation in the essential natures of things."[13]

Ockham gave to this doctrine some expressions which seem now to border on the ludicrous. Even "hatred of God, stealing, adultery and the like," he says, "may be performed by God without any sinful circumstance attached to them. They may even be meritoriously performed by man if they fall under divine precept, just as their opposites, as a matter of fact, fall under the divine precept."[14] Evil, then, cannot be seen as contrary to the nature of things, contrary to any objective order itself rational and purposive which militates against evil. It can be measured only against God's revealed will, which is not contingent on anything, but from which all contingency flows.

To look ahead for a moment, consider that the Friar in Ford's *'Tis Pity She's a Whore* informs the hero, Giovanni, that his incest accords with nature, that except for Divine revelation, which is contrary to nature, all would be well in his incestuous relation to his sister. The tragic worldly consequences of the evil done are then arbitrary and of merely conventional and social origin; sympathy with the act of the hero is not balanced against any recognition of the way in which it violates the good and intelligible natural order. There is nothing to reconcile us to tragic consequences, which are now meaningless and testify only to a hostile and incomprehensible cosmos, in which man and his nature are alien.

In the realm of human values Ockham thus dethroned reason, "by which the world was thought knowable and the strategy of salvation understandable." He severed the realm of nature from that of moral law. This was the first "emancipation" of nature, become "the only legitimate object of man's comprehension," from morality.

"The consequences for the intellectual history of Europe were immense," says Baker;[15] and in fact, without Ockham, Bacon would not have produced *The Advancement of Learning*, with its similar division, for he built upon the Ockhamite tradition which he derived through a Calvinist-Protestant intermediary. "The old instruments of discursive reason and logic were discredited" by medieval nominalism and its theological corollary, voluntarism, just as "the cosmological status of reason was [later] impugned by the voluntarism of the great Reformers."[16]

Against voluntarism, says Jacques Maritain, Aquinas had lost his "customary serenity," exclaiming his opposition to the voluntarist thesis in these violent words: "To say that justice depends upon the pure and simple will of God is to say that the will of God does not proceed according to the order of His wisdom, which is blasphemy."[17] Of all law, Aquinas says that "in order that the volition of what is commanded may have the nature of law, it needs to be in accord with some rule of reason. And in this sense is to be understood the saying that the will of the sovereign has the force of law; otherwise the sovereign's will would savour of lawlessness rather than of law."[18] "They err therefore," says Hooker, "who think that of the will of God to do this or that there is no reason beside His will."[19]

Luther, in stark contrast to this, thought that "God's free sovereignty is expressed in that his world order remains incomprehensible"[20] and that the distinction between good and evil rests wholly on the divine will. "His judgments," says Luther, "are incomprehensible, and His ways past finding out."[21] Human corruption is absolute, natural morality is an impossible blasphemy, the will is helpless, and natural man is an enemy to God. The Roman Church had "too high an estimate of the worth and potentiality of man."[22]

Luther in fact attacked the "scholastic doctors" as

authors of "pure errors . . . for by them it is taught:
That since the fall of Adam the natural powers of man
have remained entire and incorrupt, and that man by
nature has right reason and a good will, as the philosophers teach. And that man had a free will to do good
and omit evil."[23] "Why," he asked, "do we hold concupiscence to be irresistible? Well, try and do some thing
without the interference of concupiscence. Naturally
you cannot. So then your nature is incapable of fulfilling
the law." He was harshly contemptuous not only of
Aristotle and Aquinas, but of rationality itself, believing
that God and all his works are "altogether hidden to
human reason."

Calvin's influence on these issues was even greater:
"In the main stream of Christian humanism," says
Baker, "man's prestige was immense: in the theology
which Calvin had revived primarily to combat such optimism man's degradation was made the pivotal fact of
history."[24] The dark Augustinian anthropology had
"nearly slipped away in the onrushing currents of
Thomistic rationalism and scientific naturalism," but
had a powerful resurgence toward the end of the Renaissance. Calvin "wished to reduce man to a proper humility before God by challenging, out of the Scripture, the
impious errors of Thomistic rationalism."[25] "We know,"
he taught, "that there is nothing at all in our nature but
wretchedness and misery; nothing but a bottomless pit
of stench and infection."[26] The flesh is

> so perverse, that, with all its affections, it entertains a
> secret hatred against God. . . . Now, grant, that in the
> nature of man there is nothing but flesh, and elicit any
> good from it, if you can. But the name of flesh, it will
> be said, pertains only to the sensual, and not to the
> superior faculties of the soul. This is abundantly re-
> futed by the words of Christ and of the Apostle. . . .
> there is such a comparison between the flesh and the

spirit, that there is no medium left. . . . Whatever, therefore, we have from nature is carnal.[27]

The "perpetual corruption," the "ruin and destruction of our nature" is witnessed by the Scriptures, "which demonstrate our nature to be totally ruined. . . . in vain do we seek in our nature for anything that is good. . . . The will, therefore, is so bound by the slavery of sin, that it cannot excite itself, much less devote itself to any thing good."[28]

This element of Calvinism is profoundly hostile to the impression of human stature communicated in Elizabethan popular literature. Contempt of fallen humanity in the Calvinistic doctrines, which permeated even the Anglican Church, eventually helped to force the dramatic representation of man away from a realistic basis, since there could be no heroic treatment in the terms which were now so widely felt to apply to real life. Calvinism thus may have helped to foster the adoption of artificial, theoretic, and self-consciously systematic views—Senecan and Stoic, Platonic and Epicurean—in which the later tragedies abound.[29] In fact, its division of spirit from body, goodness from matter, is dramatically indistinguishable from that of Platonism. In the court of Henrietta Maria, after about 1628, drama was sometimes to be simply the exposition of the fashionable "Platonic" love, by writers like Hausted, Carliell, Davenant, Glapthorne, and Suckling. Any philosophy is an intellectual construction, but belief in the natural law had constituted a philosophy only in the sense that belief in gravity constitutes for a modern man a scientific theory. It was simply the recognition of unquestionable reality, one of those "assumptions which appear so obvious that people do not know they are assuming them, because no other way of putting things has ever occurred to them." A writer who adopts an ideological system to serve dramatic structure or shapes drama to demonstrate the system, is likely to produce something quite different.

The Calvinistic image of man degraded, impotent, and uncomprehending is admittedly also unlike the image created by "second-stage" Renaissance drama—by Chapman's Bussy, Fletcher's Amintor, Tourneur's Vendice, etc., but with this difference: whereas the earlier tragic heroes suggest the Thomistic conception rather than that of Calvin, these "later" ones (not always chronologically later, but representing a succeeding mode) often bear little relation to any Christian worldview. They fail to display the human grandeur or the optimistic world-vindication of natural-law philosophy, and they achieve heroic elevation by the artificial and hypothetical character and the systematic virtue of one or another ethical cult consciously adopted for use as a dramatic machinery. None shows the concretely apprehended causal working out of nature's retribution in a morally intelligible pattern. Of Chapman, for instance, Una Ellis-Fermor writes, "often, indeed, his figures break down into an undramatic exposition of particular doctrines (Senecan, Ciceronian, Epictetan) that were uppermost in Chapman's mind, and we see the native ardour of the Elizabethan obscured by the characteristic cast of Jacobean uncertainty."[30]

There is, of course, Stoicism in Shakespeare; but "Stoicism," like "Platonism," can mean a variety of things. One has only to compare Horatio or Brutus with Chapman's Bussy D'Ambois or Clermont to see the difference between a Stoicism compatible with the inherited Christian-humanistic view and assimilated to it, and a Stoicism inimical to that belief and to the tragic form it underlay.

Clermont, in *The Revenge of Bussy D'Ambois*, speaks of the cosmos as a rigid economy whose parts are ordained "to th' use of th' All." Men, as "Parts of that All," must keep to their given places in the fixed scheme, or "resisting th' All [be] crush'd with it."[31] This inflexible pattern, externally imposed rather than flowing from an inner nature, is a Stoic version of natural law which does not serve, like much Renaissance Stoicism, as a support, virtually a constituent, of the traditional Christian humanism. It is more akin to Calvin's voluntarist version of the moral law, as Stoic "fate" is akin to the Calvinist providence. Such Stoicism is a consciously adopted and doctrinaire substitute dramatic ethic. In his preface to the works of Seneca, Thomas Lodge makes clear, on the other hand, that Stoic principles are for him ancillary to Christian moral doctrine. The invulnerability of the will; fortitude, patience, and honesty; obedience to the rule of reason and to the cosmic order are equally Stoic and Christian. But Bussy and the "Senecal man" Clermont are each a law unto himself, in defiance or rejection of the corrupt world where Bussy's assertive "natural" greatness cannot and Clermont's philosophic integrity will not accept the terms of survival. If this is related to the Counter-Renaissance form of Stoicism which exalts the individual "nature," scorns the world, and sees the most effective assertion of moral freedom in suicide, it also connects with the Calvinistic morality, in which "nature," like Bussy, rejects all moral restrictions, and rectitude, like Clermont, rejects the world.

Chapman and those who follow him, as Hardin Craig has observed, are markedly sympathetic with the passionate sinner against the moral law.[32] Bussy D'Ambois receives a just "punishment" for his sins, but these are also his heroic virtues and are dramatically made more attractive than anything else in the play. Webster's Bosola and even Vittoria Corombana are felt to be victims more than offenders. Ford, too, as Sensabaugh has argued, absolves and approves the actions of his passion-ridden heroes, since they are driven by irresistible "natural" forces beyond the control of their wills.[33] Their sin lies in the challenging of social conventions which Ford seems to see as invalid—certainly not as "nature."

If "nature" is on the side of the sinner, rather than of the moral law, it is dramatically almost inevitable to magnify the heroic stature of the rebellion against the law. The moral intelligibility of tragedy being then utterly gone, other more sensational and escapist solutions to the tragic issues must be found, as indeed they are by Fletcher, Massinger, Ford, Shirley, and others. Thus, the end of the older natural-law tradition left a vacuum which the tragedians attempted to fill by various expedients.

Perhaps Calvinism helps to account also for the Jacobean fascination with burning and sterile lust. Shakespeare can see sexual love as in *Romeo and Juliet* or *As You Like It*. He may draw (as in this tragedy) on Platonic traditions of unworldly love, yet love is fundamentally a natural good; indeed, the sane balance between Petrarchan romanticism and cynical or unrealistic denial is a pervasive theme of the comedies.[34] There is little such love in Jacobean drama, where either depraved lust or hypothetical courtly-love extravagances generally prevail. Harbage's chapter on "Sexual Behaviour" in *Shakespeare and the Rival Traditions* pictures the prurient eroticism of the private stages as contrasting sharply with the healthiness of the public theaters. The uniformity of the difference remains perhaps somewhat debatable, but Harbage's examples do serve to demonstrate the degree of libertinism found in many of the Jacobean writers.[35]

Even in *Measure for Measure*, a play which has often been found morally objectionable, the idea of restraint as natural to man prevails. Lucio is given none of the arguments with which he would have been supplied by other and later dramatists. Angelo responds to the accusations of Isabella only by distinguishing voluntary from involuntary sins, not by pleading for sensuality on the authority of animal nature. Harbage compares to this a passage from Marston's *Dutch Courtesan,* a play which argues the irreconcilability of virtue and nature:

> O, you happy beasts
> In whom an inborn heat is not held sin!
> How far transcend you wretched, wretched man,
> Whom national customs, tyrannous respects
> Of slavish order, fetters, lames his power.
> Calling that sin in us which in all things else
> Is nature's highest virtue.
>
> (I. i)[36]

Lines like the following:

> Philosophy maintains that Nature's wise
> And forms no useless or unperfect thing . . .
> Go to, go to, thou liest Philosophy:
> Nature forms things unperfect, useless, vain.
> (*Antonio and Mellida,* III)

"express a frontal attack upon universal law and the divine plan."[37]

In the tragedy of the early Renaissance, the inherent force of the moral order exerts itself to redress distortions of its nature. In many of the Jacobeans, as Clifford Leech has said, "the final effect is antinomian—the hierarchies among men are unsound, the patterns in the world are arbitrary and anti-human."

REMEMBERING THE BITTERNESS of the Marprelate episode, Archbishop Laud's ferocity, and the whole Tudor and Stuart history of sectarian warfare, we find it hard to realize that Calvinism encroached steadily on the older tradition even within the Anglican Church (which had sought originally to accommodate both). Yet this is so. The strife, we should remember, opposed Anglican to Puritan; *Calvinist* and *Puritan* are not synonyms, the Puritan movement having other elements, and theological Calvinism (as distinguished from Calvin's presbyterian plan of church government) having penetrated much more generally than just to the Puritan churches. Some Puritans were hardly Calvinists, e.g., Milton and Henry Parker, the controversialist; and many Calvinists were not Puritans, e.g., King James himself, who "adhered to orthodox Calvinism" and "agreed with the Puritans on most theological points." There is, in fact, ample testimony that "Calvinistic doctrine prevailed in all quarters,"[38] at least until the development of Anglican Arminianism in the 1630's. "Both [Anglican and Puritan churches] were committed to Genevan theology and built their creeds around that dark dogma," says Baker, and only the "almost maniacal fervor" with which the Puritan held the same doctrines distinguished him theologically.[39] In 1540 Henry VIII had prohibited Calvin's early writings, but "the ruling theology of the Church of England in the latter half of the 16th and the beginning of the 17th cent. was Calvinistic."[40]

Indeed, Calvinist influence had early worked itself into the heart of Anglicanism, for the returned Marian exiles who had participated in the Elizabethan settlement were Calvinistic (even those like John Jewel, John Foxe, John Bale, David Whitehead, and Edmund Grindal, who had spent the time in other centers than Geneva), and the Geneva Bible of 1560 was the Bible of the Elizabethan Protestant. Before the turn of the century Hooker and his party had done something to stem the tide of Calvinism in matters of church polity; later, Andrewes and Laud restored Anglican ritual at Oxford and Cambridge. But the doctrinal cast set by Calvin's

Protestant *Summa* was ever more pervasive. Key features of Calvinism were common to all the reformed sects,[41] and it remained the dominant force in English Renaissance theology.[42]

In the 1630's Archbishop Laud and the Puritans contended fiercely; yet there was nothing in the conflict to indicate real theological difference. King James in 1622 forbade all preaching on predestination, but that muffling of controversy tells equally little of the Anglican mind. Throughout the period, Calvinist views became more generally diffused. Their theological domination was faced and fought in Restoration times by writers like Rust, Glanville, and the Cambridge Platonists, who took up for the purpose the old tradition of rationalism.

Whitgift, the Elizabethan Archbishop of Canterbury who had in 1584 suppressed Cartwright's translation of Travers' *Disciplina Ecclesia,* had yet been a vigorous Calvinist and tried, says M. M. Knappen, to "saddle high Calvinism upon the established church,"[43] quoting Calvin even against the Puritanism of Cartwright. His predecessor, Archbishop Grindal, repressed the Marprelate tracts and punished Puritan advocacy, but was theologically a thoroughgoing Calvinist.

Calvin himself had in 1548 dedicated his *Commentary on I Timothy* to the English Protector Somerset, had written to Somerset and to the king letters which were well received, and had in 1552 acceded to Archbishop Cranmer's request that he attend a theological conference directed toward uniting the reformed churches (though King Edward's death prevented this). Calvin's catechism became a university textbook; Thomas Norton translated the *Institutes* in 1561, and its influence in England was very great. Twenty-seven editions of Calvin's sermons had appeared in English by 1592.[44] In 1586 Whitgift had made Bullinger's *Five Decades of Sermons* required reading for the clergy, Bullinger like Bucer being very close to Calvin. Nowell's catechism, also translated by Norton and approved by Convocation in 1570, makes clear the Calvinistic stance of the Anglican Church on predestination and other key points, explaining that natural law, though it "as the highest reason, was by God grafted in the nature of Man," is no longer available to us. Man's nature is now so darkened and corrupted that "scarce any sparkles" of the "natural light" may be descried.[45]

Elizabethan Puritans included powerful and famous members of the Establishment: Sidney, Leicester, Walsingham, and Cecil were sympathetic not only to Calvinism but to the extreme Presbyterian Puritanism represented by Cartwright and Travers. Sidney was friend and host of Languet and Mornay, both Huguenot spokesmen, and the Sidney family had important Puritan connections. Spenser allegorized Puritan propaganda in the *Shepherd's Calendar*, Fulke Greville wrote a Calvinist treatise, Arthur Golding (the Elizabethan translator of Ovid) translated Calvin's sermons, and Thomas Norton gave much energy to the Calvinist cause.

The Lambeth Articles of 1595 were an explicitly Calvinistic Anglican counterblast to the early appearance of Arminian theology at Cambridge. The Thirty-Nine Articles of the Anglican Church, like the Forty-Two Articles which were their earlier form, are, despite Newman's Tract 90, distinctly Calvinistic. Articles IX and XVII (on original sin and on predestination and election) are clearly and explicitly so. Articles X and XI, dealing with free will and justification, are equally strong in their implicit Calvinistic denial of nature, of works, and of reason. Article XIII asserts again the utter corruption of the merely natural by its treatment of good works. Article XXIII counsels against all reliance on the "light of Nature." In Article XXVIII, the

Calvinist doctrine of election shapes the treatment of the Eucharist.[46]

John Allen, the early nineteenth-century translator of the *Institutes*, speaks of

> the high estimation in which the works of [Calvin] were held by the venerable Reformers of the Church of England, and their immediate successors, as well as by the great majority of religious people in this country. This is not a question of opinion, but an undeniable fact. Dr. Heylin, the admirer and biographer of Archbishop Laud, speaking of the early part of the seventeenth century, says, that Calvin's "Book of Institutes was, for the most part, the foundation on which the young divines of those times did build their studies." The great Dr. Saunderson, who was chaplain to King Charles I., and, after the restoration of Charles II., was created Bishop of Lincoln, says, "When I began to set myself to the study of divinity as my proper business, Calvin's Institutions were recommended to me, as they were generally to all young scholars in those times, as the best and perfectest system of divinity, and the fittest to be laid as a ground-work in the study of this profession."[47]

It is not mysterious, then, to discover profound Calvinist influence in writers who were certainly not Puritans—some of whom were in fact given to vitriolic satire of the "precisian."

Marston, despite his scathing attack on Puritanism in *The Scourge of Villanie*, is strongly Calvinistic in affirming the total corruption of human nature and the doctrine of unmerited election as the only source of righteousness, and in his obsession with loathsome and ubiquitous lust.

> Omnipotent
> That Nature is, that cures the impotent,
> Even in a moment. Sure Grace is infus'd

By divine favour, not by actions us'd.
Which is as permanent as heavens blisse
To them that have it, then no habite is.
. . . .
Yee curious sotts, vainly by Nature led,
Where is your vice or vertuous habite now?[48]

There is no free will; "impotent" human nature is raised
from congenital slavery to evil only by omnipotent divine "Nature." The Scholastic conception of virtue as
habit gives way to election according to a grace "In-
fus'd, displac'd, not in our will or force."[49] Fallen man
"hath no soule, the which the Stagerite / Term'd ration-
all":[50] he is too far steeped in "foule filthe" to possess
still that image of divinity.[51] His intellectual powers are
lost, for the soul has fled its "Land-lordes muddy slime."[52]

By the time Puritan abuse of the theater had reached
the climax of Prynne's *Histriomastix* (1633), the drama,
and especially the "tragicall stage-plays" which Prynne
particularly abominated, had been transformed by a
spirit which, paradoxically, possessed common roots
with Prynne's.

"We represent not God as lawless," says Calvin, "who
is a law to himself . . . the will of God is not only pure
from every fault, but the highest standard of perfection,
even the law of all laws. But we deny that he is liable to
be called to any account."[53] For,

> I confess, indeed that all the descendants of Adam
> fell by the Divine will into that miserable condition in
> which they are now involved; and this is what I as-
> serted from the beginning, that we must always return
> at last to the sovereign determination of God's will,
> the cause of which is hidden in himself. . . . the
> reason of the Divine justice is too high to be measured
> by a human standard, or comprehended by the little-
> ness of the human mind.
>
> (*Institutes*, III. xxiii. 4)

Who are you, miserable mortals, preferring an accusation against God, because he accommodates not the greatness of his works to your ignorance? as though they were necessarily wrong, because they are concealed from carnal view. . . . Now, examine your contracted intellects, whether they can comprehend God's secret decrees.

(Ibid., III. xxiii. 5)[54]

Thus, although Calvin speaks of "law," he denies all natural law in anything like the Scholastic or tragic sense, by identifying law with the indeterminable divine will and placing both of these beyond all hope of human comprehension. He sees that such a universe cannot fail to inspire rebellion; but this will be suppressed by denying the rights of reason, as of nature:

Foolish mortals enter into many contentions with God, as though they could arraign him to plead to their accusations. In the first place they inquire, by what right the Lord is angry with his creatures who had not provoked him by any previous offence; for that to devote to destruction whom he pleases, is more like the caprice of a tyrant than the lawful sentence of a judge; that men have reason, therefore, to expostulate with God, if they are predestinated to eternal death without any demerit of their own, merely by his sovereign will. If such thoughts ever enter the minds of pious men, they will be sufficiently enabled to break their violence by this one consideration, how exceedingly presumptuous it is only to inquire into the causes of the Divine will; which is in fact, and is justly entitled to be, the cause of every thing that exists. For if it has any cause, then there must be something antecedent, on which it depends; which it is impious to suppose. For the will of God is the highest rule of justice; so that what he wills must be considered just, for this very reason, because he wills it. When it is inquired, therefore, why the Lord did so, the answer must be, Because he would. But if you go further, and ask why he so determined, you are in search of something greater and higher than the will of God, which can never be found.[55]

The voluntarist position is stated with equal force in another passage: "If therefore, we can assign no reason why he grants mercy to his people but because such is his pleasure, neither shall we find any other cause but his will for the reprobation of others. For when God is said to harden or show mercy to whom he pleases, men are taught by this declaration to seek no cause beside his will."[56] The Puritan physician Bright describes, in his *Treatise of Melancholie* (1586), the "extreme miserie and utter confusion" of those who "grone under the burthen of the heavy crosse [i.e., divine displeasure], wherein no reason is able to minister consolation." The result of religious belief may well be "continuall distrust" or "resolute desparatnes."[57]

Arbitrariness is now the glory of divine omnipotence. The medieval view had held contrarily, that the basic axioms of reason were transcendentally the innate laws of being, and so of the very essence of God.[58] God's nature to the Scholastic might be mysterious as partly beyond human understanding; God to the Calvinist is inherently unintelligible or inscrutable, as are his justice, his grace, his election, and his Providence in the world. Repeatedly emphasized by Calvin, this is a key matter. Surely no tragedian acclimated to the Calvinist tradition would presume to show the temporal and worldly consequences of moral qualities—to trace the intelligible causality linking evil with its natural effects, as in the careers of Romeo, Othello, or Macbeth; for he habitually assigned the two to orders entirely discrete, and his whole world-view was based upon the lack of rational and moral order in nature. He might see the prosperous as the elect, but theirs was an utterly inscrutable election and showed no *natural* relation between moral will and physical consequences.

The voluntarist ethic of Scotus and William of Ockham, the notion of moral law as the expression of the divine will, of God ruling by fiat, passed over from the nominalists to the reformers: to Wycliff, to Luther, and later on to Calvin. The latter two in fact explicitly professed their allegiance to Ockham.[59] "It seems obvious enough," says D'Entreves, "that the Thomist conception of natural law as a mediatory element between God and man and as an assertion of the power and dignity of human nature would have been out of place in the reformers' theology, and actually they found little or no room for it."[60] If in fact the moral law is not grounded upon an essential human nature common to men, there is no need for the tragic dramatist to set out on his voyage of discovery or exploration of that nature and that law.

What is called "Fortune," says Calvin, is really the secret ordering of all things by God. The Calvinistic Providence was God's direct manipulation of events for his ultimate glory.[61] The world exists solely for this glory, and to it the damned contribute no less than the saved: the first show his justice, the second his mercy. Luther and Calvin, had in fact extended the voluntarism of Ockham to the point of regarding evil as divinely purposive. The Scholastic tradition saw nature as purposive, evil as the failure or thwarting of nature and the frustration of natural purposes. But Calvinistic theology was forced to make evil absolutely inscrutable by attributing it to the secret purposes of God, incomprehensibly grounded in an absolutely undetermined will. The Calvinists rejected the "crimination of God" which this suggests and insisted that justice itself was defined by the divine will. They even distinguished two such wills, one public, commanding good and forbidding evil as in revelation, the other secret. Calvin struggles mightily in the *Institutes*[62] to reconcile his claim of human moral responsibility to the iron necessity which he sees as ruling every human action.

Elizabethan history plays and the antecedent and surrounding historical literature testify to providential retribution, especially in the nemesis of wicked rulers, but this is not distinct from the working-out of divinely originated natural law, in which are found the intelligible proximate causes of things. The older tradition accepted the natural order as an instrument and intermediary of Providence: Hooker maintains that it is "inferior causes," some of which are contingent and variable, "from which, since the first creation, all things (*miraculous events excepted*) have had their being."[63] "When natural law theorists," says Gierke, "assumed that Natural Law had an external sanction in the Divine threat of penalties for its breach . . . that was [not a special act of God, but a] retribution which manifested itself as the natural course of affairs."[64] Calvin's view is different: "All events are governed by the secret counsel of God," who "has declared . . . that the daily rising and setting of the sun is not from a blind instinct of nature, but that he himself governs his course, to renew the memory of his paternal favour toward us." Of the changing seasons of the year, "it is obvious that every year, month, and day, is governed by a new and particular providence of God."[65] Not only are men wrong to ascribe events to "fortune and fortuitous accidents," but they are much to blame "who confine the Divine providence within such narrow bounds, as though he permitted all things to proceed in an uncontrolled course, according to a perpetual law of nature."[66] Equally pernicious is the belief that God enables man "to act according to the tendency of the nature with which he is endued; but that man governs his actions by his own voluntary choice."[67] Every bountiful crop is in truth God's special benediction, and every famine, storm, and illness his malediction. His retribution upon evildoers is always an intervention in nature, interrupting rather than fulfilling it.

Calvin finds it necessary to insist upon the differences between his doctrine of Providence and the Stoic doctrine of fate;[68] the differences are real, but the situation to which each consigns mankind is in fact the same. Henry More, the Cambridge Platonist, tells that although raised as a Calvinist, he could never "swallow down that hard Doctrine of Fate."[69] "God," says Nathaniel Culverwell, "set up the world as a fair, and goodly Clock, to strike in time, and to move in an orderly manner; not by its own weights . . . but by fresh influence from himself." And more explicitly, "*Fortune* [is] nothing, but a more *abstruse,* and *mysterious,* and occult kinde of Providence."[70]

The pious Calvinist goaded himself to despise the natural order, thanked God for misfortune, since it prevented him "from makeinge this world my heaven," sought "to learne to contemne the world more hartiely," assured himself, concerning his failures, that "the lord will hereby acquaint us the more with the contempt of it," reveled securely sometimes in "a comfortable and sensible feeling of the contempt of the worlde," and ever reminded himself that "no man hath grace at commaund." He made of Providence a power which brooked no natural intermediary.[71]

This emphasis on God's immediate regulation of the world is reflected in the writings of Baxter and Taylor, in the drama of Heywood and others, and probably in the dramatic theory of the Calvinistic Bacon, who considers it the business of tragedy to reveal Providence by chronicling God's punishment of sinners. Samuel Daniel's Cleopatra, in her monument, wonders if her tragic fate has been decreed by "th' heavens" to punish Egypt's sins[72]—a piece of moralizing more Calvinistic than Senecan.

Of the new strength of this absolutist idea of Providence, Cyril Tourneur's *The Atheist's Tragedy* is an extreme but not an isolated illustration. The villainous protagonist, D'Amville, is certainly punished for sin. But Tourneur, like Heywood, has no way of seeing his characters punished *by* the evil they do: like Heywood he can trace no connection between the violation of nature and the damage done to nature, but only asserts the fideistic "fact" of retributive justice as of a God who rules by fiat. D'Amville's unintended striking out of his own brains at the climax of the play is the crassest example of such assertion, but it is equally true in other Jacobean tragedies that the retribution insisted upon has none of the natural "inevitability" based on the character-effects of evil which we see, for example, in *Macbeth*. By *The Atheist's Tragedy* we are told, in a way unrelated to any observation of the root system of causes in human life, "Evil men shall be punished." *Macbeth* unfolds, on the other hand, a concrete and natural way in which evil destroys a man.

This distinction between earlier and later dramatic versions of the issue of evildoing may seem questionable in light of such early dramatic figures as Cambises, who suffer similarly arbitrary catastrophe as the wages of sin; one difference is that these were the products of a relatively naive popular drama witnessing belief in Providence in the simplest terms, struggling to create methods for the dramatic treatment of tragic fact, in an age when the popular mind saw the hand of God in every fire and plague. Tourneur writes after the point of highest refinement has been reached in the dramatic contemplation of causes in human affairs.

It is clear enough, at any rate, that a dominant strain

in England before 1600 was a rationalist optimism which traces not, like the tradition which supplanted it, through Calvin and Luther to Ockham and Scotus, but through Hooker to Aquinas, and eventually perhaps to Cicero.[73] Spenser's Redcross Knight shows his creator too much a rationalist-humanist to accept Calvin's anthropology: Redcross is holiness within its own rational control. Guyon is an Aristotelian hero of reason and moderation and self-discipline.[74] Spenser had strong Puritan sympathies, and Milton was an outright Puritan; yet both maintained, against the current of Calvinism, many of the natural-law values of the early Renaissance, *Paradise Lost* being more Arminian than Calvinist, and Milton generally a rationalist and no real despiser of the world. These poets and others felt the force of the Genevan influence without abandoning the Elizabethan humanistic optimism: the darkening after the turn of the century, the increasing penetration of Calvinist doctrine into the literary sensibility, must be assigned then to a confluence of supporting causes. It is one aspect of the well-known Jacobean mood of weariness and disillusion, the sense of disorientation and of a world passing, the feeling that "we have seen the best of our time." This episode of English social history, and the ideological counter-Renaissance which is associated with it, involved a failure of intellectual nerve, the causes of which historians may debate. It is certain that in the thought of the time, Calvinist antirationalism and voluntarism cooperated with the assaults of sectarian struggle and with the fashionable skepticism which was in part no doubt their consequence, with the disintegrating effects of Protestant individualism and with the mechanism of the new science, in the destruction of that cosmic confidence which is belief in the natural law.

Chapter Five

The Decline of
Natural-Law
Beliefs [11]

JEREMY TAYLOR, chaplain to
Charles I, represented the conservative Anglican party,
but was led to espouse both nominalism and voluntarism. As definitely as the natural philosophy preached by
Bacon and the mechanism preached by Hobbes, his
theology marks the ending of Renaissance Christian humanism. In *Ductor Dubitantium*, he

> so steadily constricts the area of natural knowledge
> while augmenting that of faith that he, like certain
> Puritans, is forced to segregate reason and goodness
> altogether. . . .
>
> But what is extraordinary—and especially in that
> tradition of post-Thomistic rationalism to which
> Taylor ostensibly belongs—is his effort to demolish
> the claims of natural reason within its own legitimate
> sphere. . . .
>
> He does so through his denial of natural law, and he
> centers his attack there because he regards natural
> law as the most sinister threat to religious truth.

Hooker had been able to construe nature in sacramental terms. . . . By the middle of the seventeenth century it was apparently no longer possible to do so. . . . Thanks to the Protestant bifurcation of nature and grace, and to the Baconian segregation of secular and religious knowledge, by Taylor's time natural truth was being cut loose from morality.

Of the natural law, therefore: "revelation and express declaring it was the first publication and emission of it,"[1] and "if we enquire after the law of nature by the rules of our reason, we shall be uncertain as the discourses of the people, or the dreams of disturbed fancies."[2] The whole basis of the natural law was thus abandoned by Taylor, as it was by the Jacobeans generally.

Sir Robert Filmer was a mid-seventeenth-century theorist of royal absolutism whose work was important enough in its time so that Locke, in his *Two Treatises of Government*, found it necessary to answer his arguments. Filmer states flatly the voluntarist belief that all law is the expression of will.[3] The king conceived by this Stuart political doctrine bears much the same relation to Thomas Smith's constitutional ruler as does Calvin's God to Hooker's. Cowley, certainly no Puritan or conscious Calvinist, reveals himself in his *Tree of Knowledge* as a solid nominalist,[4] and consistently, a voluntarist. In the disintegration imagery of Donne's "First Anniversary" there is an echo of the nominalistic repudiation of universals, the denial of the common essences on which had rested the natural law or law of "kind" uniting king and subject, father and son:

> Prince, Subject, Father, Sonne, are things forgot
> For every man alone thinkes he hath got
> To be a Phoenix, and that then can bee
> None of that kinde, of which he is, but hee.
>
> (ll. 215–18)

Nathaniel Culverwell, raised in a Puritan family but intellectually allied with the Cambridge Platonists, produced in his *Elegant and Learned Discourse of the Light of Nature* a work which begins as a "self-conscious echo of the Thomist Tradition of rationalism," yet displays the Calvinistic voluntarism in its extreme form, rendering the operations of the universe, despite Culverwell's title, morally incomprehensible to reason.[5] In the introductory address to the reader, this book is described as having been written "to chastise the sawciness of Socinus, and his followers, who dare set Hagar above her Mistress, and make Faith wait at the elbow of corrupt, and distorted Reason."[6] Culverwell nevertheless purports to defend reason from her adversaries, but his defense will be such that he can promise to say nothing "but what an *Augustine* or a *Bradwardine*, those great Patrons of Grace, would willingly set their seals unto."[7]

His explicit treatment of natural law puts him most firmly in the voluntarist camp. "Vasques," he remarks, "says that the 'formality' of natural law consists only in that *harmony*, and proportion, or else that discord, and disconvenience, which such and such an *object*, and such and such an *action*, ha's with a *Rational Nature;* for (saies he) every *Essence* is *Mensura Boni et Mali* in respect of it self."[8] This is exactly the doctrine of Aquinas, Hooker, and the Scholastic tradition. Culverwell rejects it flatly, unable to conceive law except as command. He thinks it is impossible, with a classic begging of the question in his assumed definition of law, that

> any *naked Essence*, though never so pure, and noble, lay a *Moral* engagement upon it self, or binde its own *Being*, for this would make the very same *Being Superior* to itself, as it gives a law, and inferiour to it self, as it must *obey* it.
>
> So that the *most high*, and *sovereign Being*, even God himself does not subject himself to any Law.[9]

Nor does reason, in men, have the force of law, for "that proportion, which Actions bear to Reason," though a "sufficient foundation" for law to build on, is "not the *law* it self."[10]

Culverwell fears that the Schoolmen have been so overbold in their claims for nature and reason that he is "ready to question whether it be best to repeat them."[11] They are wrong in tying natural law to rational essence, for reason binds only "in the name of its *Supreme Lord,* and *Sovereign.*"[12] Since no creature is willing or able to inflict on itself the punishment which is "answerable to the violation" of law, "it must be accountable to some other *Legislative Power,* which will vindicate its own commands, and will by this means engage a *Creature* to be more mindful of its own happiness, then otherwise it would be."[13] And of this legislative power Culverwell makes the final voluntaristic assertion: "not the understanding, but the will of a Law-giver makes a Law."[14]

Haller selects the Puritan Thomas Goodwin as an illustration of the effect of Calvinistic preaching on boys at Cambridge in the first part of the seventeenth century. Goodwin, of course, knew the *Institutes.* The great temptation which preceded his final regeneration was, he tells us, a temptation to trust natural reason, rather than revealed grace. On the day of his "crisis," Goodwin looked deeply into his own heart, "into the filth of a dungeon." There he saw "millions of crawling living things in the midst of that sink and liquid corruption." Such is human nature, and such the virtue of natural reason.[15]

Most of the continental thinkers whose influence was increasing in early seventeenth-century England are at one with the English Puritan at least in their opinion of human depravity. Pierre Charron, a recognized influence upon Jacobean thought, says that from the "generall and universall alteration and corruption it is come to pass, that there is nothing of nature known in us." Man cannot then discover what natural law is, or what it would be in an unfallen world. Charron approved the traditional idea that "the ensign and mark of a naturall law is the universitie of approbation." But this old belief combines strangely with a newer one: Charron must confess (with his master Montaigne) that "there is not any thing so strange and unnatural in the opinion of divers, which is not approved and authorized in many places by common use"; therefore "doubtless there remaineth no more any image or trace of nature in us."[16] Morality thus is necessarily legislative; from a Calvinistic estimate of man Charron is forced to a voluntaristic ethical doctrine. Reason has lost its former dignity and all religion is "strange and horrible to the common sense." There are many "misbelievers and irreligious persons," because men "consult and hearken too much to their own judgements" and attempt to "handle [religion] with their own proper and natural instrument. . . . To receive religion, to believe and live under the law, [we need] by reverence and obedience to be led and conducted by publick authority . . . *submitting our understanding* to the obedience of faith."[17] Many complaints against "atheism" (which sometimes means simply the rejection of orthodox creeds) attribute it to the presumptuous demand for rational understanding, or in Bacon's often repeated opinion, to "learned times"—a diagnosis equally antirational in its implications for religious thought.

Descartes' theological voluntarism is fully as uncompromising as Calvin's and rather more surprising in the terms chosen for illustration: it roots not only moral but also mathematical law in arbitrary divine fiat, rather than in reason or substantial nature. "It is because [God] willed the three angles of the triangle to be necessarily equal to two right angles that this is true and cannot be otherwise. . . . though it may be said that it is the merit of the saints which is the cause of their obtaining eternal life, . . . they are merely the cause of an effect of which God wished them from all eternity to be the cause." To Descartes as to Calvin, this quality of arbitrary and absolute freedom in the divine will is "the supreme proof of [God's] omnipotence."[18]

The very defense which the Cambridge Platonists found necessary in the last half of the seventeenth century, of a rational world against the voluntarist one, demonstrates the prevalence of voluntarism; and in Culverwell's case, despite his lipservice to the supremacy of reason, the enemy has penetrated within the defender's gates. Caught between Hobbesian mechanism and Calvinist rejection of nature and reason, the Cambridge men developed an eclectic Platonism which, in its relation to either extreme, is in effect a return to medieval rationalism. "To go against Reason," says Whichcote, "is to go against God."[19] Scripture confirms nature; evil is negation; sin is disease and virtue the natural health of the soul.[20]

John Smith's "truths of natural inscription" perhaps reflect Platonic archetypal ideas of goodness and beauty and may echo an Augustinian "inner light" doctrine rather than the Scholastic tradition of natural law as reason. Yet by contrast with Calvinist voluntarism, their aspect of reasserted theological confidence in human nature is marked. Cudworth's attack on fatalism in *The True Intellectual System of the Universe* and More's and Whichcote's writings resisted the new materialism, denied the opposition of rational to spiritual, maintained the natural-law basis of the state, and sought to interpret nature in vitalist and sacramental ways.

These defenses of Christian humanism are embattled, not like Hooker (whom Ernst Cassirer names as a major influence upon them)[21] primarily against an opposing system of polity, but against a fundamentally opposed conception of the world.

IN THE TRAIN of scientific "new philosophy" (which as Donne believed, placed "all in doubt") came mechanism, to join the forces revolutionizing the conception of natural law. "For the ingenious World being grown quite weary of Qualities and Formes, and declaring in favor of the Mechanical Hypothesis," reported Joseph Glanville in 1665, many "accept Mechanism upon Hobbian conditions."[22] For his own part, Glanville thought that a chief aim of the Royal Society ought to be the "searching out of the true laws of Matter and Motion, in order to the securing of the Foundations of Religion against all attempts of Mechanical Atheism."[23]

Whether one was inclined to read pro- or antireligious implication in its discoveries of inexorable pattern, the quantitative and mathematically, rather than philosophically, framed cosmology developed by Galileo and his successors involved a radical redefinition of "nature." Hylozoism gave way to the world-machine; the natural came to be identified with the physical, and the physical with the mechanical.

Bacon admired "scientific" historians like Machiavelli and Guicciardini, who wrote of what men did rather than what they ought to do. Brahe and (after some resistance) Kepler dealt with the heavens as by direct observation they were, and not as they ought to be, according to a priori deduction from classical and Christian belief. The humors theorists developed a harder and more deterministic interpretation of behavior than their predecessors. All were oriented toward the discovery of predictable, i.e., mechanical, causality. Renaissance Lutheranism and Calvinism might have been said to deal with spiritually corrupt and helpless man as he actually was, rather than as Scholastic presumption had vainly theorized him to be. The Calvinistic cleavage between the moral norm of divine command and the human corruption which gave actual behavior over to the animal passions, i.e., to physical causality, accords in this way with the views of the realist historian, the empirical astronomer, the deterministic psychologist. And in another way, the Calvinistic God, conceived as "arbitrary will laying down eternal and unchangeable laws for the creation," says one scholar, "seems ready to merge with Robert Boyle's portrait of the Divine Mechanic."[24] Calvinist voluntarism and Protestant contempt for medieval thought both facilitated the development of the mechanical conception of nature.

Matter and mind had been regarded as parts of one reality, interacting and inseparable, but to Bacon and Descartes, they became separate orders of being, as mutually isolated as body and spirit to the strict Calvinists. The new study of matter and its motions yielded a knowledge which was without moral dimension. Upon the abandonment of the physical world to utilitarian and mechanical sciences, Calvinism, Platonism, Baconian empiricism, and Cartesian rationalism converge. Matter is to the Plotinian Neo-Platonists only the ultimate darkness into which the diminishing emanations of the Absolute finally disappear. To Plato himself it is nonbeing, a principle of limitation; in the *Timaeus,* God creates soul but Demiurge creates the body, soul's prison. Virtually all rising seventeenth-century intellectual forces agreed in segregating the body and the "natural" or physical world from the order of moral value. Men were exhorted to abjure the realm of the senses and strive toward a level of Cartesian mathematical abstraction, Platonic ideas, or ascetic spiritual virtue—or to master nature by accumulating a physical knowledge to which could be allowed no moral or spiritual meaning. There had been, it is true, a long medieval tradition of the psychomachia, but this expressed the hostility of flesh and spirit as two harmonizable substantial principles, not as opposed laws or separate substances. It portrayed a conflict between elements the proper and natural state of which was hierarchical integration within a single substance.

Of the general currency and influence of the new science during the earlier part of the period, G. F. Sensabaugh gives a helpful summary: Bacon's *Novum Organum*, he reminds us, appeared in the same year as Ford's *A Line of Life;* William Harvey's *Exercitatio* was published simultaneously with *The Lover's Melancholy.*

> True scientists . . . were responsible for arousing public excitement. Galileo's announcement in 1610 of his discovery of Jupiter's moons and of countless stars in the Milky Way both fired the imagination of men and led them to bestow on the new scientists an authority formerly given only to Aristotle and Ptolemy—particularly in England, where by the first quarter of the seventeenth century handbooks and religious works had begun to refer to Copernicus, Tycho Brahe, and Galileo.[25]

Even if there was actually no organized "School of Night," there is yet a likelihood of common fascination with the recherché aspects of the new learning on the part of such men as Chapman, Marlowe, and Raleigh. Donne evidently recognized the importance of Kepler's work very early; Henry Wotton invited Kepler to continue his studies in England.

The prestige of science extended also to the humors psychology, which was now received as a genuinely scientific account of "the laws governing man's course in the world." Burton's *Anatomy* (1621) was a popular and successful work of rather pronounced scientific determinism: it is true that it dealt with cures as well as causes of melancholy, but the manipulation of physical causes is a mechanistic approach to behavior. Burton shows the passions to be of physical origin and irresistible by the rational will, so that "man's organs control his whole life, even his habits of virtue and vice."[26] When these passions conflict with society's moral codes, tragedy ensues in which the protagonist is a helpless victim of the disjunction between animal nature, or the new "natural law," and an absolute, or Calvinistic, morality to which that natural law is opposed. Calvin himself, assuming the anti-Scholastic conception of the "natural" which was to become dominant, had said that man "neither rationally chooses as the object of his pursuit that which is truly good for him, . . . nor takes the advice of reason, . . . but without reason, without reflection, follows his *natural* inclination."[27]

Burton actually suggests that the sanctions of traditional morality are cruelly unjust to those moved by the passion of "heroical" love. His mechanistic teaching on the relation between nature and morality thus corresponds with the teaching of Luther and Calvin, although it is concentrated upon the opposite side of the dilemma. God in effect predestinates men to perdition by inexorably mechanical laws of nature operating contrary to the commands which make up morality, the justice of this arrangement being inexplicable. Burton perfects the correspondence by asserting that these mechanisms of nature are based upon God's will. The medieval treatment of the humors had not made their inclinations irresistible, but had integrated the theory with a belief in free will and the retributive power of the natural. Now, says Greville, "Humours are man's religion."[28]

Thus, although the seventeenth century was much

given to talk about natural law, it meant something mechanical rather than moral. The absence of final causality from the test tubes of the new science inevitably meant the eclipse of its intellectual importance. There is an inevitability in the line of development from Bacon and Descartes to Hobbes. "The universe that reason could properly explore," says Samuel Bethell, "had narrowed to the calculable aspects of material existence: This was the real, the rest was epiphenomenon, manageable in part . . . by a 'common sense' which aped the categorical exactitude of true reason, but in the main left to . . . 'enthusiasts' and sentimentalists."[29]

Bacon's handling of religion is, not surprisingly, Scotist, Ockhamite, and Calvinistic.[30] His militantly Calvinist mother, Anne Cooke, controlled his early education, which quite evidently fixed some of the premises underlying his mature work—in particular his absolute separation of natural reason from religious morality, which, he consistently maintained, is not rationally examinable.[31]

Bacon's essay "Of Nature in Men" treats "nature" as the obstacle to be overcome in pursuit of virtue.[32] "Divinity," he believes,

> is grounded only upon the word and oracle of God, and not upon the light of nature: for it is written, *Coeli enarrant gloriam Dei,* but it is not written, *Coeli enarrant voluntatem Dei,* but of that it is said, *Ad Legem et testimonium: si non fecerint secundum verbum istud,* etc. This holdeth not only in those points of faith which concern the great mysteries of the Deity, of the Creation, of the Redemption, but likewise those which concern the law moral truly interpreted. . . . To this it ought to be applauded, *Nec vox hominem sonat:* it is a voice beyond the light of nature. . . . a great part of the law moral is of that perfection, whereunto the light of nature cannot aspire. . . . So then the doctrine of religion, as well

moral as mystical, is not to be attained but by inspiration and revelation from God.[33]

Reason's uses in religion lie "in the conception and apprehension" of revelation, and in "the inferring and deriving of doctrine and direction thereupon." "For after the articles and principles of religion are placed, and exempted from examination of reason, it is then permitted unto us to make derivations and inferences." The laws that underlie morality are "positive upon authority, and not upon reason"—or upon nature, for *"Quod Natura remittit, invida jura negant."*[34] The knowledge by which Adam fell, says Bacon, was "not the natural knowledge of creatures, but the moral knowledge of good and evil; wherein the supposition was, that God's commandments or prohibitions were not the originals of good and evil."[35]

If these Ockhamite premises came to Bacon through a Calvinist intermediary, Puritanism had in turn a part in the spreading of Baconian ideas.[36] There was a widening influence of the inductive and antimetaphysical mentality. The seventeenth century produced no novel answers to the teleological question "Why?" Instead, it increasingly neglected that speculative topic to seek factual solutions to the mechanical problem "How?"

In Bacon's time, says Whitehead, science was becoming, and has remained, primarily quantitative. It developed the conception of nature as "a dull affair, soundless, scentless, colourless, merely the hurrying of material, endlessly, meaninglessly."[37] The scientific denial of objective existence to characteristics other than quantity, figure, and motion, the denial upon which this conception is based, began with Galileo, developed in Descartes, and was completed by Locke.

Bacon's inductive method of collected instances and "exclusions," which aims by elimination to discover efficient causes and physical "essences,"[38] never became very productive of the "commodity" that he so prized, although in the nonmathematical sciences of biology and geology, the Baconian procedures did bear fruit; but its prestige contributed powerfully to mechanistic conceptions of that same nature, entirely segregated from morality, which was implied in Calvinistic thought. Baconian scientists and virtuosi came to see that while physical regularities might be discovered by such a method, the principles presumed even by Baconian science itself, e.g., the principle of causality, and all purpose or moral quality were "insensible."[39]

Bacon thus probably influenced moral philosophy more than he did the actual work of science:[40] he was a very important part of the change which led continental and English thought from a sacramental to a mechanical view of nature. On the basis of the Calvinistic alienation of faith from reason, he set out to show how the world might be comprehended in material terms. The resulting conception of nature as mechanism would provide for the eighteenth century some deistic arguments for a cosmic designer and first mover and offer analogies for human conduct, but it was essentially without axiological meaning.

When Bacon's prophecies had reached such a fulfillment as Newton's *Principia,* it was still generally thought that "natural law" supported religion—i.e., that the astonishing mechanical order of the cosmos argued an original cause which was, as Newton himself said, "not blind and fortuitous, but very well skilled in Mechanics and Geometry."[41] Newton, in fact, insisted that "when I wrote my treatise about our systeme, I had an eye upon such principles as might work with considering men for the beliefe of a Deity; and nothing can rejoyce me more than to find it useful for that purpose."[42] "Gravity," he asserts, "may put the planets into motion; but, without the divine power, it could never put them into such a circulating motion as they have about the Sun; and, therefore, for this, as well as other reasons, I am compelled to ascribe the frame of this Systeme to an intelligent agent."[43] "The cause of gravity," he says, "is what I do not pretend to know";[44] i.e., the mathematically stated law describes only a mechanical regularity, the cause of which is unseen, and is probably the action of God himself. The idea that gravity might be "innate, inherent, and essential to matter" is, says Newton, an absurdity."[45] Calvin would have applauded.

Thus Newton himself climaxed the chorus which, upon the disclosures of the *new* "natural law," urged men to "turn [their] eyes from the works to the workman." But the inexorable order of mechanical causes and effects that gave this theological testimony had nothing to do with the ethical norms referred to as "natural law" by Hooker and reflected in the dramatic world of Shakespeare. That system had appealed from what is to what ought to be; it had drawn not upon fact alone but upon standards evolved partly deductively and a priori. The limit of Baconian science lay, on the other hand, within the boundaries of actual physical fact; it could not accommodate the natural law of Cicero, of Aquinas, of Thomas Elyot, or of Richard Hooker.

After Bacon's work, and then Newton's, men might think it best to "follow nature, still divinely bright" as exemplar or extrinsic model in some respect discerned by reason, but they could no longer conceive of morality as the realizing of an internal human nature, integral with the spiritually purposive social and cosmic orders. External nature might be made a pattern as by Glanville, or denied any participation in moral law, since it taught nothing relevant to salvation. It remained in either case mechanical and divorced from morality. Bacon wanted the achievements of science to testify to the glory of God, but his whole intellectual position was utterly opposed to the traditional Christian humanism which had made of a spiritual and God-oriented human nature a main source of values and standards.

Writing of the eighteenth century, Michael Macklem says that "the idea that moral law is an imperative statement derived from the belief that the standard of moral values is provided by the will of God; the idea that moral law is an indicative statement derived from the belief that the moral standard is provided by the nature of man."[46] If moral law is "an imperative statement" in this sense, it is, he thinks, necessarily unrelated to nature and depends immediately and solely on revelation. If it is "an indicative statement" of that which follows from man's nature, it must be mechanical and unvarying, a description merely of what is. The distinction may be a valid one for the period of which Macklem writes. To Hooker, on the other hand, moral standards did indeed derive from man's nature; and yet, since the human essence was defined by its free rationality, moral law was an imperative to man, not merely an indicative. It defined what should be; it gave standards, rather than simply describing causes and effects like the "natural law" of post-Cartesian thought. It was based ultimately not on divine will but divine reason, and it was wholly conformable to human intelligence.

The Scholastics had thought that the quantitative knowledge drawn through sensation, knowledge of accidents and properties, yielded a qualitative and essential knowledge, and that sense revealed ultimately not only physical properties but something of the essence, distinct from them, to which they were truly "proper." Knowledge based on percepts ended not in the practical command of matter and motion, the "hurrying of material," but in moral and teleological truth. But the method of assigning units of quantity and submitting them to mathematical operations, although it could produce workable and useful formulations of quantitative reality, was quite unable to register the qualitative. The idea gradually weakened that the senses and understanding of men normally perceive the real world as it is, and reality became something concealed behind appearances, which are determined largely by the limitations of the senses.[47] The conception of substance was replaced by that of structure or arrangement of parts as the ultimate reality of things. The world was comprehensible in terms of mechanics, or of efficient causality. Teleology had no relevance to this knowledge and no place in nature as the new science conceived it. Moral purpose was exiled with quality, so that value-judgment became intuitive, fideistic, or merely subjective. Natural law might be pleaded as a precedent for this or that, but it could no longer refer to the demands of an intellectual and spiritual constitution.

Aquinas had entertained no doubt that what Locke would call secondary qualities did possess an existence apart from the observer. "Sense has no false knowledge about its proper objects," he said, "except accidentally."[48] This belief was bedrock in the Middle Ages and early Renaissance; there was a fixed relationship between substances and their evident qualities; by these the mind knew the substratum which supported them. But Galileo denied this, and Descartes, at the end of the Renaissance, believed that such properties as color existed only in our internal sensations, and that "there is nothing known of external objects by the senses but their figure, magnitude, and motion."[49] By 1641 he was convinced that only those things "which, speaking generally, are comprehended in the object of pure mathematics, are truly to be recognized as external objects."[50] The senses may be guides to what is "beneficial or hurtful"; they cannot be reliable sources of knowledge concerning noumenal reality.[51] We do not see a torch or hear a bell; we "perceive just the movements which proceed from them."[52]

Man, whose sense impressions were for Scholasticism the grounds of all knowledge, was now quite cut off from outer reality, which came to be thought of as quantitative structure determined by mathematical relationship, or else as unknowable. Charron asserts that the senses ("vile and corruptible") "do apprehend only the simple accidents, and not the forms, natures, essence of things, much less things universall, the secrets of Nature, and all things insensible." Some men, in fact, have deprived themselves of the use of some of the senses, so that the soul might "better, and more freely execute its own affairs."[53] Basil Willey concludes that after Descartes it was believed that poetry dealt merely with appearances and fictions, and not with truth or reality (which were available only to scientific abstraction): this is perhaps the original "dissociation of sensibility" in modern Western culture.

In his *Apology for Raymonde Sebond*, Montaigne shows the same belief that the real world and the world perceived by sense are not the same. Nature is conceived mechanically and mathematically. The actions of the human body are rigidly determined; the actions of the soul are wholly unrelated to nature. But it is Descartes, with his strange and extreme separation of *res extensa* and *res cogitans*, who most absolutely divides all of the natural from all of the spiritual and moral. The body is for him explicitly a machine, and the soul, which is the person, is *not* its life principle:[54] "This I . . . is entirely and absolutely distinct from my body."[55] Reason is as removed from nature on one hand as it is from faith on the other: "For since nature seemed to cause me to lean towards many things from which reason repelled me, I did not believe that I should trust much to the teachings of nature."[56]

The mechanistic physical world is indifferent to all morality; "look you," says Webster's Bosola, a Jacobean mouthpiece who echoes liberally Montaigne's distrust of knowledge and of natural law, "the stars shine still," despite the curses of the innocent who suffer the world's injustice. The universe of *The Duchess of Malfi* so verifies this estimate of things that Bosola's dying speech, after his repentance for misdeeds, damns "this gloomy world . . . deep pit of darkness" and urges his auditors to disregard it and willingly to suffer its inevitable penalties for doing "what is just." He has learned that virtue is better than the world, to which it remains quite foreign and opposed.

The human person was exempted from complete mechanism but was at the same time cut off from the natural world by this Calvinistic-Baconian-Cartesian division of matter and spirit. Experiential, volitional man—the only possible subject of narrative and drama—became pure reason trapped in an opaquely material universe indifferent to his values. Ethical thought on the mathematical model was ideal and abstract, dissociated from the "nature" of the animal and physical world and dictating an inflexible code. It led in drama to the tragedy of Racine, the tragedy of reason opposed to the forces of life, in a dramatic world where the "right" is a pure logical imperative. Characters do not *become,* do not take on definition under the need to respond to events not merely logically, but as persons. The basic situation of a Racinian tragedy," says Fergusson, "never changes." The tragic pattern is simply that "reason reveals with triumphant clarity its incommensurability with the merely actual world of the senses and emotions."[57] A like division underlies the passivity of Jacobean tragic heroes, whose world is riven by the same dichotomy. The mechanistic-Calvinistic tendency to see the natural and the moral as opposed generally conceives its hero as a victim, crushed between inexorable nature and imperative reason or morality. This happens, in differing ways, in the work of all the Jacobean playwrights here studied. The moral choices which confront their heroes are often as transparent as those of the morality play. The problems are not real: the "right" choice is clear to them and to us, and there is no difficulty of judgment to draw us into the dramatic issues. Suspense and surprise must bear the chief burden of sustaining our interest.

Other Calvinist features in Jacobean plays have not gone wholly unnoticed. "There is a Calvinist strain in Jacobean drama which is commonly overlooked," says Clifford Leech; "the tragic writers know little of heaven but much of hell."[58] More particularly: "Webster's theology is Calvinistic," and "what matters most is Webster's apparently unconscious acceptance of the doctrine of election."[59] Ford, in a religious tract (almost if not quite certainly of his authorship), uses "rather savage Calvinistic terms," and in his plays "has affinities with Calvinism in his notions of an aristocratic elect."[60]

In *Perkin Warbeck, The Broken Heart,* and *Love's Sacrifice,* says Leech, "the exalted human beings' actions never come in for censure. . . . suffering of melancholy or of deprivation is the dominant strain of their world." Only Giovanni (of *'Tis Pity*) is in "the tragic manner of the opening of the century."[61] But Giovanni, as much as the others, is an essentially helpless victim of a "nature" which runs counter to morality. His spiritual adviser admits that if it were not for divine revelation, his incestuous love would be permissible. Ford—or the Friar—regards incest as a moral abomination, but as perfectly natural. We are at a far remove from Shakespeare.

Giovanni is driven helplessly, acquiring what heroic stature he has by his defiance of moral convention. His artificial, irresistible passion forces us to perceive his "guilt" in a purely abstract way, never to feel it or to complicate our sympathy with any recognition of his responsibility.[62] Heywood's Mistress Frankford, in *A Woman Killed with Kindness,* displays the same phenomenon—purely mechanical guilt, kept inviolate from any feeling on our part of her accountability for it or for its consequences. We are made to see unmistakably the heroine's total helplessness: she despises her guilty action; she recoils from its moral horror; but her recognition serves only to reveal the helplessness of conscience or of reason, before contrary nature.

Again in *The Witch of Edmonton,* by Dekker, Rowley, and Ford, Frank Thorney sins helplessly and after punishment and repentance hopes piously for heaven. Malheureux, in Marston's *Dutch Courtesan,* is equally helpless before the power of lust to do what his reason clearly and insistently commands. If we find a Hippolytus-like ironic propriety in this end for his earlier priggishness, that priggishness is in fact nothing else than the moral code of Renaissance Christianity.

We witness in these plays the evil which befalls characters whom we cannot blame, because of transgressions to which we can attach no guilt by any human standard. There is an impulse on the part of the playwrights to redeem this otherwise unbearable picture by the promise of heaven. The incomprehensibility of the evil which they dramatize has much in common with the Calvinistic, little with the tragic, at least in any sense relevant to the Shakespearean achievement.[63] Something had changed radically within the traditional homiletic pattern of temptation, sin, discovery, repentance, and punishment.

The Baconian mechanistic conception of nature, on the other hand, also contained in embryo the belief that "whatever is, is right." In the older tradition, the state of things in this world was not necessarily or always their natural condition. "The natural object was that which perfectly expressed the idea of a thing. It was the perfect object,"[64] so that the only wholly natural man was, in a sense, the saint.

There are traces of mechanism in William Perkins' sermons and tracts and in Ralegh's *History*. Later, Fuller and Browne show its influence. Selden displays a "sophisticated contempt for the effort to read moral significance into the events of nature."[65] The Catholic Pascal recoiled into fideism before the implications of mechanistic thought. Glanville wrote in *The Vanity of Dogmatizing* that "how the purer Spirit is united to this *clod*, is a knot too hard for our degraded intellects to unty," and that "to hang weights on the wings of the winde seems far more intelligible" than to explain the interaction of soul and body.[66] Philosophical "occasionalism" represents a final extremity of the effort to explain how the human spirit and the mechanical world of nature can have any relation whatever.

THE INCREASING skepticism of the early seventeenth century was more conscious of its implications for treading on the heels of an unquestioned Christian rationalism. "What had once been a fashionable skepticism—Donne's youthful Paradoxes and Problems is a very fair specimen—could become the starting point of Bacon's methodology, of Descartes' metaphysics, of Hobbes' political juggernaut . . . this skepticism, which waxed as the Renaissance waned, was basically a protest against Scholastic rationalism."[67]

The decline of natural law might be considered as only an aspect of this larger shift. Certainly there developed a widespread feeling which, as Chesterton said, "is not unconnected with skepticism . . . first, that we do not really know the laws of the universe; and second that they may be very different to all that we call reason."[68] Bacon indicated his regard for several of the ancient and modern skeptics; Greville was well acquainted with systematic skepticism; Raleigh's essay "The Skeptic" employs the classic solipsistic arguments. Whether or not Ralegh and Marlowe were really atheists, the skeptical "poison of Atheisme" was increasingly present.

Sextus Empiricus was fashionable with the learned. Lucretius and the Epicureans seem to have been known in England, if not so well as on the continent. Montaigne and Machiavelli were quite familiar. Agrippa and Diogenes Laertius were read. Montaigne himself was so enthusiastic over Sextus Empiricus that he struck a medal to celebrate his discovery chiefly of that writer and decorated his study walls with mottoes taken from him. Pierre Charron (*De La Sagesse*, 1601) and Francois La Mothe Le Vayer (*Dialogues Faits à L'imitation de anciens*, 1630) were continental exponents of skeptical thought who commanded an English audience. A point of emphasis with all was the impossibility of a natural science of ethics, in light of the contradictory moral customs of diverse peoples. A passage from La Mothe Le Vayer's *Dialogues* is especially revealing.

> L'empereur Claudius ayant epouse sa niece Agrippine les incestes furent permis par authorite du Senat. Et nous sommes contraints d'advouer que ce qui est inceste aujourd'huy, estoit innocence a lanaissance du monde. Les voyages d'Americ Vespuce, nour ont appris qi'en toutes les Indes Occidentales il n'y avoit aucune acception de parente, pour cela; Marc Polo soustient le mesme des Indes d'orient, et les Druses du Liban vivent encore aujourd'huy de la sorte. Pour ce qui est semblables nous monstrent journellement le contraire.[69]

"Thus," says Bredvold, "the law of nature and of nations . . . is dissipated into a chimera."

Montaigne sometimes exalts nature over convention and artifice, particularly in discussing education. By the late part of his career, he seems in fact convinced that it is best to "follow nature." But the nature in question is largely identified with appetite, impulse, and instinct; it is connected with individuality and self-expression; it anticipates Rousseau rather than recalling Hooker.

The Calvinist revival of nominalism provided a congenial milieu for skeptics: in holding law and virtue to derive from the divine will, the nominalists placed them beyond thought. Calvinism and Jansenism, by considering the natural faculties useless with respect to virtue, further aligned themselves with the skeptical deprecation of those powers.

Science too had some impact on skepticism. Thomas Sprat, Robert Boyle, and others were constrained to defend it "in respect to the Christian Faith." Finally, the individualism of the Protestant sects generated a climate of dispute which, like the excessive controversiality of late Scholasticism, tended to wear itself out in an anti-intellectual and skeptical mood, and to produce by reaction a simplistic fideism.

All that we can know of the world, says Ralegh, is how it appears; but it must appear differently to different creatures, according to the varying constitution of their sense organs.[70] Greville's *Treatise of Humane Learning* is skeptical as well as Calvinistic. Donne, Burton, Browne, and Hobbes (who, says Aubrey, was once Bacon's secretary, and whose *Elements of Law* was circulated in manuscript by 1640) were skeptics of varying kinds and degrees. By Restoration times, skeptical thought was *de rigeur;* it was "grown the entertainment of tables and taverns."[71]

Fideism, or religious faith founded on skepticism, was common. "The more discordant therefore and incredible the Divine mystery is," said Bacon, "the more honour is shown to God in believing it, and the nobler is the victory of faith."[72] Among both Protestants and Catholics, this note was increasingly strong. A number of the continental skeptics were not attacking but defending religion. In England, Edward Stillingfleet's *Origines Sacrae* (1662) went so far as to reverse the older formula by making reason itself depend on faith. Much earlier, Marston expressed a contemporary religious mood in *What You Will:*

> The more I learnt the more I learnt to doubt.
> Knowledge and Wit, faith's fool, turn faith about.

At least one of Donne's sermons dealt with the hazards of submitting faith to "the common light of reason"—a course by which one might "sooner become mad than good," since reason was opposed to religion.[73] In Du Bartas' Calvinistic *Triumph of Faith,* reason "seekes for masks, vizards, and garments gay / . . . Of her loath'd limbs to hide the foule disgrace." The work of her tongue is "Blaspheming Heaven with filthy vanities," and since the first creation, she "Hath with mild *Faith* maintain'd continuall fight." The poem consigns to hell not only Plato and Aristotle ("Sorrie t'have led so many soules awry"), but "he that labours to conciliate them."[74] Pious skepticism proclaimed the Ockhamite-Calvinist doctrine of divine inscrutability and the darkness and helplessness of reason.

The skeptical spirit burgeoned in the later Renaissance as political and other forces converged to reinforce the Calvinist depression of man's estate. Marston's slashing seventh satire in *The Scrouge of Villanie.* Donne's *Songs and Sonnetts* which attack moral codes as dead conventions, are examples of its libertine aspect.

Finally, a mood of pessimism, the corollary of these developments, is discernible in the Jacobean period and has, in fact, long been recognized as a *leitmotif* of the age. Throughout the Renaissance there had been maintained a secondary tradition of contempt for "stinking" men—"huge impolish't heapes of filthiness," and the belief had never disappeared that "the latter daies" of the world, as of the microcosm man, must be a time of decay. More's *Four Last Things*, Baldwin's *Treatise of Moral Philosophie: The Mirror for Magistrates*, many of the satires, *The Paradise of Dainty Devices* and other volumes of somber poetry, all had carried on the background strain of *contemptus mundi*. In *Timon*, *Lear*, and *Macbeth*, Shakespeare provided glimpses of the nightmare vision of disintegration and chaos come again.

After 1600 this stream widened and darkened, pessimism growing more pervasive. There was a last efflorescence of the spirit of the *ars moriendi* and the late medieval *dans macabre* which had entered into the composition of the morality plays where Renaissance tragedy began.[75] There is in Donne's sermons a dwelling on bodily putrefaction, illuminated by the techniques of Ignatian meditation, which does not belong to the Elizabethan age: "Between that excrementall jelly that thy body is made of at first, and that jelly which thy body dissolves to at last; there is not so noysome, so putrid a thing in nature,"[76] says Donne, from an imagination touched by the forces which shaped both seventeenth-century Calvinism and the Jacobean drama. "By the second decade of the seventeenth century the subject of decay had developed a morbid fascination for some of the most sensitive poets and theologians of the age. Webster's ghastly vision of a charnel-house world is hardly separate in mood and conviction from a theological treatise published in the year of Shakespeare's death, *The Fall of Man*."[77] This book's not unfamiliar message was that the earth was in the last stages of corrupt decrepitude.

By 1600 or shortly after, the Renaissance was dying, and with its close, "the ancient tradition of human dignity as conceived in terms of Hellenic and Christian humanism, entered its long decline."[78] Jacques Maritain, T. E. Hulme, Christopher Dawson, C. S. Lewis, and others have lamented this eclipse of the integrated medieval world-view in which natural-law conceptions had formed so central a part, and have considered the period under study here as being more an end than a beginning. The general mood of disillusionment, the Lutheran and more importantly the Calvinistic theology, the Jansenist movement, the skeptic revival, the rise of Baconian science, all converged upon the withering of the old conception of natural law, and therefore of the Elizabethan tragic vision. Of these disintegrating forces, all but the last two were popular, and these two were powerful among the coterie audience to which the drama increasingly belonged.

Chapter Six

The New
Meaning of
Tragedy:
Heywood &
Webster

THE CONNECTION of the
greatest Renaissance tragedies with the spirit of medieval rationalism is unmistakable: the reconciliation to
the tragic world achieved in those plays is integral with
their realizing of medieval philosophical assumptions.
The continuity between the altered spirit of later tragedy and the dissipation of belief in a natural moral law
is more mediate and various. The fact that tragedy
changed, losing its affirmative power, is well enough
recognized. It is clear too that the medieval conception
of natural law died in the intellectual and religious revo-
lutions of the time, while the term took on a meaning
nearly opposite to its traditional one.

In the Jacobean tragedies and tragicomedies there

appear a number of alternatives to the old pattern. But a fundamental difference in moral vision and an ultimate reason for the darkness which has descended in the cosmos of Webster, Tourneur, or Ford, or the meaninglessness of the world where Fletcher's virtuosity performs its feats,[1] is not the presence, in the structure of that world, of particular other philosophies or moral systems, but the absence of the traditional natural law. And a vacuum can be hard to describe. Nor is there any exact chronology to divide the medievally based tragedy from the drama of voluntaristic, Calvinistic, and mechanistic influence. Elizabethan culture and dramatic literature were various enough to admit many currents. Some plays which bear the Calvinist stamp and witness the failure of the earlier tragic vision were written before *King Lear* or *Macbeth*.

Certain general characteristics do appear in most of the tragedies beneath which natural-law foundations have been replaced by Calvinist-voluntarist ones, or have simply collapsed. The implicit standard of judgment, the basis for the "good" actions of "good" characters, will often be a code morality.[2] What we are led to feel as virtue will be some course of action in which these characters are governed by highly mechanical ethical codes. The dilemma of Susan Mountford in *A Woman Killed with Kindness* (which in Shakespeare would have been a problem, a conflict, but not a true dilemma) is created by such a conception of virtue, accepted by Susan, by her brother Sir Charles, and by Sir Francis Acton, demurred from by no character, assumed by Heywood as a basis of action much as Shakespeare assumed the natural law. On one hand is her own sexual honor, on the other her brother's honorable duty to discharge an obligation and free himself of a debt to an enemy. There is no solution to this dilemma: the play's answer is that Susan will preserve her brother's honor by yielding to Sir Francis and her own honor by suicide. Nobility or virtue—at any rate the quality which marks sympathetic characters—is commonly incompatible with life. Virtue is not the primordial demand made by life, a guide and safeguard, a map of the terrain to be crossed; it is something separate from, and better than, the exercise of prudence; it points directions which disregard the topography of the world; its imperatives have no need of the application of reason to particular circumstances: they exist separately and absolutely.

This is a Calvinist morality of inflexible command. The Calvinistic virtues must be absolutes, because they are unrelated to the natures of things and to reason's judgments of the demands of nature. Man is not free to submit divine imperatives to reason in the face of varying circumstance, and so morality becomes a set of absolutes, an inflexible code in a sense in which Christian ethics, understood as based in the natural law, had not been a code. When two such absolutes come into play, they may well conflict, as do the two "honors" in *A Woman Killed with Kindness*, or the loyalty and honor of Amintor in Fletcher's *Maid's Tragedy*. In the morality of natural law, it was axiomatic that right reason could not conflict with itself, so that opposed virtues were an absurdity—were by definition impossible. Susan Mountford's dilemma was conceived in a mind to which virtues are fixed patterns of action rather than habits or principles by which the operation of human faculties might be developed and perfected.

In a more practical sense, virtue was, in the older ethics, the way in which reason adjusted to the world, a world ordered by reason and inherently rational. But morality abstracted from nature becomes a code the inability of which to accommodate circumstance provides some of the basis of tragedy—a tragedy in which the hero is always really a victim, and the final effect is not acquiescence in the order of nature and the conditions of life, but rebellion against a world in which all that is noblest may be alien and vulnerable.

The helplessness or passivity which this suggests is in fact a mark of the Jacobean hero. Calvin, although his central doctrine of predestination denied human control, insisted that it did not deny responsibility, which he explained by a distinction between externally constrained and internally necessitated actions.[3] But the Calvinist view gives no sense of the command of one's destiny. For dramatic purposes, a distinction between kinds of helplessness before fate can hardly be relevant. Sympathy for the fated or "necessitated" tragic sinner, and rebelliousness against the existing order and its conventions, which crush the individual whose "natural" needs drive him to violate it, are another dimension of this helpless entrapment between nature and morality, in which one's ruin can be foreordained.

Scientific determinism provided a convenient, congruent picture of the tragic sinner as victim of involuntary forces. Behavior is largely controlled by amoral influences suggested by the psychological symptomology of humors, not only in the plays of Ford, but to some extent in those of Heywood and Webster. Morality and nature are thus disjoined, the first becoming oppressive, the second irresistible. The individual may suffer because nature compels him to violate the absolute edicts of morality, and society punishes him (as with Giovanni and Annabella in Ford's *'Tis Pity*). Or he may suffer the inner torments of outraged nature because he adheres to orthodox morality, as do Fletcher's Amintor in *The Maid's Tragedy* and Ford's Penthea in *The Broken Heart*. He may render himself fatally helpless by adherence to a virtuous code which ignores the demands of reality, like the title-hero of Greville's *Mustapha*. Or, as in many of the Beaumont and Fletcher plays, the tragic issues may be based entirely on misunderstandings and false reports (in which the audience is deceived equally with the characters) which can be dispelled in act five by the introduction of previously concealed facts, to provide by a happy ending the relief which is otherwise no longer possible.

A strong element of satyr-satire persists in Jacobean tragedies and tragicomedies. Revulsion at the general depravity of fallen man, a horror for "the flesh," for man the animal, pervades the period. Chapman, Marston, Tourneur, and Webster are as Calvinistic in this respect as the conventional "false Puritans" whom they satirize. Rotten sensuousness and prodigality, sycophancy and guile, cruelty and selfish ambition are everywhere in their fictional worlds.

Chapman and Webster concentrate upon the evils of courts; Tourneur rails continually against "the age." But Chapman is certainly not making a narrowly special study of court conditions; he does not interpret human experience as he does because he is writing of the court as an isolated and special situation. Rather, he writes of the court because it is a suitable vehicle for his interpretation of life. Courtly experience may have influenced that view, but that is another matter. Tourneur fulminates, on the note of satyr-satire, against "the age"—the sustaining theme of the cankered muse. But he does not present humanity as vicious, and the world as a jungle where virtue is an universal prey, because he thinks of those conditions as peculiar to the time, contrasted with an actual past. The denouncing moralist focuses by definition on his own time. The norm against which it is measured (and one must exist before he can denounce) may be, as to the Calvinist, a set of divine commands which can never be realized by the world. Yet it will easily appear as a better state of things located in the past.

A true dividing line lies between the high Renaissance, which endorsed and celebrated things as they are, which accepted and embraced the universe and its order, and the following ages, whose literature very often rebels against or laments the way things are. If such a rebellion is inseparable from our idea of romanticism, then a greater part of the time from the early seventeenth century to the present has been to a considerable degree romantic in its literary sensibility.

Some Jacobean dramatists, notably the four mentioned above, use the properties of the Senecan and Machiavellian "blood" tradition as modern Southern novelists have used those of a gothic tradition in the novel: as a tropology for their sense of the world, a psychological symbolism in which to embody a nightmare vision of the essential human situation. One may point to the ecclesiastical proscription of formal satires in 1599 to explain the appearance of this sort of social criticism and of the railing malcontent "satyr" character in the drama;[4] but this provides the history rather than the cause of a powerful sense of corruption in Jacobean tragedy and tragicomedy. A glance at Lutheran and Calvinist teaching and a reminder of the ubiquity of its influence may be more to the essential point.

There is, again, no single point at which to mark the displacement of natural law in the drama. In Wever's morality play *Lusty Juventus*, written about 1550 "to expose the superstitions of the Romish Church, and to promote the Reformation," moral instruction is given to the hero by "God's Merciful Promises":

> For me his mercy sake thou shalt obtain his grace,
> And not for thine own desertes, this must thou know;
> For my sake alone, ye shall receive solace.
> For my sake alone, he will thee mercy show.[5]

The Augustinian and anti-Scholastic feeling is clear enough in this. Much of the play, in fact, is devoted to arguing against justification by works. In John Bale's very Protestant moralities, the presentation of Providence—of God's vengeance—fits the Calvinistic pattern.

The Sidney family figures almost as prominently in the history of English Calvinism as in that of English literature. Sir Philip Sidney's aunt, the Countess of Sussex, in 1596 founded Sidney Sussex College for the training of preachers, and the school contributed substantially to the Puritan movement.[6] Both Sidney and his sister, the Countess of Pembroke, were interested in Calvinist religious works. Lady Mary translated Philippe de Mornay's *Discourse of Life and Death* in 1592, and Sir Philip began a translation of another work by the same Huguenot writer, a project completed by Arthur Golding. The English version of the *Discourse* appeared as a sort of preface to Garnier's classical tragedy *Marc Antoine*, written for the Countess.

The wicked Cecropia, in Sidney's *Arcadia*, urges defiance of parental authority with the argument that when man "strives to things supernaturall, meane-while he looseth his owne naturall felicitie."[7] Pamela replies with a four-page theological assault on this libertinism, but the Calvinist opposition of natural to supernatural is never questioned.

Another of the dramatic circle gathered around the Countess was Samuel Daniel, whose *Complaint of Rosamund* (1592) is, in its moralizing, much engaged by Calvinistic problems:

> But Fate is not prevented, though Foreknown.
> For that must hap, decreed by heavenly powers,
> Who Worke our Fall, yet make the fault still ours.[8]

Fulke Greville, Sidney's friend and biographer, Bacon's friend and intellectual debtor, produced two Senecan plays under the influence of the movement led by Daniel and Alexander. In *Mustapha*, his petrifyingly sententious characters sometimes echo the Scholastic tradition that "God, even to himselfe, hath made a law" (II. ii. 128).⁹ But the play has "no soul / Diffus'd quite through, to make [it] of a piece": incoherently mixed with and overbalancing these (perhaps mechanical) pieties, are Greville's expressions of another spirit, a stronger feeling that "The Earth drawes one way, and the skie another" (IV. i. 38). It is *tyrants* who, refusing to abide the will of heaven, "Make wisdome conscience; and the world their skie"; to Greville this is gross usurpation, arrogating to the world and mundane wisdom the offices of opposite and superior things. A sympathetic character laments that "Nature is lost, our being onely Chance, / Where Grace alone, not Merit, must advance" (IV. iv. 8–9). These terms are aimed particularly at the quixotic rule of the tyrant, "Solyman," but no reader in Greville's time could have avoided their primarily theological meaning, nor acquitted their speaker of protest against the Calvinist God. A Mohammedan priest complains

> O wretched Flesh! in which must be obeyed
> God's law, that wills Impossibilities,

and the sentiment does not seem to be "placed" as a pagan or infidel one. A chorus near the play's end (*Chorus Quintus, Tartarorum*) speaks in defense and praise of the law of nature. This perhaps belongs a little more clearly to pagan "Tartars." Otherwise we hardly know how to consider it, especially as it is followed by the better-known *Chorus Sacerdotum*, whose feeling, whatever its dramatic placing, could hardly have occurred outside the Calvinistic intellectual experience in which Greville prominently shared:

> Oh, wearisome condition of humanity,
> Born under one law, to another bound,
> Vainly begot, and yet forbidden vanity,

Created sick, commanded to be sound.
What meaneth nature by these diverse laws?
Passion and reason self-division cause:
Is it the marke, or Maiesty of Power
To make offences that it may forgive?

The interest in religious and philosophical discussion which is so awkwardly evident in Greville's plays produced also the *Treatie of Humane Learning*, a didactic poem in which he voices strong and unmistakable Calvinistic contempt for human nature and human knowledge, together with a Baconian insistence upon the materially useful. His poetic *Treatie of Warres* is equally stern about human depravity, which is always "striving to disfashion / Order, Authority, Lawes, and good," for "by our fall, wee did God's image leave."[10]

There was, in short, a strain of Calvinistic feeling running directly counter to the traditions of natural law, but co-existing with it in Renaissance literature, which was to rise to dominance in the Jacobean period.[11]

THOMAS HEYWOOD, the most prolific of all the Renaissance playwrights, is called by his biographer "a royalist presbyterian."[12] His plays deal incessantly in sin, lust, virtue, chastity, heaven, hell, Providence, and divine vengeance—the currency of the pulpit. An explicitly religious morality is in fact the preoccupation of all his work, dramatic and nondramatic. His assumptions about human nature, moral law, and divine Providence are distinctly Calvinistic, and from his tragedies the Shakespearean patterns of the natural law are demonstrably absent.

Heywood was born in 1573 and entered Cambridge (probably Emmanuel College, which was, with Christ's, a stronghold of Puritanism) in the early 1590's, when the Calvinistic current there was strong.[13] He was evidently the author, a half-century later, of two Calvinist pamphlets (*Brightman's Predictions* and *A Revelation of Mr. Brightman's Revelation*) expositing the religious prophecies of a Puritan preacher and magnifying the Genevan accomplishment.[14] Calvinist associations were apparently co-extensive with his career.

He has sometimes been overrated since Lamb referred to him, in the precritical spirit of an age when the "old plays" were being rediscovered, as a "prose Shakespeare." Despite a few characters who have real vitality, a relatively clear and natural style which sometimes rises to achieve considerable power, and a journeyman's dependable sense of point of view, there is nothing Shakespearean in Heywood. The way in which he sees human conflicts is basically different from Shakespeare's way and leads to other dramatic patterns. He has, too, a relentless passion for pathos which is un-Shakespearean. Above all, Heywood has but one or two strings to his bow. A dozen of his plays, read through together, coalesce in memory into a few basic situations and even fewer central themes. The recurring ethical and philosophic speeches are much alike from one to another; the pathos, including that of the recurrent sinner-victims really more sinned against by the cruel facts of a nature which leaves them no strength against evil, are the same in chronicle, romance, tragedy, and even comedy. Rarely do we pass many pages without a sermon.

Heywood's nearest approach to greatness, and the "type" of the domestic tragedy, is *A Woman Killed with Kindness* (1603). Yet this play, despite its bourgeois realism, is prophetic of the decline from Shakespeare to the heroic and sentimental drama of the eighteenth century. It fails as tragedy because it fails to crystallize any vision of intelligible law: Anne Frankford's downfall does not follow from a significant exercise of her will, although it is mechanically a consequence of her action. This is evidently what Eliot meant when he wrote that the play is weak because the fate of the heroine "is not a vindication of inexorable moral law";[15] certainly he intended more than the usual observation that Mistress Anne is inadequately characterized. Heywood's didactic concern with morality[16] (in a sense smaller than the Shakespearean one of natural law) leads him to observe the letter of Aristotelian tragedy; his instincts lead him to violate its spirit. The play never achieves a satisfactory unity.

The heroine's crucial action is insufficiently related to her character because Heywood does not (nor does he want us to) feel her responsible, as Shakespeare does with his heroes, despite our continuing sympathy with most of them. Heywood intends that our emotional response to Anne's suffering be one of unalloyed pity, like that inspired by the pathetic heroine of later sentimental tragedy. Whatever we would think were we coldly to judge the morality of her pivotal action by the play's declared moral canons, we are not permitted to feel her guilt emotionally.

In a scene which has occupied much criticism, Anne is seduced by the villain, Wendoll. Not only does she recognize the heinous folly of her act; it is she who voices every possible objection. Arguing powerfully against her own submission, she makes no attempt at self-deception or justification and manifests not the slightest desire; the only feeling she expresses is horror. There is no hint that "reason panders will." It is not, in fact, desire which is emphasized in her fall from virtue, but (unless we impose some unjustified and oversubtle interpretation upon what Heywood plainly says) confusion or helplessness.

> What shall I say?
> My soule is wandring, and hath lost her way.[17]

In her next speech, in which she consents more explicitly, Anne manages in eight lines to refer to her act as a "fall," a "fault," and an "offense"; to assure us that she is ashamed; to "pray God"; to predict that she will have reason to curse Wendoll's eloquence; to refer to her situation as a "maze"; and to make the first of many sorrowful references to "sin." Her adulterous act is in no way related to her character as developed previously: her arguments against it, on the other hand, fit that character perfectly. It is exactly the docile wife of act I who speaks here, full as ever of the pieties of conventional bourgeois virtue. This is her perfectly consistent character throughout the play. The act of adultery is mechanically superimposed on that character, its improbability being a part of Heywood's conscious or unconscious intent.

The abruptness of Anne's fall is usually referred to Elizabethan stage conventions of instant character reversal, or dismissed by the observation that neither Heywood nor the drama had yet achieved much psychological subtlety, and that the swift passage of events on the Elizabethan stage required different methods than those of the novel.[18] Craig assures us that in the light of Renaissance psychology and moral philosophy, such a leap from grace would be quite credible; other critics remind us that because of the conventions, there was no need for it to be credible at all (in *A Warning for Fair Women*, the same event is presented merely in dumbshow). Neither argument covers all of this case. Heywood might have been able to show a very swift temptation and fall (like Angelo's in *Measure for Measure*) for either or both of these reasons, but that is not what he chooses. He has rather gone out of his way to contrast what Anne is with what she does. By emphasizing her clear and intense consciousness of all the objections at the very moment of Wendoll's success, Heywood heavily underscores her helplessness. When Anne tells us that her "soule is wandring," we know pityingly that she, poor thing, is lost!

If we regard her consent as a free act, Anne's punishment is not tragically disproportionate; it is in fact hardly adequate to the crime. (The play has not a thoroughly tragic ending, but a sentimentally indulgent one, the heroine figuratively floating upward like Little Eva.) Heywood designs a pathetic effect, not a consideration of responsibility. There is ample evidence in the dramatic particulars: first, there is Wendoll's striking eloquence. His crucial seduction speech is easily the best in the play. In really Shakespearean fashion, he turns the outrageousness of his proposal to his own persuasive advantage. Second, the nature of Anne's protestations, mentioned above: there is no reason for interpreting these in any other way than the literal one in which Heywood has written them. Third, following the celebrated card-game scene, Anne tries persistently to keep her husband from leaving on his (feigned) business trip. She offers to arouse him early in the morning and gives every evidence of really wanting him to stay at home. When he refuses, she entreats Wendoll to "beare him company." Since she always speaks of her adulterous relationship as a horror which she passionately wishes to escape, this plea to her husband must be taken literally and as contributing to the pathos of her role. Fourth, left alone with Wendoll, she speaks to him in this vein:

> Oh! what a clog unto the soule is sin?
> We pale offenders are still full of feare;
> Every suspitious eye brings danger neare;
> When they whose cleere hearts from offence are free,
> Dispise report; base scandals do outface,
> And stand at meere defiance with disgrace.
> . . . .
> You have tempted me to mischiefe, Master Wendoll:

I have done I know not what. Well, you plead custome;
That which for want of wit I granted erst,
I now must yeelde through fear.

It would distort the text to assume that she has any
reason to dissemble here. Finally Anne, dying, expresses
her certainty of heaven. She is a sinner in her own eyes,
but one of the most elaborately penitent the stage has
seen. So sure is Heywood of our sympathy with her
goodness of heart that he lets her speak confidently of
her imminent heavenly beatitude.

Anne has been the pathetic victim of circumstances
beyond her control; this is the emotional rather than the
rational value of her role. The crucial failure of the play
is that the two are not inseparable, as they are in Shakespearean tragedy.

To say that she is inadequately motivated is, then, to
see only an effect and not the central cause of the failure. Heywood did not want her motivated in the way we
tend to demand, preferring our pity for her fall unmarred by any emotional realization of her own hand in
it. Where pathos is a chief element in drama, as here,
conflict becomes external, and character is either noble
or wicked. In terms of emotional values, Heywood has
done this; he retains the plot of the Aristotelian tragedy,
yoked to the characterization of the sentimental drama.

The subplot of *A Woman Killed with Kindness* has
usually been thought a structural botch. Clark considers
it an alien Italian romance, strained and silly when
dressed in English manners to accompany the Frankford story.[19] Yet there are correspondences which link
the two actions thematically. In the main plot, Wendoll
is deeply indebted to his friend Frankford, but repays
him with dishonor by seducing his wife. The heroine's
sinfulness causes disaster for herself, her husband, and
Wendoll. In the subplot, Mountford is indebted to his
enemy Acton and seeks to repay him with a code

"honor" by proposing Susan's Mountford's surrender of her chastity. Susan's virtue leads to salvation for herself, her brother, and Acton. In the Frankford plot, the two friends are separated and ruined by the viciousness of one, because Anne is morally weak; in the subplot, the two enemies are reunited and saved from the viciousness of one, because Susan is morally strong. There are mechanical plot-links: Sir Francis Acton's injustice to Mountford is a remote cause of Anne's ruin, for it drives Wendoll, Mountford's follower, to refuge in Frankford's house.

Many of Heywood's double plots show a similar paralleling. Although critical tracing of these analogies presents procrustean temptations, it does appear that attention to the moral issues in the joined plots—and such issues are conscious and important to this playwright—reveals their unity and illuminates the play.

The English Traveller is virtually a rewriting (ca. 1625–1630) of *A Woman Killed with Kindness*. The pathetic heroine here is Mistress Wincott, wife of Old Wincott. Her childhood friend, young Geraldine, returns from Jerusalem to become a familiar guest in her house, as Wendoll in Frankford's. The two exchange vows of fidelity and even a promise of marriage after Old Wincott's death. The heroine, however, betrays both her husband and Young Geraldine with the villain Delavil. She is discovered and accused, suffers the same abject repentance as Anne Frankford, quickly dies of grief over her sin, and is forgiven by her husband, who learns of her guilt from her dying letter of confession.

There is the same acutely religious feeling which suffused the language of *A Woman Killed with Kindness* and led Heywood there to violate the traditions of the revenge play by Frankford's Christian forgiveness of his wife. The sentiment expressed in the first scene by Old

Wincott—"Heaven hath will in all things"—is never long unvoiced in any of Heywood's plays.

The subplot of *The English Traveller* is a Plautine-Jonsonian intrigue involving the profligate Young Lionel, his father, and the wily servant Reginald. Young Lionel, a sympathetic character, is a sinner of Anne Frankford's stamp: in the midst of his lusts and riots he delivers a sermon on these courses, convicting himself of "sloth and negligence, / Lust, disobedience, and profuse excess / . . . every riotous sin!" When his mistress enters, he exclaims

> Oh heer's that Haile, Shower, Tempest, Storme, and
> Gust
> That shatter'd hath this building; Let in Lust,
> Intemperance, appetite to Vice; withall,
> Neglect of every Goodnesse; thus I see,
> How I am sinking in mine owne disease,
> Yet can I not abide it.
>
> (I. ii)

He is quite helpless before his own nature:

> In Youth there is a Fate, that sways us still,
> To know what's Good, and yet pursue what's ill.
>
> (I. ii)

This articulates neatly enough the central theme of both stories, which gives them some affinity despite their remoteness by other standards.

The offenses of Mistress Wincott in the tragic main plot and Young Lionel in the comic subplot violate the decalogue, not any natural law. No errors—or problems —of judgment are involved, only the opposition of nature to the perfectly clear and absolute dictates of religious morality.

Geraldine's arrangement with Mistress Wincott instances the hypothetical character of Heywood's ethical world. The way to her bedchamber, we are told, is a path that he has "frequently trodden . . . at midnight, and all hours"—in perfect innocence, although he is filled with "fiery love." On such a visit, Geraldine discovers the lady's adultery; he has, fortunately, left his sword in his own room and so is prevented from doing execution on the adulterers in the first moment of his anger, just as Frankford failed happily to act his first impulse of vengeance, giving him time to recover his sober Christian principles. Geraldine leaves the lovers with a muttered assurance that although they "sin securely," "Heaven will find time to punish."

Good Mistress Wincott's "fall" to sinfulness is entirely unexplained. Like that of Heywood's other central characters, it is perhaps best understood as requiring no special motivation in the light of Calvinistic assumptions, as Iago's malignity needs little particular reason in light of the conventions of Vice and Machiavel. We witness simply the "perpetual corruption of our nature,"[20] which is "so completely alienated from the righteousness of God, that it conceives, desires, and undertakes every thing that is impious, perverse, base, impure, and flagitious."[21]

Geraldine accuses Mistress Wincott, and she repents so violently that her sudden restoration to virtue proves fatal. She dies within minutes, but not before assuring her auditors that "my peace already I have made with Heaven."

If we ask what has destroyed the tragic heroine, the answer may well be "nothing"; in a play-world where theological considerations fill every mouth, the emphasis on her assured ascent to heaven guarantees that the dramatic effect of her death, although luxuriously pathetic, is hardly that of her ruin or destruction. If we ask more concretely what has caused her death, the answer is not "sin," but "penitence." Until the moment when she first looks upon this "sin" through the eyes of spiritual regeneration (which comes like a stroke of quite unmerited grace, to secure a spiritual salvation based wholly on faith) Mistress Wincott suffers no natural or worldly discomposure because of her wickedness. Her situation, one might argue, has its practical risks; but there is none of the poison of evil familiar in Shakespeare—none of the spreading ill effects and unforeseen complications which follow the missteps of a Richard, Romeo, Lear, Othello, or Macbeth. This "sin" exists in a world where its consequences are all "spiritual"; it can, everyone asserts, damn a soul eternally, but it is not apprehensible as an assault on a natural order of things, having physical, social, and psychological consequences. Whatever worldly effects it has depend entirely upon its discovery by one of the righteous, who can abominate it in the name of religious morality, or upon a pious grief which the sinner feels precisely because of his religious consciousness of sin.

To sum up: in *The English Traveller* there is no motive for Mistress Wincott's treachery, only the motiveless malignity of "the flesh" and the irresistibility of concupiscence. The tragic heroine sins against religious morality, not against nature in any visibly evidenced way. By the play's end she is made wholly sympathetic and is felt to be a victim of evil.

Heywood's early and loosely made *Edward IV* (1599) uses essentially the same plot in its treatment of the story of Jane Shore. In that play, King Edward struggles manfully ("down, rebel, back, base, treacherous conceit") against his passion for the beautiful wife of Shore, but to no effect. Poor virtuous Jane is "sicke with paine" at the hard choice of being false to her marriage vows or rebel to her king. She has really no choice, of course:

> If you inforce me, I have nought to say;
> But wish I had not lived to see this day.

Upon the king's insistence that she come to court, Jane gets briskly, if a little prematurely, about her chief business as a Heywood heroine: repentance.

> Well, I will in; and ere the time beginne
> Learn how to be repentant for my sinne.

Our glimpses of her as Edward's mistress show her busy at her renowned works of charity: our sympathy must not weaken. In a tearful interview with the queen, Jane confesses "my sinne" and is forgiven. Meeting Shore, she pleads to return to him as his "slave," and he stoutly replies

> Thou go with me, Jane? Oh, God forbid
> That I should be a traitor to my King.
> Shal I become a felon to his pleasures,
> And fly away, as guilty of the theft?

This unconditional, mechanical virtue of duty to an absolute royal right belongs to Heywood's general ethical machinery, rather than to specifically political doctrine. In the last scene, Shore forgives his wife and, reunited, they die together.

Not all of Heywood's helpless sinners are women. Sextus, in *The Rape of Lucrece* (1608), belongs to the type. Collatine, Sextus, and a company of other Roman captains visit the heroine in the course of a wager as to which has the most dutiful wife, Sextus is abruptly seized by irresistible passion, to which he alludes, "aside," as "our hot lust." Returning alone, he speaks of himself (in another address directly to the audience) as "love lunatic, love mad . . . my blood / Boils in my heart, with loose and sensual thoughts." At Lucrece's hospitable courtesies, he exclaims, still in the vein of soliloquy and authentic self-revelation,

> O impious lust,
> In all things base, respectless, and unjust!
> Thy vertue, grace, and fame I must enjoy,
> Though in the purchase I all Rome destroy.
> . . . .
> Preposterous Fates what mischiefes you involve
> Upon a caitiffe prince, left to the fury
> Of all grand mischiefe!

In four lines following, he refers to his "sin," "lust," and "treason"; declares himself "worst then what's most ill"; and admits that he is "depriv'd all reason." About to rape Lucrece, he moralizes, voicing like Anne Frankford all the most potent arguments against his crime, in a tone of anguished sincerity. He grieves that he "must wound virtue," talks again of his "sin" and "lust," but protests his helplessness:

> O fate! thou hast usurpt such power o're man,
> That where thou pleadst thy will no mortall can.
> On then, blacke mischiefe hurry me the way,
> My selfe I must destroy, her life betray.

Afterward he pleads "if I have done thee wrong, / Love was the cause." And in the inevitable death scene, we are shown again his hatred for the rape, and the curious separation of what he has done from what he is. He is as much victim as any other character in the play. Sin has purchased ruin, but there is no comfort in the mechanical justice done.

The helpless sinner is to become a permanent fixture in later tragedy and tragicomedy: Roderigo in *The Spanish Gypsy* commits a rape against his will; Frank

Thorney of *The Witch of Edmonton* is irresistibly driven to bigamy and murder; Malheureux in Marston's *Dutch Courtesan* loves a prostitute helplessly; Giovanni in Ford's *'Tis Pity* and Arbaces in Fletcher's *King and No King* are helpless before incestuous lust. In each we see the device of portraying "sin" without locating the cause of evil in the hero. Virtue fights against nature, and the struggle is unequal.

Even Heywood's rollicking adventure-romances contain these elements. In the early *Fortune by Land and Sea*, there are the same heavy pathos, the same incessant religious monition and attribution of "punishments" to a Calvinistically conceived Providence, the same ethical values. Young Forrest, the unpleasantly priggish hero, kills his brother's murderer in a duel fought in the name of code "honor." Over the murderer's body, he attributes his brother's death to

> . . . heavens will that for some guilt of his
> He should be scourged by thee; and for that guilt
> In scourging him thou by my vengeance punisht.
>
> (II. i)

His sister, Mrs. Harding, gives him sanctuary from the "law's griping power," reminding him that ". . . we all must yield to fate / He casts us down that best can raise our state" (III. i). The play has a double plot, and again the parts are related by a parallelism of themes. Old Harding, in one action, disinherits a son for loving nobility more than money; Old Forrest, in the other, loses a son who wastes money out of mere profligacy. The young men, in other words, disregard wealth from opposite motives. The plots are mechanically joined, as in *A Woman Killed with Kindness*, by a marriage connection and by Young Forrest's receiving sanctuary from his sister, Mrs. Harding. If one were to draw a moral, it would be the Puritan one to seek first the bourgeois virtues, for wealth, worldly honor, and the assurance of true spiritual worth shall follow.

In *The Fair Maid of the West*, Part I, the hero Spencer is provoked into killing a man innocently at Bess's tavern in Plymouth. Later he tries to prevent a sword fight in a tavern in the Azores, where he has fled. He is, for his friendly concern, wounded—mortally, as he thinks. His companion Captain Goodlack promises him, "Noble friend, / I will revenge thy death," and Spencer replies,

> He is no friend
> That murmurs such a thought. Oh gentlemen.
> I kill'd a man in Plimouth, and by you
> Am slaine in Fiall. Caroll fell by me,
> And I fall by a Spencer. Heav'n is just,
> And will not suffer murder unreveng'd.
> Heaven pardon me. . . .
>   (II. i)

In this event, like the death of Frank Forrest in *Fortune by Land and Sea*, the inhabitants of the play world see divine punishment for sin. But no natural connection joins the guilt with its consequence; God administers his judgments directly, and the significance of the events which realize them must be taken on religious faith. Very differently founded is, for example, Edgar's comment on his father's mutilation: "The dark and vicious place where thee he got / Cost him his eyes." So in visible fact it has; the unfolding of events in *Lear* reveals a natural continuity between the transgression and its eventual cost.

The second part of *The Fair Maid of the West* was written in 1631, in a different era from the first. Here the hero is trapped in a Fletcherian dilemma of opposed vows. Having sworn to the Duke of Florence to abjure all familiarity with the lady whom he is to woo in the

Duke's behalf, he discovers that she is his wife. A "code"
fidelity to the later promise forces him to be unfaithful
to his marriage vows.

A similarly hypothetical moral situation provides the
matrix of plot in *The Royal King and the Loyal Subject*.
The early part of the play pictures a moral potlatch, a
contest of magnanimity in which the king is, for a time,
angered to be outdone by the Marshal, his "loyal subject." The valiant Marshal, traduced by envious courtiers, is with brutal injustice stripped of honors and
offices in penalty for being more magnanimous than his
king. A messenger is dispatched commanding him to
send to court his most beloved daughter; the king intends, as his letter announces, to "strumpet" her. The
Marshal submits with meek patience: "The King commands, / I must obey."

Code ethics provides Heywood a situation in which
every extremity of the king's injustice and tyranny is
greeted by the Marshal as a benefaction, another welcome chance to show his submission to the sacred
crown. The absurd points of "honor," the ludicrous
"charge" brought against the Marshal that he has "dis-
loyally sought to exceed the king" (in virtue); these
belong to the same never-never land of moral unreality
as the abstractions of the Senecan *Controversiae* from
which Beaumont and Fletcher drew inspiration for similar plays.[22]

We are, finally, rather told than shown by Heywood's
very moral tragedies that sin has ruinous consequences.
The doom that falls on sinners comes in one of three
ways:

1. As God's punishment. Characters do evil, meet with
evil. There is no visible or natural causal connection
between the evil action and its alleged consequence,
which is simply announced by the characters to be
God's direct chastisement.

2. Other characters consciously punish sinners, exactly because they are recognized as such, to the accompaniment of much religious moralizing. 3. Repentance proves fatal. Righteous grief over "sin," rather than the unavoidable disruption which flows from evil, causes characters to suffer acutely and to die. Anguish in Shakespearean tragedy may redeem and regenerate those who suffer, but it originates in evil or error—in the unnatural, never in a return to virtue. In the natural order, penitence is in Heywood's world far more perilous than sin. Of course that world is much concerned with a narrowly religious view—with the blackening of immortal souls. But the soul which is said to be damned by sin is no effective part of the worldly person attached to it; i.e., its mortal wounds do not visibly alter any natural operation: a soul is something other than the vital principle of a person.[23]

Eternal damnation is dramatic only in the responses which contemplation of it may arouse in living persons. It is in itself nondramatic, unavailable to drama. It seems at times that spiritual salvation and damnation are what Heywood really longs to dramatize, and that he strains to do so by having his characters talk about these things. His plays, at any rate, present a thoroughly voluntaristic world where we will search in vain for the tragic patterns of the natural law.

JOHN WEBSTER's two best plays provide some of the effect of great tragedy, but in a distinctly Jacobean mode. His cynical imagination constructs a world whose realities contrast bitterly with its official and public pieties. Our pleasure in the macabre tragedies of *Vittoria Corombona* (1611–1612) and *The Duchess of Malfi* (1613–1614) centers partly in Webster's rich and supple poetry, but finally in the exaltation to which they raise defiance of an utterly corrupted world. Stoical independence and extreme individualism or "emancipation" become the instinctive response of the clear-sighted to a universe where no ultimate questions can be answered, and where docility to conventional codes is either hypocrisy or stupidity. There is the virtuous individualism and Stoicism of the unconventional Duchess of Malfi—the final superiority of her strength to the worst of her brothers' cruelties, and there is the "vicious" strength of Vittoria Corombona—her equally splendid defiance of a world contempt and defiance of which are not unreasonable or unsympathetic. Our emotional satisfaction in these tragedies is stronger and more bitter than the brief confectionary effect of tragicomic endings. Webster's is a world ruled by the individual wills of the powerful, themselves ruled largely by their passions; its actual order is that of a jungle, Webster's picture being in this respect not unlike Machiavelli's, Hobbes', Swift's, or Calvin's. A satisfaction stronger for its grimness and of greater conviction for its cynicism lies in the rebellion which is in Bosola and Flamineo close to despair, in Vittoria a reckless wantonness, in Brachiano a Machiavellian contempt of all restraints, in Antonio a soberly measured rejection of social convention, and in the Duchess of Malfi simply the even and confident pulse of health in a sickly world; a strong, uncorrupted affinity with life which offends the arid and morbid petrification of her surroundings.

Unable to prevail, or even to survive, Webster's empathetic characters, both "good" and "bad," "die game," go down undeceived, undefeated, still defiant and invulnerable in a Stoic integrity. The plays may contain an occasional reflection by their characters that "sorrow is held the eldest child of sin," but they show no evidence of a rational cosmic order. The traditional beliefs, of which Webster's villains are the chief (hypocritical or ironically paradoxical) voices, become only the illusions of the impotent—pitifully fragile ramparts against the real anarchic forces that rule the world. In *The Devil's Law Case,* we find almost an exact quotation from Hooker's expression of the old belief that

> Obedience of creatures to the Law of Nature
> Is the stay of the whole world.
>
> (IV. ii. 276–77)

Yet the whole of the tragicomic plot of this play, insofar as it can be said to have any meaning, shows a world entirely without a discernible natural order such as Hooker's, governed by a Providence which arranges poetic justice, in which no natural or causal connection can be discerned between action and nemesis.

In both of the tragedies there appears a specially qualified guide to Webster's cosmos. Bosola in *The Duchess of Malfi* and Flamineo in *The White Devil* are curious figures. In their relation to plot they resemble the puppet-master who presides over or "conducts" the action, like Marston's Malevole, or Jonson's Mosca or Asper-Macilente; they fill also the role of the satyr, master of the poetry of invective and railing scourge of the corrupt world—a character who becomes a pivot of Jacobean tragicomedy; Flamineo shows, too, some vestige of the traditional courtly-love mediator. More obviously, each is a Machiavel, but this convention has been adopted to Webster's special uses. Each is a ruthlessly ambitious follower of evil, yet each is the central figure of the drama, the choric interpreter of its meaning with whom the audience can identify itself as much as with anyone else in the play, partly for the reason that they share with us a more complete knowledge of the purposes and events of the plot than is given to the other characters. They move in a world where traditional belief in the inexorability of the moral law is discredited by the shape of events and by assigning the expression of the intellectual pieties of religion and of the natural law to the most consummately shrewd and vicious "politicians," such as Monticelso and Francisco de Medicis of *The White Devil*, who actually conduct their actions on very different premises.

Bosola and Flamineo are spectators of this world, aware as the other "bad" characters are not, of its monstrosity, and exacerbated by it. Each, although he is old in cynicism, looks for something to justify goodness and hope. Flamineo finds only courage. Bosola finally recognizes in the Duchess something better than the world to which it is foreign. In such a fictional universe, the frustration, hatred, and contempt which the characters embody are, in fact, vicariously the emotions of the audience; these plays are more fiercely of the world-hating art *de contemptu mundi* than are the tales of Chaucer's Monk, and in Bosola and Flamineo that contempt is distilled. They are true believers of Calvin's doctrine that the natural world is to be despised.

It is not only this shared emotion, which they articulate for us, which makes them surrogate for author and audience. There is also their reflective consciousness as observers; each is himself an audience to a drama, like us considering the meaning of what passes, questioning which of two wisdoms is best, evaluating and commenting. Weighing the evidence, each allies himself with the villains; they recognize the goodness of the "good" characters[24] and sympathize with it (the sympathy is only latent in the cynical rage of Flamineo, for his world shows no goodness but the impotent conventionality of Marcello and Cornelia), yet they side with raw force, with guile and evil. It is a world where cold intelligence leaves them no alternative to this course but that of self-destruction. There are the two wisdoms—"While we look up to heaven" says Flamineo, "wee confound /

Knowledge with knowledge"[25]—and one is in this world the most suicidal folly. Flamineo turns savagely on his mother's moral protest at the assignation he has arranged for his sister Vittoria and Duke Brachiano (I. ii. 301–25). Virtue, he instructs her, is an excellent luxury which, being at the world's mercy, he cannot afford, for it has no place whatever in the world's real functioning.[26] Both Bosola and Flamineo are defeated; yet that is because chance or fate or an inscrutable Providence—there is no clue as to which and much talk of each—renders all men ultimately impotent to govern their fates.

Each of these characters, unlike the Machiavel, feels some tormenting doubts over his course, Bosola to the extent finally of real remorse and of shifting his allegiance from realism to goodness. Each finally recognizes his own and all men's helplessness before fate and chance. Each is granted a superior eloquence with which to manage our feelings. The role is a new one; it is rather as if Edmund has moved to the very center of action in *Lear*, and been set in a world which exhales depravity and in which nature is indeed wolfish, a world where his cynicism is rather borne out than repudiated by the issue of actions.

The White Devil is a duel between two sets of rogues. On one side, the criminal lovers, Brachiano and Vittoria, free themselves from unwanted marriages, she to a fool, he to a tiresome wife. Flamineo, vicious on principle, has eagerly pandered his sister Vittoria as a means to the worldly advancement which is frankly his guidestar. He murders Vittoria's husband in one of Webster's garishly theatrical horror scenes, and Brachiano's duchess is killed by poison on her husband's portrait, which it is her ritual custom to kiss before retiring.

On the other side, the Cardinal Monticelso, cousin to Vittoria's murdered husband, and Francisco de Medicis, brother to Brachiano's murdered Duchess Isabella, arraign Vittoria for her husband's death and for her adultery (they do not yet know of Isabella's death). Vittoria is convicted by an official "justice" which is a mockery, clearly an instrument of Monticelso's revenge for a family injury and Francisco de Medicis' anger at his sister's dishonor.

The trial scene is a brilliant, rather strangely operatic one: there is no better instance of the highly developed freeom of Renaissance drama from any naturalistic servility to the irrelevant. We see the great lords of church and state, the representatives of order, as ruthless members of a power elite at the disposal of whose private passions lies the machinery in which the social order is institutionalized. The court gives the mere appearance of justice which the world requires and under which these great men prefer to effect their purposes.

The lovers are tricked by Francisco into a rash flight which plays into their enemies' hands; finally, Brachiano, Vittoria, and Flamineo are killed by Francisco and his Machiavellian followers in a savage private vengeance achieved by superior skill. There has been a contest between equally vicious antagonists, in which those who may be identified with "the world" and the forces that govern it have crushed the deliberate rebels —fully as evil but more magnificent—who chose to defy the world and live by their own wills. The unworldly villains Brachiano and Vittoria perish. The worldly villains Monticelso (now Pope) and Francisco prevail. Only the "slave of Greatness" Lodovico and his fellow hireling assassins are caught after the last murders. Brachiano's son Giovanni succeeds his father, voicing an orthodox, and typically precocious, lesson of the catastrophe:

> Let guilty men remember their blacke deedes,
> Do leane on crutches, made of slender reedes.
> (V. vi. 302–303)

But the moral is only perfunctory; the play has shown us not the purgative convulsion by which natural goodness asserts its dominion, but a world of irrational will whose highest birth is an evil and fatal grandeur. Conventional virtue has shrunk to gray wisps like Cornelia and Marcello, feeble irrelevancies leaning on crutches of the slenderest reed.

Brachiano and Vittoria answer the world's underlying lawlessness by a wild courage which raises them above their antagonists. Their love, to which both are faithful even at death, emerges as the one genuine if sinister value given dramatic prominence. Rooted in lust and murder, that passion flowers in an undeniable and autonomous greatness which lifts Brachiano's death scene and Vittoria's character throughout the later part of the play strangely above the sordidness of their crimes. Vittoria gives testimony of human greatness, but her viciousness is the paradox of greatness; the two are identical.[27]

Webster's best showcase of his heroine's grandeur is the trial scene. Here he is first at pains to show us her superior learning (III. ii. 14–18); then with quiet disdain Vittoria silences the farrago of "grammatical elocution" which is put into the mouth of the prosecuting lawyer as a foil to her wit. Of her demeanor in her own defense, the English Ambassador is moved to remark, "Shee hath a brave spirit" (III. ii. 144). Lamb's is still the classic description of her unterrified eloquence: "This White Devil of Italy sets off a bad cause so speciously, and pleads with such an innocence-resembling boldness, that we seem to see that matchless beauty of her face which inspires such gay confidence into her, and are ready to expect, when she has done her pleadings, that her very judges, her accusers, the grave ambassadors who sit as spectators, and all the court, will rise and make proffer to defend her, in spite of the utmost conviction of her guilt."[28] And the rhetoric of this scene does in fact create an aura of nobility about Vittoria which is dramatically as real as if it emanated from the purest virtue.

Webster reinforces our attraction to his heroine in her speeches to Brachiano (e.g., IV. ii. 103–29), in Brachiano's dying words to her (V. iii. 18–19), and in her religious horror at Flamineo's fratricide and proposed suicide (V. vi. 14–15, 57–65). Even her bizarre behavior at Flamineo's feigned death (V. vi. 120) does not quite forfeit this effect. The defiant courage of her own death assures our admiration, as Brachiano's fidelity to her and to himself even in his last agonies commands a kind of respect.

The "politic" Cardinal Monticelso is one of Webster's portraits of the Italian churchman of popular English tradition. In his "black book" are listed "pandars . . . pirates . . . base rogues that undo yong Gentlemen . . . Impudent baudes that go in mens apparell . . . usurers . . . Lawyers that will antedate their writes . . . murderers" (IV. i. 51–67). He counsels Francisco to

> Sleep with the Lyon,
> And let this brood of secure foolish mice
> Play with your nosthrils, till the time bee ripe
> For th'bloudy audit and the fatall gripe.
> (IV. i. 18–21)

His is a "divinity" which "draws swords, swells battles, and o'erthrows all good." But it is Francisco de Medicis, Duke of Florence, who is the complete Machiavel: master intriguer and strategist of revenge, poisoner, and suborner of rogues.

> in all my plots
> I'le rest as jealous as a Towne besieg'd.
> Thou cans't not reach what I intend to act.
> (IV. i. 42–43)

These are the figures with whom Webster associates most of the play's verbal expressions of traditional morality and faith in a just governance of the world. Monticelso is the more complex villain. He defends his intriguing against the imputation of dishonor (II. i. 386–89) and refers to Vittoria's passion as her "lust" or "blacke lust" (III. i. 7; III. ii. 168, 232). There is a grotesque metaphysical vigor of imagery in his denunciation of the ruin done by whores—"the trew matteriall fier of Hell" (III. ii. 82–105)—a charge of invective energy against the works of the flesh which seems hard to account for in any way that is consistent with his character. Speeches in Webster's plays sometimes belong more significantly to the continuous poetic fabric than to the special point of view of an isolable character. Still, religious talk of the vice which charms preachers silent (III. ii. 259–60), of the "blessed" dead (III. ii. 329), of God's governance (III. ii. 337), is quite unaffected with him. He respects the confessional seal (IV. iii. 113) and is, in short, both a voice of religion and a "politician"-revenger quite aware of the futility of virtue.

Francisco de Medicis, at the Cardinal's urging to revenge against Brachiano, piously replies:

> Shall I defye him, and impose a warre
> Most burthensome on my poore subjects neckes,
> Which at my will I have not power to end?
> You know; for all the murders, rapes and thefts,
> Committed in the horred lust of warre,
> He that unjustly caus'd it first proceed,
> Shall finde it in his grave and in his seed.
>
> (IV. i. 7–13)

Later, he inquires if his confederate Lodovico has yet "tane the sacrament to prosecute / Th' intended murder?" Several characters give lipservice to the idea of divine retribution. Marcello, killed by his brother Flamineo, sees his death as God's direct punishment of the family (V. ii. 22–23). One of the play's few "good" men, he dies meaninglessly, quite unfitted by his virtue for worldly survival, as Flamineo had warned him (III. i. 38–57). Dying, Vittoria confesses:

> O my greatest sinne lay in my blood.
> Now my blood paies for't.
>   (V. vi. 240–41)

But nothing is vindicated by Vittoria's death except her own courage—certainly not the order of things that has made disaster inevitable for her; she dies because she has antagonized a Machiavellian duke.

There is moralizing by Cornelia, Marcello, Monticelso, and finally young Giovanni, but their world is not innately moral. Both virtue and greatness are clearly antagonistic to it, and Webster's and our sympathy is with the heroic sinner. Individual assertion and defiance provide all the great moments of his tragedies. He conceives the highest human magnificence always in a character brought to bay, defying the world out of a courage which is beyond hope and feeds only on itself. His heroic murderers and adulterers, like his heroically independent "good" character, the Duchess of Malfi, silence with scorn the fatuous moralizing of their adversaries.

The real choric voices of the two plays are Flamineo and Bosola. Flamineo has a withering realism, a cynical honesty and freedom from all cant. His satiric portraits of Camillo (I. ii. 131–39) and of the French and Spanish Ambassadors remind us that Webster also wrote "characters." The tone of his plentiful comment on women and sex is epitomized by a habitual use of animal imagery and especially eating imagery. Used by other characters as well (e.g., I. ii. 20–24, 41–44, 125–26, 170–71, 188–89, 336–38; II. i. 50–52), this sustains an atmosphere of rank appetite, such as Shakespeare raises only in the nightmares of Lear's madness or in the insinuations of Iago.

Lodovico's outburst against "courtly reward and punishment" opens the play; a dialogue follows painting out the corrupt court-world in monstrosities of waste, extravagance, lust, and injustice (I. i. 1–62). The exiled Lodovico is told that

> Your followers
> Have swallowed you like Mummia, and being sicke
> With such unnaturall, and horrid Phisicke
> Vomit you up ith kennel.
>
> (I. i. 15–18)

Flamineo takes up both motifs, turning repeatedly to the theme of "Court promises! Let wisemen count them curst" (III. i. 38–57; IV. ii. 59–63, 224–35; V. i. 130–38; V. iii. 66–67, 191; V. vi. 261–62, 265–68). The great men who control preferment are great devils (IV. ii. 61–62). There is no justice (III. i. 38–57). He will outface a vile and senseless world by a rapacity greater than its own: to Lodovico, in a "confrontation" scene, he promises in mockery never to part

> till the beggerie of Courtiers,
> The discontent of church-men, want of souldiers,
> And all the creatures that hang manacled,
> Worse than strappado'd, on the lowest fellie
> Of fortunes wheele be taught in our two lives
> To scorne that world which life of meanes deprives.
>
> (III. iii. 87–92)

Flamineo sometimes adverts to the broader social order: "There's nothing so holie but mony will corrupt and putrifie it, like vittell under the line" (III. iii. 24–25) and "If there were Jews enough, so many Christians would not turn usurers; if Priests enough, one should not have sixe benefices; and if gentlemen enough, so many earlie mushromes, whose best growth sprang from a dunghill, should not aspire to gentilitie" (III. iii. 41–45).

Beyond the treacherous wills of great men, the governance of the world lies with a fate that renders our actions ultimately meaningless.

> Fate's a Spaniell,
> Wee cannot beat it from us: what remaines now?
> Let all that doe ill, take this precedent:
> *Man may his Fate foresee, but not prevent.*
> And of all axiomes this shall winne the prise,
> *'Tis better to be fortunate then wise.*
>
> (V. vi. 178–83)

The play's first lines have declared that "Fortun's a right whore" (I. i. 4), and at the end Flamineo dies with the thought that only in death do we "cease to be fortunes slaves" (V. vi. 252). Clearly enough, neither by virtue nor Machiavellian skill does any man in Webster's dark world become the master of his destiny.

Flamineo's aura of mortality is such that his death is the action most in character, most natural for him. It is the moment, too, which will test his defiant "emancipation" and validate or expose it. What has Webster husbanded against this climax? "I am ith way to study a long silence" (V. vi. 204) and

> Farewell glorious villaines,
> This busie trade of life appeares most vaine,
> Since rest breeds rest, where all seeke paine by paine.
>
> (V. vi. 272–74)

These are characteristic testimonies of the "Lucretian blankness" into which man looks when he looks deeply, and of the futility of human effort in a chaotic world.

So also in *The Duchess of Malfi* Daniel de Bosola dies

expressing the contrariety between the world and the goodness which inhabits it only at fearful risk. He ends in that nescience which is all these most acute questioners can win from the Websterian cosmos:

> Oh this gloomy world,
> In what a shadow, or deepe pit of darknesse,
> Doth (womanish, and fearefull) mankind live!
> Let worthy mindes nere stagger in distrust
> To suffer death, or shame, for what is just—
> Mine is another voyage.
>
> (V. v. 124–29)

Bosola's career in part parallels that of Flamineo. We hear in the opening lines of the play that he is an ambitious, rapacious worldling who "rayles at those things which he wants" (I. i. 26). His first words raise again the theme of courtly reward and its bitter and treacherous injustice (I. i. 32–33, 36–40, 59–69). Honesty in such a world is not possible; none can direct the way to it (I. i. 41–42). His prospective patron is a devil (I. i. 45–48). Describing Duke Ferdinand and the Cardinal, he begins at once by imagery like Flamineo's to fill the play's atmosphere with a miasma of bestial rankness. "He, and his brother, are like Plum-trees (that grow crooked over standing-pooles) they are rich, and ore-laden with Fruite, but none but Crowes, Pyes, and Catter-pillers feeds on them: Could I be one of their flattring Pandars, I would hang on their eares like a horse-leach, till I were full, and then droppe off" (I. i. 50–55). Delio says of Ferdinand that "the law to him / Is like a foul black cobweb to a spider" (I. i. 180–81).[29]

Bosola lacks some of Flamineo's satanic glee in doing evil, his vindictive pleasure in being more perverse than the world. A savage moral hatred lies very close to the surface of Flamineo's limitless Machiavellian commitment to evil. Bosola, too, hates the world, but unlike

Flamineo he functions as a kind of bewildered Jacobean Everyman within whom the clash of the two laws will not be stilled. He is articled to a course of evil which he despises; he despises himself for submitting; but the world, which he knows well, will not be changed by a wish.

When Ferdinand first enlists him as a "familiar," a "devil in the flesh" to spy on the Duchess, Bosola refuses:

> Take your Divels
> Which Hell calls Angels; These curs'd gifts would make
> You a corrupter, me an impudent traitor,
> And should I take these they'll'd take me to Hell.
>
> (I. i. 285–88)

But on hearing that Ferdinand has secured him an honorable office in the Duchess' court—one he is unable to refuse—Bosola can only lament

> . . . oh, that to avoid ingratitude
> For the good deed you have done me, I must doe
> All the ill man can invent: Thus the Divell
> Candies all sines o'er: And what Heaven termes vild,
> That names he complementall.
>
> (I. i. 298–301)

Cynically recognizing his loyalty to the world, he submits:

> What's my place?
> The Provisorship o' th horse? Say then my corruption
> Grew out of horse-doong: I am your creature.
>
> (I. i. 311–13)

When Duke Ferdinand reveals his cognizance of her secret marriage, the Duchess protects Antonio (not yet identified as her husband) by pretending to dismiss him for embezzlement. Bosola, suspecting the truth, traps her into granting confidence by his (accurate) praises of Antonio and his denunciation of "so changeable a Prince's favour" (III. ii. 283–98, 300–14). The multiple ironies of the scene involve our recognition that although Bosola's tributes to virtue are a Machiavellian trick, he means them sincerely, at least to the extent of recognizing their truth. His goodness, throttled by the world, survives to make his necessary viciousness a torment. Having made his discovery, he feels a twinge of revulsion—a temptation to virtue—which must be suppressed by reflection on the world's realities:

> . . . what rests but I reveale
> All to my lord? Oh, this base quality
> Of intelligencer! Why, every Quality i'th'world
> Preferres but gaine, or commendation.
>
> (III. ii. 374–77)

During the Duchess' last torments, Bosola begs pity for her (IV. i. 141–45), refuses to see her again (IV. i. 159), and being told that he must, resolves that his business then shall be comfort (IV. i. 164). Without quite suffering Ferdinand's paroxysm of remorse, he recognizes, after the murder, the horror of the act ("Murther shrieks out"). Faced with the inevitable fact that for his pains he will be "neglected," reward for his services denied by "so changeable a prince," he abandons all hope in the world:

> I stand like one
> That long hath ta'ne a sweet, and golden dreame.
> I am angry with myselfe, now that I wake.
>
> (IV. ii. 349–51)

Like Flamineo he concludes that

> While with vaine hopes, our faculties we tyre,
> We seeme to sweate in yce and freeze in fire.
>
> (IV. ii. 353–54)

He shifts his allegiance in the conflict between the world and goodness, and although he comes briefly to think that

> The weakest Arme is strong enough that strikes
> With the sword of Justice,
>
> (Iv. ii. 353–54)

in the final scene, he mistakenly stabs Antonio (whom he is trying to save) thinking him to be the Cardinal. At this last maddening proof of human impotence before the blind forces which impel the world, Bosola despairs.

> We are merely the Starres tennys-balls (strooke and banded
> Which way please them).
>
> (V. vi. 63–64)

The Duchess, tormented by Bosola before her death, cries out

> I could curse the Starres.
> . . . .
> And those three smyling seasons of the yeere
> Into a Russian winter; nay, the world
> To its first Chaos.
>
> (IV. i. 115–19)

His answer is a perfect Jacobean summation: "Looke you, the Starres shine still" (IV. i. 120). The verse is justly famous: it chills by its glimpse of a universe without human affinities, without place for values and virtues, with only the ultimate malignity of mechanical indifference. At his death Bosola tells that he

> . . . was an Actor in the maine of all,
> Much 'gainst mine owne good nature, yet i'th'end
> Neglected.
>
> (V. v. 106–108)

The heavenly knowledge of what is good does not easily prevail over the opposed earthly knowledge of what will serve the world. No one here makes the old assumption that the two are really one. "You would looke up to Heaven," Antonio has said to Bosola much earlier in the play, "but I thinke / the Divell, that rules i'th'aire, stands in your light" (II. i. 97–98).

There is no better expositor that Bosola of the world's foulness, although others in the play declaim on the corruption of nature and the evils of the flesh. His speech to the Duchess before her death is a Donnesque set-piece: "Thou art a box of worme-seede, at best, but a salvatory of greene mummey. What's this flesh? A little cruded milke, phantasticall puff-paste. Our bodies are weaker than those paper prisons boyes use to keepe flies in: more contemptible: since ours is to preserve earthwormes" (IV. ii. 123–27). This has been compared to the Duke's speech to the condemned Claudio in *Measure for Measure* (III. i. 5–41), but the two are different. Shakespeare's Duke uses an ingenious logic to arrive, with a "Q.E.D." flourish, at the conclusion that life's attractiveness is deceptive ("thou are Death's fool; / For him thou labour'st by thy flight to shun / And yet runn'st toward him still"). Bosola needs no paradoxes; he states flatly the loathsome and contemptible nature of life. The dirge which follows asks

> Of what is't fooles make such vaine keeping?
> Sin their conception, their birth, weeping:
> Their life, a generall mist of error.[30]
> (IV. ii. 188–90)

"The nature which begets is corrupt," said Calvin; all that is carnal is evil. (Children, he reminds us, are of purely carnal descent.) "Guilt is from Nature."[31] Infants newborn are so corrupt that they "cannot but be odious and abominable to God."[32] The human will "cannot ex-

cite itself, much less devote itself to any thing good."[33]
Antonio's dying speech sums up his estimate of life:

> In all our Quest for Greatness . . .
> (Like wanton Boyes, whose pastime is their care)
> We follow after bubbles, blowne in th'ayre.
> Pleasure of life, what is't? Onely the good houres
> Of an Ague.
>
> (V. iv. 75–79)

Sensuality is repeatedly seen as filth in *The Duchess of Malfi:* "I would sooner eate a dead pidgeon, taken from the soles of the feet of one sicke of the plague, then kisse one of you fasting" (II. i. 39–41). Man is ugly, deformed, revolting:

> . . . we account it ominous,
> If nature doe produce a Colt, or Lambe,
> A Fawne, or Goate, in any limbe resembling
> A Man; and flye from't as a prodegy.
> Man stands amaz'd to see his deformity,
> In any other Creature but himselfe.
> But in our owne flesh, though we beare diseases
> Which have their true names only tane from beasts,
> As the most ulcerous Woolfe, and swinish Measeall;
> Though we are eaten up of lice, and wormes,
> And though continually we beare about us
> A rotten and dead body, we delight
> To hide it in rich tissew.
>
> (II. i. 48–60)

"They are most luxurious," says Ferdinand, "Will wed twice . . . Their livers are more spotted / Then Labans sheepe" (I. i. 325–29).

> And those Joyes, [of second marriage]
> Those lustfull pleasures, are like heavy sleepes
> Which doe fore-run mans mischiefe.
>
> (I. i. 362–64)

The effect of such lines is not contained within the limits of characterization; their spirit permeates the play's atmosphere beyond the boundaries of Ferdinand's motives and point of view. Asceticism as well as libertinism appears in the absence of the natural-law recognition of sensuality as a good. Ferdinand speaks the language of Calvin, who treats marriage as a divine concession to human depravity—a sop to evil carnality, to be indulged only so much as is unavoidable and never sought as a worthy end.[34]

Bosola's comment on courts and courtiers (e.g., II. i. 3–12, 19–21) recalls Flamineo's and is borne out by the behavior of the Duchess' courtiers (III. ii. 252–66; III. v. 8–16). Much of this is conventional matter of the Renaissance satires, but such literary descent is not very significant. What counts is what Webster fabricates, from whatever sources: the innately corrupt and anarchic tragic world which serves as the foil, rather than the measure, of human value.

The play retains at least a vestigial pattern of guilt and retribution. Painter's version of the story, Webster's probable source, is openly moralistic, insisting that Antonio has invited his own ruin by culpable presumption, since there can be no excuse "secretly to marry, especially hir upon whome hee ought not so mutch as to loke bit with feare and reverence."[35] "Shall I be of the opinion" asks Painter, "that a household servant . . . a vile and abject person dare to mount upon a prince's bed? No, no, policy requyreth order in all, and eche wight ought to be matched according to their qualtye . . . a goodly thinge it is to love, but where reason looseth place, love is wythoute his effecte, and the sequels rage and madnesse."[36]

This is not Webster's view, but he allows it rather full expression within the play. After receiving her brothers' warning, and before her wooing scene with Antonio, the

Duchess speaks of the planned marriage as "this dangerous venture" and notes that by taking Cariola into her
confidence, she has entrusted the waiting-woman with
"More than my life—my fame" (I. i. 392). Antonio refers
twice in this scene to the "ambition" of which such a
marriage would convict him (I. i. 471, 483). Even dis-
counting Webster's tendency to inflate the rhetoric of
some lines irresponsibly, Antonio clearly thinks it
dangerous: "he's a foole / That (being a-cold) would
thrust his hands i'th'fire / To warm them." He admits by
his assurance of care for the Duchess' "good name" that
the match would be scandalous in the world's eyes (I. i.
527–28). After the marriage is made, Cariola closes the
scene with lines somewhat overcharged and self-consciously ominous:

> Whether the spirit of greatnes or of woman
> Raigne most in her, I know not, but it shewes
> A fearefull madnes. I owe her much of pitty.
>   (I. i. 576–78)

When Delio, the "loyal friend," finds that Antonio's
marriage has been discovered, his response is in the
same vein, blaming both Antonio and the fates: ". . .
how fearefully / Shewes his ambition now! (unfortunate
Fortune)" (II. iv. 105–106). A pilgrim, provided as chorus, comments on the banishment of Antonio and the
Duchess,

> . . . who would have thought
> So great a Lady, would have match'd her selfe
> Unto so meane a person? Yet the Cardinall
> Beares himself much too cruell.
>   (III. iv. 25–28)

We could be tempted to think that Webster sees justice in the catastrophe which overtakes the principals.
But such a conclusion disregards the actual effect of the

play. The Duchess is not Juliet; she is a widow, a "great prince" who has borne her office well. She is not properly subject to Duke Ferdinand or to the Cardinal, and neither of these is a benevolent guardian. Antonio is a man somewhat skeptical (V. ii. 136–37), somewhat melancholic (e.g., I. i. 456–61), honest by his enemies' testimony (I. i. 242), accustomed to responsibility, restrained to the point of scruple—"this precise fellow" (II. iii. 81). His caution even affords his adversary a chance to taunt him with the charge of cowardice (III. v. 64–66).

Social conventions and the system of rank have little part in the vital substance of these characters. We are at the farthest remove from the literature of manners, for the reality of persons is to Webster something outside of or transcending the categories of the social order. In her wooing, the heroine sheds the character of duchess and appears to Antonio, "a yong widow / That claimes you for her husband" (I. i. 523–24). Antonio, in the same scene, is intrinsically "a compleat man." However his merely extrinsic and accidental rank divide him from his mistress, the division is false, a fetter laid on living reality by convention and interests of rotten privilege.

The two contract a marriage based on mutual love and respect, a union with no impediment other than society's refusal to accept it. This marriage results for both in torment and death, which they suffer with steadfast and virtuous dignity. Why is it imprudent? On which side does the folly lie? Not the lovers' surely, but their enemies'—broadly, the world's. Defiant rebellion, not reconciliation to the world, is the ultimate distillate of *The Duchess of Malfi*. Antonio and the Duchess are prisoners of a social order which legislates against life. The Duchess feels that this is so:

> the Birds, that live i'th'field
> On the wilde benefit of Nature, live

> Happier than we; For they may choose their Mates
> And carroll their sweet pleasures to the Spring.
>
> (III. v. 25–28)

A strong sense of inscrutable and irrational fate permeates the tragedy. Bosola dies in the belief that "we are the Stars' tennys-balls." Ferdinand speaks of the

> . . . Most imperfect light of humaine reason,
> That mak'st us so unhappy, to foresee
> What we can least prevent.
>
> (III. ii. 90–92)

To "Fortune" the characters assign many of the crucial events of the plot (e.g., II. iv. 106; III. v. 112–13; III. iv. 48–49). Delio most nearly articulates the view developed by the play:

> Though in our miseries, Fortune have a part,
> Yet, in our noble suffrings, she hath none—
> Contempt of Paine, that we may call our owne.
>
> (V. iii. 70–72)

The idea of fate is diffused throughout not only by the planting of portents and omens (II. iii. 58–62; III. v. 19–24, 102–105, 108; V. iv. 21–57, especially 56–57), but by a series of "predictive" ironies: images or propositions later to be realized in tragic ways unsuspected by those who express them, or predictions so specifically contrary to the event that they are clearly ironic (I. i. 393–96, 443, 483–87, 537–40, 549–50; III. ii. 160–62; III. v. 79–80; cf. IV. ii. 125–26, 185). Most of these could hardly be noticed by a theater audience. The reader who detects them follows the spoor of a strong ironic sense; moving through the events of the plot, Webster is often conscious that if our thoughts are ours, their ends are none of our own, and all human effort to make them so is, in such a world, deluded.

If Fate is important, an equal role is assigned to chance in Bosola's recovery of the horoscope dropped by Antonio, and in the mistakes by which both characters die. Muriel Bradbrook would find the key to the play in its treatment of these two forces: "The alternative views that Fate or Chance rule the world are never set in open opposition to each other, and the omens might be interpreted as the work either of the one or the other. It is precisely this uncertainty at the heart of the play which is the heart of its darkness: either explanation, if it could be accepted as an explanation, would give some relief."[37]

It is the unintelligibility of the world, the impossibility of final answers and the absence of unassailable standards, which leaves in Webster's plays only the comfort of Stoic strength, "The gallant splendour, the ironic laughter of a humanity that is braver and cleverer than the blind Universe which drags it down."[38]

In Ferdinand and the Cardinal, Webster at least permits his audience the revenge-play satisfaction of seeing total villainy receive a proper come-uppance. Each admits the Providential justice of his end: rather a hollow concession in a play where this justice cannot be taken seriously, nor can anything resembling it be found in the deaths of the protagonists. The wages of virtue and of sin are paid by the same inscrutable fortune. The ethic of Talio, of scale-balancing and retribution in kind ("Blood asketh blood and death must death requite")[39] present in the Kydian genre, was more a structural machinery than a moral philosophy: it probably should not be extrapolated beyond the dramatic events which define it. Serious dependence on the *lex talionis* in post-Shakespearean tragedies of any pretension constitutes evidence of bankruptcy.

The Cardinal is a remote figure and not centrally important to the play. About Ferdinand, the real antag-

onist, there is something strange. He combines wickedness hardly short of caricature with elements of helplessness and pathos. In one scene (III. ii. 107–13) he refuses
a chance to meet the Duchess' husband, whose identity
he has sought for years: he is trying to avoid a plunge
into insanity. His frantic rage does not survive its object, and the stunned and broken eloquence of the great
line spoken over his sister's body ("Cover her face;
Mine eyes dazell: she di'd yong") has an effect not
far from pathos. From here he lapses into complete
madness.

Webster's treatment of Ferdinand is in fact a more-
or-less deterministic "humors" study.[40] Avarice and injured pride are the ostensible motives of both villains,
but have often seemed inadequate to the savagery of the
revenge: in any case, neither has an obvious connection
with some of Ferdinand's behavior. This seeming weakness has been sharply attacked by journalistic criticism
of modern productions.[41] Scholarly writers generally
solve the problem either by referring Ferdinand's role to
the notion of "motiveless malignity,"[42] by interpreting
the tragic action as stemming largely from incestuous
desire on his part,[43] or by dismissing strict consistency
of motivation, or of causation in general, as subordinate
in Webster's peculiar dramatic technique.[44]

Other details, not usually seen as having significant
connection with Ferdinand's character, contribute to
the impression that the structure of the play is "hope-
lessly loose": the long passage of time between acts II
and III is usually explained as pure bungling, probably
due to an injudicious regard for the facts of the source.[45]

The plot of *The Duchess of Malfi* makes considerable
use of seventeenth-century psychology. Like other Renaissance authors, Webster presumes the audience's understanding of humors, but he also provides in the play
some comments that help to diagnose Ferdinand's char-

acter. Antonio observes near the beginning of the play
that

> Want of action
> Breeds all black malcontents: and their close rearing,
> Like moths in cloth, do hurt for want of wearing.
>
> (I. i. 80–83)

This is spoken of Bosola, but is more widely relevant.
Any of Webster's generalizations on character is likely
to state a theme occurring in several variations. He is
inclined to the "symphonic" treatment of complemental
character groups.[46] The catalog of melancholy types in
Malfi is particularly impressive: there is, first, the acute
and "adust" melancholy of Ferdinand. The Cardinal's
melancholy humor, explicitly mentioned by Antonio
(I. i. 158) and by Bosola (V. ii. 213), displays such orthodox symptoms as hallucination (V. v. 5–7). Bosola, a
malcontent, represents one of the classical melancholy
types;[47] he too suffers hallucination and is described as
having been a "Fantastical scholar" who "hath studied
himself blear ey'd" (III. iii. 50–54), inevitably recalling
Burton's celebrated account of melancholy as the scholar's occupational disease.[48] Lawrence Babb concludes,
finally, that "Webster makes it very clear, in *The Duchess* of *Malfi*, that the unfortunate heroine is melancholy."[49]

Also in the first scene, there is talk of a tournament
which has just been held, and Ferdinand inquires,
"When shall we leave this sportive-action, and fall to
action indeed?" (I. i. 93–94). A few lines further, he
complains that a man might as well delegate the functions of eating and sleeping as that of fighting, since,
"this might take idle, offensive, and base office from
him, whereas the other deprives him of honour" (I. i.
103–104). In the same scene, Antonio remarks that "Out
of brave Horse-man-ship, arise the first Sparkes of grow-

ing resolution, that raise the minde to noble action"
(I. i. 145–57).

Close on this echoing praise of action, which is set
against Antonio's earlier stricture on the psychological
danger of inaction, the idea is summed up in the draw-
ing of an explicit opposition between vigorous action
and, on the other hand, "melancholy" and mental disorder. Delio asks,

> What's that Cardinall?
> I mean his Temper, they say he's a brave fellow,
> Will play his five thousand crownes at Tennis, Daunce,
> Court Ladies, and one that hath fought single Combats.
> (I. i. 153–56)

Antonio replies that "some such flashes superficially
hang on him, for forme: but observe his inward Character: he is a melancholly Churchman" (I. i. 157–59).
Functions of this "melancholy" are jealousy, intriguing,
and the patronizing of "Flatterers, Panders, Intelligen-
cers, Atheists, and a thousand such politicall Monsters."
The psychological doctrine is sufficiently clear: it is especially useful with Ferdinand.

The time-lapse between acts II and III has psychological significance. In the last scene of act II, Ferdinand
receives the news that his sister has borne a child. Maddened by her "looseness" and supposed notoriety, he
writhes in the grip of "choller," which by his own testimony overwhelms him (II. v. 19). His brother the Cardinal chides repeatedly the ungoverned rage which makes
him "fly beyond [his] reason" (II. v. 23–24, 61, 65, 73–80,
86). Ferdinand closes the interview by promising to

> . . . go sleepe—
> Till I know who leapes my sister, i'll not stire:
> That knowne, I'll finde Scorpions to string my whips,
> And fix her in a generall eclipse.
> (II. v. 99–102)

Yet in the following scene, after Antonio's expository revelation that at least two years have passed, we hear this exchange:

> *Delio.*   Pray Sir tell me
> Hath not this newes arriv'd yet to the eare;
> Of the Lord *Cardinall?*
>
> *Ant.*   I feare it hath,
> The Lord Ferdinand, (that's newly come to Court,)
> Doth beare himselfe right dangerously.
>
> . . . .
> He is so quiet, that he seemes to sleepe
> The tempest out (as Doremise do in Winter)—
> Those houses, that are haunted, are most still,
> Till the divell be up
>
>   (III. i. 17–27)

Here is the brooding inaction of whose perils Antonio has told. Ferdinand's career bears out the claim that "black [i.e., melancholic] malcontents" and mental unbalance are caused or increased by such a stifling of action. Choler, says Bacon, is "an humour that maketh men active, earnest, full of alacrity, and stirring, if it be not stopped. But if it be stopped, and cannot have his way, it becometh adust, and thereby malign and venomous."[50] The same idea appears in Lodge's *Rosalynde* and in other Renaissance works. Nashe, in *Four Letters Confuted,*[51] mentions that "a man must not take knowledge of an injury till he be able to avenge it." Excessive quietness was a symptom of melancholy, which is also connected with a long obsessive dwelling on something, an *idée fixe.*[52] Webster dramatizes some of the episodes in the long effort of Ferdinand and Bosola to identify the Duchess' husband. This we see at its inception and in the events which lead to its climax in the Machiavellian stratagem by which Bosola induces the Duchess' disclosure (III. ii). The rest is left to inference.

Webster's handling of time does not follow his source. In Belleforest's story, the brothers make their discovery after the Duchess has borne her second child, and they set directly about their revenge. They meet with difficulties and suffer delays; but there is no secret waiting or enforced inaction. The delay does not stretch over years, as in Webster; Ferdinand's long-seething, suppressed anger is a deliberate addition. The conversation that opens the third act is especially designed to impress on the spectator that several years have passed. This is true not only because of Antonio's explicit announcement, "since you last saw her / She hath had two children more, a sonne, and daughter" (III. i. 6–7); the whole focus of the scene is on the long passage of time since the events of act II. There is, first, Antonio's greetin to Delio: "Our noble friend (my most beloved *Delio*) / Oh, you have been a stranger long at Court" (III. i. 1–2). Even more telling is Delio's reply:

> Me thinkes 'twas yester-day: Let me but wincke,
> And not behold your face, which to mine eye
> Is somewhat leaner, verily I should dreame
> It were within this halfe houre.
>
> (III. i. 8–11)

Here is a meeting of old friends after long separation, one remarking the print of time on the other's face. "It seems like yesterday": nothing could convey more emphatically the extended lapse.

This is not, then, an instance of "double" dramatic time, compressing events to create an illusion; nor can it be a careless slip, an inconsistency which has crept into a line or two. Webster deliberately forces our awareness that the marriage has continued over a period of years, and that Ferdinand, for all his ominous threats, has in that time failed to identify the Duchess' husband and has only brooded over his anger. The effect aimed at surely involves our consciousness of his sinister patience, and his increasing dangerous melancholy.[53]

Comprehending all degrees of madness and many kinds of bodily affliction, melancholy displayed symptoms ranging from flatulence to hallucination.[54] What, specifically, is the nature of Ferdinand's melancholy? Something in the way of an excessive humor, some obsession or temperamental disposition must account for his irrational rage at his sister's marriage. Late in the play, the mad Ferdinand himself remembers in a moment of sanity the causes of his passion (IV. ii. 300–306). He alludes to his hope of eventually inheriting the Duchess' estate, had she remained a widow,[55] but this is parenthetical to something more important:

> For let me but examine well the cause;
> What was the meanenes of her match to me?
> Onely I must confesse, I had a hope
> (Had she continu'd widow) to have gain'd
> An infinite masse of Treasure by her death:
> And that was the mayne cause; her Marriage—
> That drew a streame of gall quite through my heart.
> (IV. ii. 300–306)

To regret having acted on a provocation which is named as too slight is surely to identify one's motive. Ferdinand tells us that it is the "meanenes" of his sister's match, or from our point of view, his pride of family and reputation, his "fantastic Spanish punctilio" together with a choleric disposition,[56] which is his motive for revenge. "Onely," in the third of these lines, has the parenthetical sense of "except." "That," in the sixth line, points backward to the key phrase "the meanenes of her match" and forward to its appositive, "her marriage."

Warning the Duchess against remarrying (I. i. 323–24), the brothers exhort her not to let "youth . . . high promotion, eloquence . . . nor anything without the addition, Honour, Sway your high blood," thus introducing the dual theme of "blood" and "honour." When they discover her secret, the subject of Ferdinand's tirade is clearly the damage to family honor (II. v). He shows a humorous pride of "blood" and a morbid concern for reputation, for the great family name of "a sister dampn'd . . . Growne a notorious Strumpet." The Cardinal enjoins him to "Speake lower": He answers "Lower? / Rogues do not whisper't now, but seeke to publish't . . . To marke who note them" (II. v. 8–12).

Racked by the idea of this stain on the indivisible family glory, Ferdinand threatens to "lay her generall territory as wast, / As she hath done her honours" (II. v. 28–29). He laments "Foolish men, / that ere will trust their honour to a Barke, / Made of so slight, weake bull-rush, as is woman" (II. v. 46–48). The Cardinal adds, "Thus Ignorance, when it hath purchas'd honour, / It cannot wield it" (II. v. 50–51). Ferdinand feels himself personally injured: "I do thinke / It is some sin in us, Heaven doth revenge / By her" (II. v. 83–85). He takes his part in her scandal with terrible seriousness.

The motif of public opinion (this is what honor amounts to) is in fact begun in the first act when Ferdinand speaks of the corruptions of the court; he warns the Duchess of "a kind of honney-dew, that's deadly: / 'twill poyson your fame" (I. i. 340–41). Sounding her out, he proposes that she marry one Malateste, and she answers "when I choose / A husband, I will marry for your honour" (III. i. 52–53). Antonio reports to Delio that "The common-rable, do directly say / She is a strumpet" (III. i. 29–30), and in the scene where Ferdinand finally confronts his sister, his climactic address takes the form of a speech on reputation:

> You have shooke hands with Reputation,
> And made him invisible: so, fare you well.

I will never see you more.
(III. ii. 157–59)

Some critics find in the play hints of incestuous passion. When Bosola asks mercy for the Duchess, that her punishment might end with her being put to a life of religious penance, Ferdinand replies,

> Damne her, that body of hers,
> While that my blood ran pure in't, was more worth
> Then that which thou wouldst comfort call'd soule.
> (IV. i. 146–48)

The hint of sexual interest here has been seized on to solve the difficulties of motivation. But in view of Ferdinand's obsession with honor, these lines surely concern "that body of hers" as a vessel of the family blood so often invoked.

Can this be the reason that Webster's Ferdinand refuses to admit the reality of the Duchess' marriage, although he has no evident reason to doubt it? She is in fact joined to Antonio by a genuine sacramental bond, concluded according to canon law. Antonio's first verbal feint in the proposal scene refers to "the sacrament of marriage," and both he and the Duchess declare before Cariola the intention necessary to that contract.[57] The Duchess explicitly tells her brother "I pray sir, hear me: I am married." Yet when Ferdinand comes to her in her imprisonment, he asks "Where are your cubs?" She replies, in anger and indignation, with the single word "Whom?" and Ferdinand answers,

> Call them your children;
> For though our nationall law distinguish Bastards
> From true legitimate issue: compassionate nature
> Makes them all equall.

The Duchess exclaims,

> Doe you visit me for this?
> You violate a Sacrament o'th' Church
> Shall make you howle in hell for't.
>
> (IV. i. 41–47)

It is possible to think that her outraged question is occasioned by some action of Ferdinand's, some sexual advance, for which our text gives no direction. An incest theme is again a convenience to the critic. But what relevance would the idea of a sacrament then have to her protest? It is less conjectural to see Ferdinand as characteristically refusing, as he does in Bandello, to admit that any children not the heirs of a prince or duke could conceivably be regarded as legitimate issue of the Duchess of Malfi. The Duchess' indignant reference to his violation of a sacrament—that sacrament which has legitimatized her children—is then a perfectly natural mother's response. The difficulty is resolved by an appeal to the theme of excessive family pride.

Injury to an obsessively regarded honor has aroused Ferdinand to rage. Because he is disposed by temperament to choler, and because his anger, finding no outlet, continues over a long period, choler becomes melancholy adust, and he descends into criminal madness. These steps accurately reflect the humors psychology. In the Galenic system "just as the temperament influences the passions, so the passions may affect the temperament."[58] Burton says of the role of imagination in the engendering of melancholy: "If the imagination be very apprehensive, intent, and violent, it sends great store of spirits to or from the heart, and makes a deeper impression, and greater tumult; as the humours in the body be likewise prepared, and the temperature itself ill or well disposed, the passions are longer and stronger; so that the first step and fountain of all our grievances in this kind is a distorted imagination, which, misinforming the heart, causeth all these distemperatures,

alteration, and confusion, of spirits and humours."[59]
This will gloss the vivid fantasies of Ferdinand:

> . . . talke to me somewhat, quickly,
> Or my imagination will carry me
> To see her, in the shamefull act of sinne.
>
> (II. v. 53–55)

"Passions," says Babb, "are very likely to produce black bile: 'nothing certainly engenders melancholy more quickly, or more readily causes existing melancholy to linger than passions of the mind, for they both dry the body and disturb the spirits and humours beyond nature.'" Finally, and most significantly, "Hot passions, if they are excessive, engender adust melancholy by burning the humours. Anger is very likely to do so. If anger continues long, the choler in the system 'becometh Blacke, and seething strongly, dries up and burnes, whereby oftentimes it happens that some become frantique, mad and desparate.'"[60] Burton, explaining anger and "desire of revenge" as causes of madness, touches several times upon the idea that long duration exacerbates their ill effect and may be a condition of their malignity.[61]

Dying, Ferdinand exclaims

> My sister, oh! my sister, there's the cause on't.
> "Whether we fall by ambition, blood, or lust,
> "Like Diamonds, we are cut with our owne dust.
>
> (V. v. 90–92)

Surely Webster does not allow him, in this catalog of fatal vices, to exclude his own fault, the cause of his fall ("we are cut with our owne dust"). Possibly he is guilty of all the sins he names. "Blood" means anger, or lust, or passion generally; it can mean kinship or murder. Here it likely refers to anger ("ambition" and "lust" name passions, not acts; Ferdinand is thinking of the

unruly forces which drive men, not of the acts committed because of them). By implication at least it refers to
Ferdinand's morbid pride of family, the cause of his
hysterical anger.[62] Perhaps we would be justified in
seeing also an intentional ambiguity alluding to kinship.

A choleric nobleman whose passion for family reputation inflames the rage excited by his sister's marriage,
Ferdinand is driven to insanity and murder by the long
frustration of his anger. Recovering briefly after the
Duchess' death, he is allowed a pathetic remorse before
he plunges into lycanthropia.[63]

The Cardinal's share of responsibility for the murder,
declared by him in V. ii. 278–79, cannot be accounted
for in exactly the same way as Ferdinand's. But although his motives might in a case at law be of equal
significance with his brother's, in the play they have
small importance. Ferdinand is the central antagonist.
The Cardinal, furthermore, is a legitimately "melancholy" character, though not of the same type as Ferdinand, and his behavior is explicable and consistent in
light of the humors psychology.

Anyone who knows this much about Ferdinand's character will not, at least, find in the motivation of the play
so complete an enigma that he is compelled to build up
from slight hints an elaborately Freudian interpretation,
to be forced upon the play as a main theme.[64]

The Duchess of Malfi would still require, for any modern production, some translation into twentieth-century
terms. But recognition of Webster's intent with respect
to Ferdinand would enable a reviser to know what it is
that he must translate. The treatment of the key character has been a "case study" of melancholy adust, tracing
the causes of tragedy to the operation of mechanical
natural forces which he cannot control. Not even with
the play's guiltiest villain, then, may we fix an unequiv-

ocal responsibility for events. Behavior is governed by "natural" (involuntary and physical) forces.

The finest spirit, resolution, and intelligence in Webster's tragedies lies with Vittoria, Flamineo, Antonio, Bosola, and the Duchess of Malfi; these characters are moved, in differing ways, to set the world at defiance. It is a late Renaissance world, an unmapped waste, where the only natural law even dimly adumbrated is that of irrational and ungovernable forces. It is a voluntaristic world, for the moral norms which its inhabitants profess are not based on an observable natural order: mankind is so depraved and society so chaotic that, in Charron's words, "from this generall and universall alteration and corruption it is come to passe, that there is nothing of nature known in us."[65] The noblest thing in this world is the spirit and courage of exceptional persons, and tragedy offers what vindication of life it can by exhibiting that spirit's unbreakable defiance of the world to which it is fatally alien.

Chapter Seven

The New Meaning of Tragedy: Tourneur, Beaumont & Fletcher, Ford

THE TWO TRAGEDIES attributed to Cyril Tourneur conduct us through a charnel darkness lit by the phosphorescence of moral decay and the glare of Juvenalian rhetoric. The tone of *The Revenger's Tragedy* (1606–1607) and *The Atheist's Tragedy* (1610–1611) may be in part the inevitable response to a recurring theatrical situation—the excess of the writer who comes late to a familiar and too well-worked dramatic genre. Much of the gloom and revulsion, however, is Calvinistic.

The plot of *The Revenger's Tragedy,* too intricate to rehearse in full, turns on the machinations of the hero,

Vendice, to avenge his betrothed Gloriana, poisoned by the lecherous Duke whom she rejected. He appears holding before him the lady's skull as he rails against court viciousness. Gloriana, he recalls, was so beautiful

> That the uprightest man (if such there be,
> That sinne but seaven times a day) broke custome
> And made up eight with looking after her.
>
> (I. i)[1]

Depravity is total and universal. The sour comment on Scripture and the outraged idealism which it implies announce the spirit of the tragedy. This, at its most intense, passes into savage relish for the most appalling demonstrations of vice, into a lust for the exposure of evil which gloats over every revelation of the world's perversity. Vendice is a Jacobean "reality-instructor." His intelligent response to the spectacle of Tourneur's world provides us at least an anchor for sympathy: we have from him the satisfaction of truth; one voice gives adequate expression to the outrage such a world should inspire.

Disguised as Piato (a malcontent in the mold of Bo-sola, Flamineo, or Marston's Malevole), Vendice serves as bawd to the Duke's heir, Lussurioso. In this capacity he solicits his own mother, Gratiana, to pander his sister. Even as Vendice, he addresses to Gratiana such comment as his thought that "Wives are but made to go to bed and feed"; his speeches as Piato are even more strongly flavored. After a series of intrigues filled with rape, incest, and murder, Vendice succeeds in killing the Duke: conducting him to a darkened place of assignation, he bids the old lecher kiss the bashful lady there presented—a puppet topped by Gloriana's skull, the mouth poisoned. But Vendice and his brother Hippolito are careful that the Duke does not die before he has seen his Duchess incestuously embraced by his bastard son.

After their final murder of Lussurioso (the succeeding Duke), Vendice and Hippolito are led to execution, satisfied with their accomplishments, which have included their mother's reform and the proving of their sister's chastity.

The play harps incessantly on the corruption of the time. Of Piato it is said that "This our age swims within him / . . . He is so neere kinne to this present minute." He offers his credentials to his patron:

> I have beene witnesse
> To the surrenders of a thousand virgins,
> And not so little,
> I have seene Patrimonyes washt a peices,
> Fruit-feilds turnd into bastards,
>
> . . . .
> Some father dreads not (gonne to bedde in wine) to
>   slide from the mother
> And cling the daughter-in-law,
> Some Uncles are adulterous with their neeces,
> Brothers with brothers wives. O howre of Incest!
> Any kin now next to the Rim ath sister
> Is mans meate in these dayes; and in the morning
> When they are up and drest, and their maske on,
> Who can perceive this? save that eternall eye,
> That see's through flesh and all? Well: —if any thing
>   be dambd,
> It will be twelve a clock at night; that twelve
> Will never scape;
> It is the Judas of the howers, wherein,
> Honest salvation is betrayde to sin.
>
>   (I. iii)

Lussurioso professes to be "past my depth in lust" and speaks of rubbing "hell o'er with honey": in sophisticated drama we reencounter the self-recognizedly evil villain, hardly explainable here by morality-play or even Machiavellian stage convention. Advancing a step past Heywood's characters into the Calvinist milieu of invincible carnal depravity, he perceives himself and his actions as evil, but persists with undisturbed appetite. (Heywood's sinners too are irresistibly driven, but they voice incessantly their moral horror.)

The name of bawd, says Lussurioso to his new factotum, "Is so in league with the age that nowadays / It does eclipse three quarters of a mother." The courtier Antonio relates that Lussurioso raped his (Antonio's) wife "amidst a throng of pandars" and that she died a suicide. Hippolito replies

> A wondrous Lady; of rare fire compact,
> Sh'as made her name an Empresse by that act.
>
> (I. iv)

Virtue consists largely of refusal to be part of this world. It stands always isolated, absolute, wholly unrelated and out of tune with all about it, as in the dead Gloriana or the chaste sister Castiza. No judgment falls on the rapist, for "Judgment, in this age, is near kin to favour," and "Tis no shame to be bad, because 'tis common."

The satyr-satirist Vendice wonders "Why does not Heaven turn black, or with a frown / Undo the world?" A constant chorus to the scene, he is afflicted by a sense of the incredible corruption lying just beneath the surface of the world about him, and a shocked awareness of evil which issues in sensational and fascinated imagery somewhat akin to that of the mad Lear. There is a sting not felt in the satyr-rhetoric of Beaumont and Fletcher:

> Night! Thou that lookst like funerall Heraulds fees
> Torne downe betimes ith morning, thou hangst fittly
> To Grace those sins that have no grace at all.
> Now tis full sea a bed over the world;
> Theres jugling of all sides; some that were Maides
> E'en at Sun set, are now perhaps ith toale-booke;
> This woman in immodest thin apparell

Lets in her friend by water, here a Dame
Cunning, nayles lether-hindges to a dore,
To avoide proclamation.
Now Cuckolds are a quoyning, apace, apace, apace,
    apace.
And carefull sisters spinne that thread ith night,
That does maintaine them and their bawdes ith daie!

(II. ii)

Vendice's musings over the skull of Gloriana (to cite these as an echo of the words spoken over Yorick's skull would be to single out one from many Shakespearean echoes) include some remarkable lines:

Are Lord-ships sold to maintaine Lady-ships
For the poore benefit of a bewitching minute?

(III. v)

But here their tone and the atmosphere they generate are exactly those of the whole play, just as the "hidden imposthume" of Hamlet's world has become the world itself, the body of the time. A review of, for instance, the Calvinist Thomas Goodwin's account of his spiritual awakening[2] will suggest the affinities of such an imagination. Dialogue between the bastard Spurio and his stepmother at their assignation is especially revealing:

Spurio	Had not that kisse a taste of sinne 'twere sweete.
Duchess	Why there's no pleasure sweet but it is sinfull.
Spurio	True, such a bitter sweetnesse fate hath given; Best side to us, is the worst side to heaven.

(III. v)

Seen against the Calvinistic background, this opposition of human nature to moral law requires little comment. "When the bad bleeds," says Vendice, "then is the tragedy good." In *The Revenger's Tragedy* "the bad bleeds," but through the agency of a revenger who enjoys our assent in his motives only because of the extreme viciousness of the world he scourges. We feel no hope of general justice in his punishment of evil: it bespeaks no natural retribution and restoration; it brings only a vindictive pleasure in seeing these particular wretches get what they deserve.

The Atheist's Tragedy is a slightly later comment on the "world order inherently evil," the city of dreadful night, which is Tourneur's dramatic arena. The general scene is, again, one of unabated lusts and incests, leering prurience and depravity, greed and murders, graves and death-heads; still it does not reach to that poetic joining of sexual desire with death and decay which in *The Revenger's Tragedy* intimates to the imagination an utter and universal corruption. D'Amville, the title character, is a peculiarly Jacobean "atheist"—a "naturalist" or materialist. In his attempt to seduce his chaste daughter-in-law Castabella, he urges the supremacy of "nature" in lines reflecting faithfully the Calvinist-voluntarist separation of natural from moral laws.

> Incest? Tush.
> These distances affinitie observes;
> Are articles of bondage cast upon
> Our freedomes by our owne subjections.
> Nature allowes a gen'rall libertie
> Of generation to all creatures else.
> Shall Man to whose command and use all creatures
> Were made subject be lesse free then they?
>
> (IV. iii)

The heroine rebukes him for arguing "merely out / Of Nature," which for the virtuous as for the vicious has now this meaning. His follower Borachio is a mechanist "read / in Nature and her large Philosophie":

> . . . there's nothing in a Man, above
> His nature; if there were, consid'ring t'is
> His beings excellencie, t'would not yeeld
> To Natures weakenesse.
>
> (I. i)

Levidulcia, the "lascivious gentlewoman," counsels her daughter that "Nature" is not only opposed but preferable to reason.

> . . . If Reason were
> Our counsellour, wee would neglect the worke
> Of generation, for the prodigall
> Expence it drawes us too, of that which is
> The wealth of life. Wise Nature (therefore) hath
> Reserv'd for an inducement to our sence,
> Our greatest pleasure in that greatest worke.
>
> (I. iv)

And of her own adulterous passion, muses that "though it seemes to be the free effect of mine owne voluntarie love; yet I can neither restraine it, nor give reason for 't" (IV. v). "Compact of lust," she is never "so powerful or so convincing a figure," says Una Ellis-Fermor, "as when she rationalizes it as natural law."[3]

As in *Lear*, the implications of "nature" reverberate through the play, but moral causes and effects form here into a very different pattern. D'Amville and Levidulcia are the votaries of nature, their behavior at once morally wicked and perfectly natural. Living "merely out / Of Nature" and in defiance of moral rules may be perilous, but only because of the risk that an angry God will intervene.[4] After all his plots and murders, D'Amville is prevented from killing Charlemont and Castabella, the radiantly virtuous hero and heroine, by a providential stroke quite unrelated to anything that has gone before. Raising a weapon to execute them, he accidentally strikes out his own brains, leaving the "good" characters to a happy ending. The playwright has exhausted the dramatic potential of his materials in a display of wickedness and nobility, in the excitement of horror and admiration; he concludes with a nakedly perfunctory assertion of the wages of sin. Whatever relief that conclusion affords to the spectacle of suffering can hardly reach beyond our superficial engagement with this particular fictional scene.

The hero Charlemont is satisfied that

> . . . by the worke of Heavin; the men that thought
> To follow our dead bodies without teares;
> Are dead themselves.
>
> (V. ii)

And D'Amville's dying words,

> . . . Nature is a foole. There is a power
> Above her that hath overthrown the pride
> Of all my projects. . . .
>
> (V. ii)

set out with absolute clarity the final dissolution of the medieval synthesis and express the terrifying Jacobean conviction of total enmity between goodness and the law of nature.

Tourneur's frequently splendid poetry (a little rigid sometimes in its rhythm, perhaps with the need to contain Tourneur's teeth-gritted rage) has realized a very substantial natural world of indomitable corruption and evil. Only the intervention of Providence defends in it the weakness of human virtue.

Charlemont is in fact quite disabled by his goodness for the contest with the vicious world; his heroism is to submit with passive fortitude to the fate from which he is saved by D'Amville's death. To liken this inactivity to Hamlet's (as has been done) is quite misleading, for Charlemont's passive and permanent helplessness is the measure of his virtue. Yet he is, unlike Vendice, in some sense a noble hero, meant to engage our sympathies, so that the unrelieved debacle which concludes *The Revenger's Tragedy* would here become intolerable. Carried to its natural conclusion—the murder by D'Amville of Charlemont and Castabella—*The Atheist's Tragedy* would inspire only horror and despair. The tragic relief, the reconciliation of the viewer to the world of trial and suffering where such drama must take place, is counterfeited by a happy ending. The play remains a tragedy despite its deus ex machina rescue of the virtuous: five acts have been devoted to producing the experiences of tragedy. The final one, however, is unattainable on Tourneur's terms: tragic catharsis becomes a mere evasion in the tragicomic ending. This does not make of *The Atheist's Tragedy* a Jacobean tragicomedy in the mode of those produced by Beaumont and Fletcher, but provides a hint which may help us to understand the relation of those plays to the genre of tragedy.

Tourneur seems still to feel that morality is at least theoretically practical; if men obeyed their consciences, things would go as they should. But those consciences are defied by everything which must be called "nature," and the moral norm, the function of rulers for the common good, the devotion of husbands and wives, parents and children, to their proper purposes, is so remote as to be only a pious rhetorical reproach or a pastoral idyll. In *Macbeth, Hamlet, Othello,* or *Edward II,* the natural moral order of things is felt barely to tolerate the rash and presumptuous interruption of its working. Cosmic realities are engaged, and there is a thrill of human magnitude. We are made to feel that man wields enormous powers of good and evil, and that his acts are central to all of the vast creation. Order has overcome at the end of tragedy, the power to evade or pervert it. But in these two plays, that teleological order of nature is nowhere visible or tangible and certainly does not shape events, as in *Lear* or *Hamlet*. Violence and evil are destructive, and even self-destructive; but only by the vindictive counterviolence they arouse in the injured or by the will of a power from beyond the boundaries of the natural world. In place of the retributive working of the natural law there is a merciless avenger and a demonstration that whoever indulges himself at the expense of others will meet his match among his intended victims (as in *The Revenger's Tragedy*) or be blasted by divine lightning (as in *The Atheist's Tragedy*).

It is gratifying to be shown that wolves, if they become rapacious enough, devour each other. There is some satisfaction of the need for justice (and perhaps of less admirable instincts) in seeing a Vendice, the maddened agent of a reprisal emotionally justified by the enormity of the offenses he suffers, exact a savage measure of payment for crime. Evildoers get all they deserve, and a revenge that balances the books does allay in some sort the stormy emotions aroused by the play. We consent to Vendice's death, as he does himself in his final speech. But it is a bitter conclusion and hardly distracts us from the injustice of his world. We cannot be much comforted by mere retaliation; and to "set" the hero's revenges, to prepare us for his symbolic reprisal upon life, Tourneur deepens the horror of the world's corruption beyond all hope. Vendice is in effect a more theatrical and sensational Hamlet whose only problems are those of opportunity and ingenuity. But if, in Shakespeare's play, our final feeling were to depend solely on the success of the tyrannicide, Claudius and Gertrude would have to be far worse than they are, and far more of a piece with their world.

The tragicomic alternative naturally suggests itself. Having had the thrills of four and a half acts of *The Revenger's Tragedy*, let us have a complete relief from its rigors. The present ending leaves us with a sour taste; it dissipates too little of our well-aroused horror, or of our pity for the innocent victims. We have small comfort in Vendice's end or in the world left by his extermination of these particular villains (despite the conventional appearance at the end of a new and virtuous duke). Therefore, let Vendice's dead mistress, Gloriana, be revived by some plot contrivance, in which we shall willingly be complicit. Tell us that she has secretly been held prisoner, and bring her forward now to Vendice's arms. This will relieve our emotions and allow us to feel, at least momentarily, that the worst storms can be weathered and that it is darkest before the dawn. We can, by such devices, enjoy the spectacle of seeing nobility under stress, but resign what has become the hopeless and painful struggle with ultimate questions. Give the audience at least the ending of *The Atheist's Tragedy;* better still, give them the tragicomedy of Beaumont and Fletcher.

THE PLAYS traditionally assigned to Beaumont and Fletcher, despite the undoubted presence of other hands, do share important and distinctive characteristics. The collaboration began its popular success with *Philaster* (1609), which was therefore uniquely important to the development of Jacobean drama. Probably the most familiar of its type, *Philaster* is almost, although not completely, representative of the genre. This sort of tragicomedy was approached by Chapman in *The Gentleman Usher* and by Marston in *The Malcontent*. It provided the main pattern for plays by Shirley and Massinger. It influenced the courtly drama which dominated the Caroline theater in the time of Charles' French queen, Henrietta Maria,[5] and which affected in turn the heroic drama of the Restoration. It had often a slight basis in known history, to help the realism of its language give substance to its fairyland characters.

Eugene Waith, in his fine study of the Beaumont and Fletcher plays,[6] has traced their technique of characterization and the rhetoric of virtuous denunciation which, he says, creates in them an "atmosphere of evil, vivid but not actual," to a double origin in the traditions of pastoral and of satire. The satyr-figure borrowed from the satires, a protean character who assumes different qualities in different scenes, is, however, common to the tragicomedies and to the plays of tragic ending which Beaumont and Fletcher also wrote. In both kinds of drama, consistency of character is repeatedly sacrificed to theatrical expediency arising in individual scenes. The connection of the railing satyr with the genre of tragicomedy is, on Professor Waith's evidence, strong in Renaissance dramatic theory. But in the actual plays the satyr is so transformed that neither characters nor plot-patterns are adequately accounted for by his influence; he is too much altered from his conventional origin to be explained entirely by it. Equally, the semi-allegorical characters of pastoral, the details of the corrupt world depicted by the satires, the extravagant and "hypothetical" plot situations taken from romance and from the *Controversiae* of Seneca the Elder[7] seem to have come as grist to a mill that was already turning.

There are of course characters in other Renaissance drama who have been seen as inconsistent. The Cressida whom Troilus envisions as two persons, Bosola, Malevole, Vendice, Edgar, all play double roles. They join, says Muriel Bradbrook, extreme and unreconciled opposites; such a combination of conventional types was itself a convention.[8] But such conventions are only shortcuts, tacitly agreed-upon substitutions to free the drama from mechanical necessities of literal verisimilitude. Their particular uses are not explained by their existence. Nor does the availability of a given source material explain why a playwright turned to it, nor what he made of it. The deeper question is that of what it was that made the *Controversiae* and the satyr-figure congenial to these writers' purposes, and why the earlier drama did not make a similar use of available materials. What, in short, really caused the shift to tragicomedy?

The crucial fact is that Fletcherian tragicomedy is actually a variety of tragedy, a substitute, attempting to continue the experience of tragedy in the face of the bankruptcy of the tragic vision. When the conception of natural law had undergone that transformation which has here been traced, there was no longer any basis for the study of character in the aspect of its causal moral relation to event. For the tragic writer, plot was freed from significant character and character from plot, which concentrated increasingly on the exploitation of pure incident. The determining moral will was no longer the nucleating element in serious drama. Characters in the Beaumont and Fletcher plays do not develop from within by responding to events that unfold from self-initiated moral choice. They change violently, but mechanically, under pressure of the dramatic exigencies of individual scenes; the changes are inexplicable except theatrically. Even the events of the tragicomic plot do not unfold in a causal sequence, but are arranged in a series of striking theatrical moments, constituted chiefly by impassioned rhetorical encounters. The elements of reversal, contrast, and surprise are more important to the direction of events than is that of tragic inevitability.[9] Character becomes, in any scene, a donnée, a postulate like geographical setting, and often the postulated character is manufactured from the tenets of the courtly-Platonic love code or of an aristocratic "honor" compounded of absolute virtues whose measure is their irreconcilability to the demands of ordinary life.

Shakespearean tragedy involves the existential struggle of judgment, the demand laid on reason to forge an application of its principles to circumstances. Choice and consequent action are shown in a causal relation to tragic event, a relation based on the underlying conception of natural law and inherent moral order violated by defect of rationality through error or perverseness. Virtue therefore does not appear in Shakespeare as an aprioristic fact, absolute and apart from the generation of action out of circumstance. The most significant evil lies in the rational failures of good men. But in the code ethic which creates and measures the heroes of these tragicomedies, virtue is absolute and disconnected from the world of natural forces which control events. It appears embodied clear and complete in Philaster, Amintor (*The Maid's Tragedy*), even Arbaces (*A King and No King*), despite the fact that the last of these heroes has character defects and is not made seamlessly admirable.

A character can now be virtuous in a static and final sense. Hooker's or Shakespeare's "good" man must be unendingly engaged in creating his virtuousness, striving against impediments to achieve his nature, to act rationally. The struggle of the Beaumont and Fletcher hero is not like this, but is a conflict with outer circumstances against which his virtue is pitted, generating a rhetoric of grandeur or pathos, but not of deep questioning, meditation, or introspective discovery. His goodness or chivalric nobility is complete in him, for the code virtues, being absolute, require no obscure struggle of judgment. They are fixed, complete, and do not proceed from but conflict with the demands of nature. Where there is internal conflict, as in Arbaces' temptation to a supposed incest, it is merely the resistance by reason to clearly opposed and simply evil desire; no problem arises of moral recognition or discovery. The ethical questions are not real. We and all the characters know exactly what is right, what the tragic hero is obligated to do; in this the tragicomedy is like a morality play.

It is natural that there should arise a tendency to depict character chiefly as the embodiment of such virtues, or of their corresponding vices, in a gamut of types which resemble the characters of allegory. The influence of the pastoral tradition, with its allegorical or semi-allegorical figures manifesting the conceptions of a systematic ethics, flows naturally into this stream of dramatic development. Thus, the figures of Spenser's fairyland (animated by changed ethical conceptions) materialize among the more substantial scenes of tragedy, speaking now the language of the real world. Here they approach the personified type because the axiology which is the basis of choice and action is a code, enhancing nobility by extremity and exaggeration. When loyalty is an absolute value, detached from natural prudence and the rational regard of circumstance, then the more exaggeratedly loyal the hero, the more noble and heroic. But one whose hypothetical loyalty reaches such unwavering absoluteness and remoteness from the natural and ordinary course as that of Amintor in *The Maid's Tragedy* must inescapably become something like a personification of loyalty, a near-allegorical figure.

This is another path to such characterization than (to make the obvious comparison) Ben Jonson's. "The tendency toward moral abstraction implicit in the romantic tradition is strongly reinforced," says Waith, "by the tradition of satire, and Jonson's dramatic practice is suggested by the frequent clashes between characters who represent polar extremes."[10] There certainly is the likeness of technique. But the impulse which produces it in Jonson's moral satire is quite different from that of the tragicomedies. The "abstraction" of Jonson's characters with its simplification and clarification of realistic motive was a perfect tool for the exposition of behavior perverted from the rational norm against which it is measured by Jonsonian satire. Beaumont and Fletcher produce their almost Theophrastan characters (and engage them in rhetorical clashes) for different reasons; their creations are infused with another life. Instead of a dramatic means to Jonson's satirical end, they are a result of code ethics employed as a basis for the treatment of tragic fact.

Nor is it the presence of allegorical characters which removes these plays from reality. It is, again, the ethical conceptions which the characters personify. Jonson's humor figures are even more nearly personifications than Fletcher's, yet Jonsonian comedy is richly, recognizedly realistic, bearing more of the flavor of the daily life of Renaissance London than any other drama. Jonson was dismissed in the "Parnassus" trilogy as a mere "empiric," and his name still connotes a vivid fidelity to the actual life of his time and place, minutely observed and recorded. His abstract characters can reasonably be said to bring us closer to that reality, to hold the mirror up to nature and show the time its form—its essence. Face and Subtle embody fraud and take on the particular colors of fraud in the London of 1610, each gathering into a universalized figure a vivid concentration of the real. Sir Epicure Mammon is greed, seen every day in real life, and he bears its familiar marks, isolated and compacted. A whole class of men of our world, and a daily and familiar aspect of most men, is comprehended in a glance in the clarity and realism of the "humor" character. If the tragicomic world is unreal, it is because of the animating code or cult values, unrelated to the practical considerations of the natural world. They are mothered by Senecal, Platonic, courtly, and chivalric traditions, and fathered by Jacobean skepticism.

Jonson's morality characters, like the near-allegories of Hawthorne or of William Golding, are a result of his interest in the relations between ideas overriding his interest in his imaginary persons. They are abstract because of the didactic intent which produces allegory by subordinating everything to theme, employing character merely to enact relations between ideas in the service of systematic doctrine. Thematic elements—the general meanings which the actions of the plot manifest—here so dominate character as to reduce it to an instrument of theme, which in allegory absorbs character and itself becomes the structural frame. The type-characters who people such literature are distinguished, like Jonson's, by their rigid self-consistency and decorum. The tragicomic "abstract" characters such as Philaster and Arbaces are, despite their abstraction, grossly inconsistent, assuming almost opposite natures in successive scenes: their abstraction is not the result of any particular overall meaning or thematic design. In the manipulation of such character-conceptions into a drama of tragic incident and tragic poetry, the interest of Beaumont and Fletcher's "tricky, stilted, and artificial" plots and the melodramatic force of the scenes of confrontation, surprise, and code heroics, of which they are masters, replace the interest of the serious moral issues which were at the heart of earlier tragedy.

Except in its reflection of the manners of the familiar world (the "conversation of gentlemen" by which its authors earned Dryden's praise), *Philaster* is not modeled on either of the two satirical plays which Beaumont had written before entering the collaboration, but on Fletcher's unsuccessful first production, *The Faithful Shepherdess* (1608). Adapted from Guarini's *Il Pastor Fido*, this stylized, masque-like Arcadian charade is more reminiscent of the mythical and pastoral courtly drama of Lyly and Peele than of anything that had appeared in the theater in the intervening decades. Clorin, the "faithful Shepherdess" whose life is dedicated to the memory of her beloved, represents the ideal of chaste and spiritual love. The other characters form a descending series of gradations measured by this ideal. Through disguises and misunderstandings, impersonations and deceptions, a series of scenes are contrived in which the characters' emotions are strained to the highest pitch, and their dominating qualities are afforded the fullest verbal expression. The denouement secures a happy ending for the faithful lovers Perigot and Amoret by the removal of misapprehensions.

Fletcher soon discovered that these same elements of character and conflict could be used to create something more realistic and, ostensibly at least, more serious. Waith traces the increase in verisimilitude and, in general, the development from the ostentatiously stiff artifice of the pastoral to the deceptive naturalness which conceals essentially the same machinery in *Philaster*. The intermediate step is *Cupid's Revenge* (1608), the first of the Beaumont-and-Fletcher plays. Here there is the same set of character-types, embodiments of love ranging from bestial to ethereal. As *The Faithful Shepherdess* is a parable of the power of chastity, the theme of *Cupid's Revenge* is the power of love. Nothing better shows the artificiality of the ethic upon which dramatic issues turn in these plays than the plot of *Cupid's Revenge*. The initial tragic flaw of Leucippus, the hero, is his complicity in the sacrilege of destroying Cupid's statues. The love god punishes Leucippus' excessive devotion to chastity by causing his infatuation with the lustful Bacha. When Bacha, married to his father, later tempts the now-repentant hero, his recovered pure virtue confronts her total viciousness in one of the rhetorical encounters characteristic of tragicomic method. From this nemesis of excessive chastity, Shakespeare might have produced a symbolic treatment of love as a natural good perverted in defect as in excess. But its treatment in *Cupid's Revenge* is at once ethically artificial and realistic in style (even in the scenes in which the god descends upon the stage). The quality of dialogue, including much cynical ribaldry, and the whole manner of presentation, make this simply a world where a different set of laws apply, a world where a literal Cupid's power is terrible enough to visit tragedy on whoever offends it. Here where the eye is stopped by the bright enameling of every surface, we are very far from the (essentially medieval) symbolic and allegorical mode of Shakespeare's late romances.

All the chief characters of *Cupid's Revenge* die; the play is a "tragedy." But the deaths yield only rhetoric; they have no meaning. The nature of the play's characters (love-cult abstractions) and the nature of its plot conflicts are closely related. Neither has within it the potentiality of a genuinely tragic interpretation of experience. We are from the start in a postulated romantic world whose laws are not those of the real world; the mirror is held up not to nature but to Arcadia and the realms of ancient Greek and modern French romance.

The opening situation of *Philaster* is exposited by three Sicilian courtiers (a clumsy first-and-second-gentlemen device for such theatrical virtuosi as the authors): the Sicilian King, seeking in a Spanish alliance securer power over his own subjects, has promised his daughter Arethusa to the Spanish Prince Pharamond. He is justifiedly fearful of his people's affection for Prince Philaster, whose father was by the present King's father unrighteously deposed. Philaster is permitted his freedom only out of fear of popular revolt.

Three court ladies enter and are described in turn by the nobleman Dion. The first is Galatea, "a wise and modest Gentlewoman that attends the Princess"; the second is "one that may stand still discreetly enough,

and ill favour'dly Dance her Measure; simper when she
is Courted by her Friend, and slight her Husband"; the
last is Megra, "a lascivious lady." "She'll cog and lie
with a whole army. . . . She loves to try the several
constitutions of men's bodies. . . ."[11] The King enters
with his retinue to announce the betrothal. Pharamond
displays his character by a series of absurd pomposities
("This speech calls him *Spaniard*, being nothing but a
large inventory of his own commendations"). Philaster
appears and with magnificent daring declares his right
to the throne and braves the popinjay prince:

> When thou art King, look I be dead and rotten,
> And my name ashes; For, hear me Pharamond,
> This very ground thou goest on, this fat earth,
> My Fathers friends made fertile with their faiths,
> Before that day of shame, shall gape and swallow
> Thee and thy Nation, like a hungry grave,
> Into her hidden bowels: Prince, it shall;
> By Nemesis it shall.
>
> . . . .
>
>   If thou wert sole inheritor to him,
> That made the world his; and couldst see no sun
> Shine upon any but thine: were *Pharamond*
> As truly valiant, as I feel him cold,
> And ring'd among the choicest of his friends,
> Such as would blush to talk such serious follies,
> Or back such bellied commendations,
> And from this present, spight of all these bugs,
> You should hear further from me.
>
> . . . .
>
> . . . my Father's spirit; It's here O King!
> A dangerous spirit; now he tells me King,
> I was a Kings heir, bids me be a King.
>
>   (I. i)

Here is the first of an endless series of such "brav-
ings" and confrontation scenes, which charge the stage
with emotion and exhibit the extravagant virtue of

"good" characters by providing occasion for its impassioned rhetorical expression. True Nobility has faced Bragadoccio.

As Philaster and Pharamond clash, the ladies comment on them: the virtuous Galatea recognizes Philaster's worth; the aggressively salacious Megra prefers Pharamond, the "prince of wax": virtue is wise and sweet, gifted with discernment and taste; vice is stupid, clumsy, and foolish. The spectrum of personified types of love is later extended by the development first of Pharamond as another exemplar of promiscuous lust; then of Euphrasia as an example of spiritual devotion (loving Philaster, she follows him in boy's disguise, but has vowed never to marry, desiring only the worship of her beloved); and finally of Princess Arethusa as an instance of chaste and faithful love (for Philaster).

Dion and his friends approach the hero to speak of their sympathy with his "wrongs and virtues." The heroes' wrongs and virtues are in fact essentially the matter of each of these tragicomedies, and the phrase suggests their passive role and the cause of their suffering. Philaster explicitly classes himself with "men disgrac'd for virtue."[12]

He is called to an interview with the Princess Arethusa, who unexpectedly declares her love for him in another set-piece theatrical scene (I. ii) skillfully wrought to its surprising climax. She first announces her determination to enjoy "both these kingdoms," and upon Philaster's reply that honor will not permit him to surrender his right to the crown, she reveals that she "must have them and thee." Philaster's page Bellario is appointed to attend Arethusa, serving as messenger between the lovers. Pharamond enters and insults the hero, affording another *coup de théâtre* to close the scene, as Philaster cows the blustering Spanish prince by the force of rhetoric:

know Sir, I can grasp
You, and your greatness thus, thus into nothing:
Give not a word, not a word back: Farewell.

(I. i)

Bellario's report to Arethusa displays Philaster's flaw-less propriety as courtly lover:

If it be love,
To forget all respect of his own friends,
In thinking of your face; if it be love
Do sit cross arm'd and sigh away the day,
Mingled with starts, crying your name as loud
And hastily, as men i'the streets do fire:
. . . .
If when he goes to rest (which will not be)
'Twixt every prayer he saies, to name you once
As others drop a bead, be to be in love;
Then Madam, I dare swear he loves you.

(II. i)

The contemptible and comic Pharamond arranges an assignation with Megra, his female counterpart in lust, in a scene of "daring" salacity. Galatea reveals this to the King, and the lustful lovers are trapped together. In retaliation, Megra publicly accuses the Princess Arethusa of adultery with Bellario, who has been her constant companion. Honest Dion, as the scene ends, disclaims belief in Megra's "strange found out antidote to cure her infection" (II. i). Then, with striking irony, the following scene (III. i) opens on a courtier's words, "Nay doubtless 'tis true," and Dion's answer "I, and 'tis the gods / That rais'd this Punishment. . . ." Convinced of Arethusa's guilt and anxious to persuade Philaster that he should seize the throne from her father, Dion falsely claims that he has himself discovered the two in adultery (an action thoroughly inconsistent with his character). Philaster cannot but accept such evidence; he is a victim not of his own passions, but of an invincible deceit.

Philaster confronts Bellario in a sensational inter-view, seeking to trick him into confession.

> I bad her do it; I charg'd her by all charms
> Of love between us, by the hope of peace
> We should enjoy, to yield thee all delights
> Naked, as to her bed: I took her oath
> Thou should'st enjoy her: Tell me gentle boy,
> Is she not paralleless? Is not her breath
> Sweet as Arabian winds, when fruits are ripe?
> Are not her breasts two liquid Ivory balls?
> Is she not all a lasting Mine of joy?
>
> (III. i)

Unsatisfied by Bellario's denials, he casts the page off. Another such scene follows between Philaster and Are-thusa, and the lovers part in great distress. The princess, called to hunt with the King and court, wanders dis-tracted into the forest. Bellario finds her unconscious and is trying to revive her when Philaster happens upon them. Frantic at this seeming evidence of their guilt, he wounds Arethusa with his sword. A "Country Fellow," stumbling on the scene, drives Philaster away; the mag-nificent hero must here become a coward, beaten off by a rustic, to facilitate the movement of the complex plot. When Bellario, to save Philaster, falsely confesses to having wounded Arethusa, Philaster realizes the boy's fidelity and creeps from hiding to admit his guilt and be sentenced to death. There is an altogether suffocating reconciliation scene, Bellario protesting:

> Alas my Lord, my life is not a thing
> Worthy your noble thoughts; 'tis not a life,
> 'Tis but a piece of child-hood thrown away:
> Should I out-live, I shall then out-live
> Vertue and honour.
>
> (V. i)

Arethusa, moved by the same code virtue, also swears not to outlive her love. Forgiven, Philaster finds that "it is my joy to dye / I find a recreation in 't" (V. i). Hearing of Philaster's sentence, the Sicilian people mutiny. The hero is freed, and we find that he has been married to Arethusa while imprisoned. This catastasis is dissolved when Megra repeats her accusation, and Philaster, swearing to grant the King one request, finds himself bound in honor to permit the inquisitorial torture of Bellario. At this, he threatens suicide, but Bellario assures a happy ending by revealing himself to be Euphrasia, Dion's daughter, in disguise. And Philaster ends in secure possession of both his kingdom and his bride.

The King has previously expressed some repentance and the belief that he cannot escape retribution or hope to enjoy an ill-gotten throne. Even he can now be seen as more a victim than an offender. The emotion excited by the picture of "men disgrac'd for virtue" is relieved by this happy conclusion, as it could hardly be by any other.

A King and No King (1611) is much the same. King Arbaces of Iberia has conquered King Tigranes of Armenia and leads him home a prisoner. Arbaces plans that his sister Panthea, whom he has last seen as a child, shall be married to Tigranes. But the captive King is betrothed to Spaconia, who arranges to follow her lord to the Iberian court. Tigranes, protesting his fidelity to Spaconia, employs a suggestively easy equation of sexual attraction with deadly sin, insisting that he could not love Panthea "had she so tempting fair, / That she could wish it off for damning souls" (I. i). When the reverend guardian Gobrias presents the beautiful Panthea to her long-absent brother, Arbaces is struck dumb by sudden, passionate love. Recovering, he refuses to believe that she is his sister, then laments the "ungodly sickness" with which fate has afflicted him.

> he that undertakes my cure, must first
> O'rethrow Divinity, all moral Laws,
> And leave mankind as unconfin'd as beasts.
>
> (III)

Again the tragic offender is a victim, driven protesting by irresistible "natural" impulse against unmovable law. "I wade in sin," he says, and reproaches the gods, who "punish [him] / With such unmanly sins" (III)—a conception which breathes the atmosphere of Calvinism. Moral law is imposed from without upon a human vitality which beats against its confines. Arbaces asks,

> Is there no stop
> To our full happiness, but these meer sounds
> Brother and Sister?
>
> (IV)

He begs Panthea to pray for his death, as the only escape from the crime to which he is drawn, and cries out in protest against his entrapment.

> Accursed man,
> Thou bought'st thy reason at too dear a rate,
> For thou hast all thy actions bounded in
> With curious rules, when every beast is free.
>
> (IV)

Arbaces is composed of opposites: magnificence and egregious self-regard. Yet he is really a rudimentary character, a simple and mechanical juxtaposing of conventional valor and vainglory. He speaks of heaven's having "laid this punishment upon [his] pride," but his vainglorious "humor" is structurally irrelevant. It adds emotional complication, but has no connection whatever with the genesis of his tragic situation; it contributes nothing to the causes of his misery or the threat of his destruction. In his tragic relation to Panthea he is innocent and noble; it is not his excessive pride which is attracted to her virtue and beauty.

As Arbaces is about to kill Gobrias because the old man is in some part responsible for the hero's love of his sister, the Counsellor reveals that Panthea and the King are not related; Arbaces is really Gobrias' own son, a subject, while Panthea is the true inheritor of the throne. All difficulties evaporate in a happy ending like that of *Philaster*. Arbaces has suffered a trial for which we cannot see him as significantly responsible. There is nothing to be vindicated by a tragic consequence, and nothing to be won from it except a display of rhetorical sentiment, which may be more acceptably employed upon a happy ending.

Tragedy has become limited to the function of entertainment. Not that *A King and No King* is more of a dramatic entertainment than *Hamlet;* only that, unlike *Hamlet*, it is nothing else. The last-act felicity of the sympathetic characters suits this purpose better than their destruction.

These two tragicomedies represent a drama left with no central public myth to celebrate. Had there been, in the preceding seven centuries, no more profound interpretive response than this to the spectacle of suffering, great tragic drama would not have evolved. But the Elizabethan years bequeathed a flourishing tragic theater, and such playwrights as Beaumont and Fletcher continued to supply the demand which it generated. What they provide for the now chiefly aristocratic and coterie audience has all the sound and gesture of Renaissance tragedy (the constant Shakespearean echoes ring strangely through these plays) but not the soul that gave life to the body, which is animated now by the gears and wires of contrivance.

Tourneur's tragedy had gone farther than Webster in Webster's own direction and reached a complete Calvin-

istic *contemptus mundi.* In this next step tragedy re-
cedes almost out of existence, yet leaves behind a highly
developed theatrical tradition. What criticism has
called the "theoretic" form of tragedy is moribund; its
technical or "executive" form remains, undergoing consequent adaptations.

The Maid's Tragedy (1610), a showpiece of Beaumont-and-Fletcher's (or at least of Beaumont's) royalist
political doctrine, is in many respects like these tragicomedies, although technically a tragedy. At the command
of the King of Rhodes, the hero Amintor abandons his
betrothed, Aspatia, to marry Evadne, the sister of his
friend Melantius. He discovers on his wedding night
that his nominal wife is the King's mistress, to whom he
has been married "to Father Children, and to bear the
name / Of Husband" (II). This revelation is handled
with typical polish. First we are impressed by Evadne's
modesty with her waiting-ladies and her maiden-coyness
with Amintor, which evokes his affectionate indulgence:

> If you have sworn to any of the Virgins
> That were your old companions, to preserve
> Your Maidenhead a night, it may be done
> without this means.

Then there is the theatrical thrill of her reply: "A
Maiden head Amintor at my years?" (II).

The hero resolves to "know the man that wrongs me
so, / That I may cut his body into motes." But when
Evadne convinces him that it is the King ("What, did he
make this match for dull Amintor?") he is subdued:

> Oh! thou hast nam'd a word that wipes away
> All thoughts revengeful.
>
> (II)

Amintor is trapped between the claims of loyalty and
honor—the true dilemma of heroic drama. His role is

from here entirely passive, consisting mostly of pathetic speeches. He sees his disgrace as a merited punishment:

> The faithless Sin I made
> To fair *Aspatia*, is not yet reveng'd,
> It follows me
>
> . . . . . .
>
> This 'tis to break a troth.
>
> (III)

But he has left Aspatia only at the King's command, his loyalty forcing him then to sacrifice love, as now honor. The real origin of his trouble appears when he protests to the King that "you might have ta'ne another": The King replies "No; for I believe thee honest, as thou wert valiant" (III). Amintor suffers, of course, because of his virtues.

In another emotionally tempestuous dialogue, Melantius forces the truth from his friend. After outbursts of disbelief and anger, then expressions of grief and sworn loyalty, he goes to plan revenge. Intending to kill the King and escape to the palace fortification, he reveals his scheme to Calianax (Aspatia's father), hoping that the old man will surrender his command of the stronghold out of resentment for the King's wrongs to his daughter. But Calianax betrays the plot, and in a banquet scene the King confronts Melantius with the truth before his accuser and the court. By brilliant and brazen outfacing of Calianax, Melantius makes him seem the liar. In whispered asides to the old man during this exchange, he still urges him to surrender the fort. Calianax tells the company of these overtures as they are made, but Melantius and the rest laugh at him as a dotard. The audience can enjoy the spectacle of superb Machiavellian dexterity, while sympathizing with the deceiver as well as his victim.

After the banquet, the King commands Amintor to

send Evadne to him. The hero is so desperately outraged that he means to slaughter his tormentor instantly, but Melantius quiets him with a reminder that he knows will awaken Amintor's holy dread of regicide: "But 'tis the King, the King, the King, *Amintor*" (V).

Melantius' plan proceeds: Evadne, awakened by him to an abject, pathetic repentance, stabs her seducer. Announcing the reason for the King's death from the walls which Calianax has at length surrendered to him, Melantius wins an amnesty from Lysippus, the new king, for himself and his confederates.

Aspatia now assumes as a disguise the identity of her own young brother and challenges Amintor. She forces him to kill her, despite his extreme reluctance to lift his hand against the kin of his beloved. The sword-thrust by which a hero, under some misapprehension, wounds or kills a heroine is a remarkably persistent feature of these sexually oriented plays. Perigot wounds Amoret, in *The Faithful Shepherdess;* Philaster stabs both Arethusa and Euphrasia; Amintor kills Aspatia. Other heroines are stabbed, like Urania in *Cupid's Revenge,* when they come between the hero and his assailant. These writers have an unmistakable and suggestive fondness for this particular Freudian melodramatic piquancy.

Evadne returns with bloody hands, expecting Amintor's praise, but the absolute virtue which has condemned the hero to passive suffering can permit him to view her act only with horror:

> Why, thou hast rais'd up mischief to his height,
> And found out one to out-name thy other faults;
> Thou hast no intermission of thy sins,
> But all thy life is a continual ill;
> Black is thy colour now, disease thy nature.
> Joy to Amintor! thou hast toucht a life,
> The very name of which had power to chain
> Up all my rage, and calm my wildest wrongs.
>
> (V)

The mortally wounded Aspatia reveals her identity, and Amintor implores the gods to spare her life (out of mercy, "Since out of justice we must challenge nothing"). She dies, and Amintor kills himself. Melantius enters with members of the court and, viewing the bodies, vows his own death.

Just as a merely illusory tragic flaw was provided in Amintor's breaking of his troth, the play's last lines present a false moral, giving, like the assumption of the throne by the just Lysippus, a perfunctory appearance of tragic justice:

> on lustful Kings
> Unlookt for sudden deaths from heaven are sent!
> But curst is he that is their instrument.
>
> (V)

Unlike Hamlet, Amintor has *not* been an instrument of the King's death, nor has Aspatia. The nexus between the King's lust and the catastrophe is Melantius' revenge, motivated by honor: Evadne is its instrument. The tragic principals Amintor and Aspatia are purely passive victims of evil, immobilized by virtue. Even Evadne is made over emotionally into a victim by the poetry of her repentance, which is presented as an awakening of the "real" Evadne from the hypnotic influence of the King. Her pathetic mourning of her loss of virtue and her devotion to Amintor place her among the injured. Pathos is all that can be wrung from the catastrophe. The tragic situations have not evolved by causal processes related to character, but have been imposed on character and so arranged as to provide a pageant of surprises and dramatic showcases for noble sentiment.

It is only in its ending that there is a difference between such tragedy and tragicomedy. The logic of this play is such that it could easily be revised into something resembling *Philaster* or *A King and No King*. Calianax, for instance, might stop Melantius' plot by revealing Amintor as true heir to the crown, dispossessed in infancy by Calianax and the King. Amintor then could be made to disavow his unconsummated marriage, assume his throne, take Aspatia as his queen, and send Evadne and the false King off in disgrace, like Pharamond and Megra in *Philaster*.

Waith is quite correct in saying that in *Philaster* "the threat of tragedy is more immediate" than in *The Faithful Shepherdess*, but perhaps we should substitute "disaster" for "tragedy," as a caution against a misleading equivocation. Tragedy as a literary mode is present throughout *Philaster*, until the last few lines. The play portrays serious and violent action and unhappy circumstances; it deals with suffering and evil; its characters speak in the style of tragedy. Until Evadne's fifth-act murder of the King, *The Maid's Tragedy* differs in no important way from *Philaster* or *A King and No King*. The only basis for accurate distinction between them lies in the surprise ending of the tragicomedies, which evades a tragic outcome by revealing that key "facts," which we learned previously, were false, although our acceptance of them has served for over four acts to permit the same sort of dramatic experience as in *The Maid's Tragedy*.

Fletcher's famous definition of tragicomedy, prefixed to the first quarto of *The Faithful Shepherdess*, says that it "is not so called in respect of mirth and killing, but in respect it wants deaths, which is inough to make it no tragedie, yet brings some neere it, which is inough to make it no comedie: which must be a representation of familiar people, with such kinde of trouble as no life be questiond, so that a God is as lawfull in this as in a tragedie, and meane people as in a comedie."[13]

The first clause is meant to correct a popular misapprehension and distinguish Fletcher's first play from the native "mongrel tragicomedies," with their kings and clowns, "hornpipes and funerals," Huff, Ruff, and Snuff. It fits *The Faithful Shepherdess*, which lacks both mirth and killing, far better than it does the later, characteristic Jacobean tragicomedies, like *A King and No King*, to which the definition has often been applied. These, like the tragedies, frequently do include a mixture of low comedy. (They are like the tragedies, too, in presenting characters of both high and low estate.)

More to the point, these tragicomedies do not always "want deaths," except in a sense which might satisfy the letter of Renaissance literary law, but has little to do with the realities of drama. Crimes, and in several play deaths, are believed by the audience to have occurred, and are therefore completely real, dramatically speaking, until a trick ending cancels their existence. In *The Mad Lover*, we are made to think that the character Polydore is dead. This tragic turn almost causes the suicide of another character, but Polydore rises from his coffin, and we find that our fears were based on our ignorance of a fact concealed by the authors. Alphonso, in *A Wife for a Month*, is thought to have been poisoned. But we discover at the happy ending that the poison meant by the villain to kill him has instead cured his melancholia (a motif which pervades Cavalier drama, where intended poisons which restore to health and assassins' thrusts which cure are used to solve innumerable plot problems). *The Lovers' Progress* and *Sea Voyage* both contain deaths, so far as the audience knows, until their final scenes. It is, however, usually not crucial to a play's effect, although it was pivotal to some humanistic dramatic theory, whether or not it "wants deaths." The tragic situations which threaten death and inflict anguish are quite as harrowing; the difference is purely mechanical.

It is, finally, quite false to say of these plays that in

them "no life [is] question'd." Their continual questioning of noble lives—Philaster's threatened execution and later threatened suicide, Arbaces' almost-accomplished murder of Gobrias (and his own inevitable death to follow)—are of their very essence. In some comedies too, of course, lives are imperiled, characters thought dead, trials suffered. But peril, suffering, and the threat of death do not dominate the atmosphere of comedy, as they do here, despite the fact that an audience acquainted with the tragicomic genre might suspect that all would yet turn out well. Even in *Much Ado about Nothing*, *All's Well That Ends Well*, and *Measure for Measure*, for instance, there is no (or the very briefest) time when the audience believes irreversible tragic situations to exist. We know that Hero is innocent and alive and that her false accusers have been caught; that Helena is plotting her reconciliation with Bertram; that the disguised Duke is watching Angelo.

Some Beaumont-and-Fletcher tragicomedies really mix comic matter with the lofty and heroic, in such a way as to be actually a blend of comedy and tragedy. But this is not the method of *Philaster* or *A King and No King*. The difference between these plays and the "tragedies" of Beaumont and Fletcher lies, again, only in the technique of denouement. When the outcome of the play is to be "tragic," the crimes and outrages in which we have been the chief characters become involved are allowed to remain genuine crimes and outrages; the insuperable dilemma presented to us in acts I and II was really insuperable. We have been given all the facts; we were not fooled. Evadne is indeed the King's mistress, and she really has become Amintor's wife, through treachery which remains treachery even in the light of act V. The tragic resolution is genuine to this extent at least.

The typical tragicomic resolution is not genuine. It is

not a working out of the things we have known about and watched. It does not in fact resolve; rather, it dissolves the plot problem which provided the motive force of the action, by its introduction of concealed facts. In act V we discover that Bellario is a girl (and one who values Philaster's welfare above her own life). Philaster's life has not really been "questioned," although we surely thought it was. Arethusa has, of course, been innocent and assured of exoneration all along. Arbaces in *A King and No King* is not really Panthea's brother; yet it is this supposed fact which has held lives in the balance. His father has all along had the intention of revealing the secret at a proper time. If we had known these things in act I, the proceedings would have been absurd. So, in *The Island Princess*, Captain Ruy Dias, who has been developed as a dangerous villain, turns out in the end to be noble and valorous and amply redeems what we now see as his slight lapse. The same thing has been done earlier in the play with the character of the heroine Quisara. There is a trace of this method in *The Elder Brother;* in one scene (III. iii) we see Andrew's wife, Lilly, arrange an assignation with Brisac; but we find later (IV. iv) that she was not really guilty of any illicit intent, although we were led to think so.

Dramatically speaking, then, lives are certainly "questioned," although the evil conditions which threaten catastrophe turn out to be an illusion, and things are not what they seem. It might be noted that surprise is also used, for example, in Jonson's comedy *The Silent Woman*. (Obviously, much of the plot technique of the tragicomedies is like that of romantic comedy: transvestite-disguised heroines, mistaken identity, heavy use of coincidence.) But in Jonson's play things are what they seem; the truth of the basic situation (Morose is being cozened by marrying him to a "planted" bride) is known to the audience all along. That the bride turns out to be a boy adds a fillip to the denouement, but does not reverse the situation or dissolve the problem; it is a part of the expected cozening.

Fletcher's definition of tragicomedy was borrowed from the theoretical defense of the genre by the Italian Guarini, whose *Il Pastor Fido* had provoked a great deal of critical controversy. Guarini defended the form as not a juxtaposition of the elements tragedy and comedy, like the English plays of the *Cambises* type deplored by Sidney, but a "mean between the austerity and dignity of the one and pleasantness and ease of the other."[14] Modern critics have found this a satisfactory account of the Jacobean tragicomedies also, and speak of the form as midway between comedy and tragedy, combining some of the qualities of each into a distinct third form. Actually, if a scale of style is postulated extending from comedy to tragedy, Fletcherian tragicomedy should occupy a position at the opposite extreme from the comic, sharing with tragedy its most impassioned and, by aim and sometimes achievement, most elevated rhetoric. The emotions aroused are those of tragedy—exactly those of the mode seen in *The Maid's Tragedy*. Affectively (and the essence of these plays lies in their emotional appeal) they are a form of tragedy specified by the happy ending. This is not true of all the mass of earlier English plays that can be ranged under the heading of broadly defined tragicomedy, or which were so called in their own time. But the characteristic type developed by Beaumont and Fletcher, continued by Massinger and others, is both historically a successor and intrinsically a subvariety of tragedy.

There is little special insight into the Jacobean plays to be gained by pursuing tragicomic theory and practice back through the Spanish cloak-and-sword drama and the theoretic works of the Italian humanists, to the

Amphitruo of Plautus and the *Cyclops* of Euripides. Nevertheless, some observations by early critics are helpful even with the plays of Beaumont and Fletcher. In 1590, Giasone de Nores, a Paduan professor engaged in controversy with Guarini, made in his *Apologia* a point that modern criticism might do well to consider in its application to Jacobean tragicomedy. He denies that one can decrease the terror of tragedy by admitting no deaths, but only the danger of death. " 'How,' he asks, 'can there be danger of death unless there be terror?' "[15] And in fact, if the form were a blend of comic and tragic elements, as is still generally maintained,[16] why might it not as well portray happy events, with an unhappy end; or a moderated conflict, not involving extreme emotions of fear or pity, with a conclusion neither wholly happy nor unrelievedly tragic? But what in fact we have in the Fletcherian plays is a lofty and serious treatment of the most extreme tragic issues, conducted suddenly to an unmixedly happy conclusion: not a blend of the comedy and tragedy, but a special treatment of the latter. In fact, the seventeenth-century Italian writers of the "tragedy of happy ending" "jealously guarded the claim of their productions to the title of tragedy" and invariably cited the authority of Aristotle to support the legitimacy of the form.[17]

Some of the dramas labeled as tragicomedies in the seventeenth century are merely chronicle romances: e.g., *Dick of Devonshire,* a play with a profuse wealth of adventure and a happy conclusion. Some might best be called problem plays (*The Fair Quarrel*); some are genuinely satirical in impulse (*The Malcontent*). Definitions of tragicomedy which seek to include all these and to encompass early popular and religious drama such as *Apius and Virginia* and *Christus Redividus,* and to make room for plays like Lyly's *Campaspe* or like Greene's *James IV,* together with the plays under discussion here, must end by creating an imaginary genre. In many earlier plays virtue is rewarded and vice punished, and this sometimes produces a happy ending for a treatment of tragic matter. But the happy ending of Jacobean tragicomedy has nothing to do with simple didacticism. If, to define tragicomedy, we must find what *Dick of Devonshire* and *A King and No King* have in common, the resulting definition will be false to both, for the features which they share are not of the vital essence of either.

One aspect of the "decadence" of Jacobean tragicomedy and coterie tragedy is its extreme imitativeness, its relentless exploitation of the successful, not merely in the manner of the popular Elizabethan stage, but with a constant heightening of sensational effects, an increasing audacity and a straining for novelty which betray the exclusively theatrical preoccupation of the writers. The same situations, particularly sexual ones, recur again and again; Leucippus, in *Cupid's Revenge*, is ardently courted by his lustful stepmother, as was Spurio, in *The Revenger's Tragedy*. In Massinger's *The Bondsman*, the scene is repeated, and by now the boundary of restraint is pushed back considerably. Incest is a favorite motif. The ladies in male disguise killed by their lovers are legion. The theme of sexual frustration, complicated by the need for secrecy and dissembling, is very common: Brachiano, in *The White Devil*, vows never to lie with his wife; the Duchess, exiled from his bed, pretends the vow was hers, to prevent violence between Brachiano and her brothers. Castabella and Rousard, of *The Atheist's Tragedy*, cannot consummate their marriage because of Rousard's impotence. In *The Maid's Tragedy*, *A Wife for a Month*, and Shirley's *The Doubtful Heir*, characters newly married are unable to consummate their marriages for reasons which become increasingly more complex, and are remarkably so in *The Doubtful Heir*. Plot devices of surprise and reversal—

false reports and false deaths, apparent crimes which are actually innocent, miraculously restorative medicines, murderous assaults which effect cures—are characteristic of the tragicomedies of Beaumont and Fletcher, and their regular imitation figures largely in the "petrifying" of the genre by the Cavalier drama of Cartwright, Killigrew, Carlell, Davenant, Gough, Habington, Hausted, and the others who followed in Fletcher's well-worn footsteps.

The type of *Philaster* and *A King and No King* is, then, best considered as a response to the failure of the earlier tragic spirit. It is drama for an audience which, like the authors, no longer shared the vision of law which had made Shakespearean tragedy possible. The older form could bear as its motto "the fault lies not in our stars"; above the central group of Jacobean tragicomedies we might substitute, from Beaumont and Fletcher, "Some ships reach port which are not steered." The happy ending which dismisses the tragic issues seems, patently, a merely theatrical substitute for the tragic reconciliation and acceptance that had once been based in the affirmation of the natural law.

Questions concerning *Pericles, Cymbeline,* and *The Winter's Tale* hover about such an interpretation of dramatic history. If Shakespeare's *Cymbeline* was not modeled on *Philaster,* surely *The Winter's Tale* and *The Tempest* were influenced by the success of the rival playwrights. Whatever the direction of influence, if Shakespeare wrote even two or three tragicomedies like those of Beaumont and Fletcher, is it reasonable to view the many Jacobean tragicomedies as essentially a continuation of tragedy by men incapable of the Shakespearean solution to the problem of suffering? It is. The point is not that Shakespeare was unable to write tragicomedy; he wrote it well, as *Cymbeline* proves. The point is that Beaumont and Fletcher could not write

Shakespearean tragedy; *The Maid's Tragedy* is sufficient evidence for this.

It might be maintained, too, that there is nothing in the world of Shakespearean tragicomedy to prevent its author from dealing satisfactorily with a tragic outcome. There is an appearance of what might (mistakenly, I think) be called "code" ethics in Posthumus Leonatus' swaggering venture upon his faith in his wife's virtue and in the extravagance of King Leontes' jealousy and repentance. Yet the action of *Cymbeline* and *The Winter's Tale* might still be said to take place in the Shakespearean world where evil can be shown intelligible.

There are, to begin with, mechanical differences in Shakespeare's handling of the genre. Even in *Pericles* (for portions of which it is very hard to believe him responsible) it is only the characters and never the audience who think Thaisa and Marina dead, and for whom the events of the story are tragic. We also share the author's omniscience in *Cymbeline*, where we know throughout that Imogen is both innocent and alive. Nor are genuine tragic tensions created in *The Winter's Tale*. Shakespeare's late romances are the comparatively relaxed work of a man who had repeatedly and successfully confronted the greater challenge.

Radically more hostile to my thesis is the critical belief, common enough, in Shakespearean cynicism and rebelliousness. After reading *Macbeth*, *Othello*, and *Lear*, thinks Leech, "we cannot feel other than at odds with the great scheme of things in which these events occur."[18] Una Ellis-Fermor speaks for another school, seeing in the tragedies "Shakespeare's fundamental belief in ultimate co-ordination and in an ordered universe."[19] She thinks, however, that in *Troilus and Cressida*, *All's Well*, and *Measure for Measure*, "the glory that is an inseparable part of tragic vision has gone,"[20] and Shakespeare sees with the eyes of a Tourneur. This is, to Miss Ellis-Fermor, especially true of *Measure for Measure*, where "the lowest depths of Jacobean negation are touched. Cynicism has taken on the kind of diabolic vigilance; with the exception of the kindly, timid Provost, there is no character who is not suspect, and those whose claims to goodness or decency seem most vigorous are precisely those in whom meanness, self-regard and hypocrisy root deepest. The theme of the main plot is Isabella's triumphant preservation of physical chastity against Angelo's cunning and at the risk of Claudio's life."[21] This goes too far. Angelo, in fact, is the only really corrupt character in the main plot of *Measure for Measure* (except perhaps for the fop Lucio), and the Duke leads him from his vice quite credibly, as Jonson's Asper brings men "out of their humours." The perfectly healthy treatment of sexual union as the basis of marriage in the Mariana-Angelo story is in accord with the natural-law ethic, and need offend no one. Neither Julietta, Claudio, nor Mariana violates more than custom. The cohabitation of "handfasted" lovers, who are in fact considered as canonically married, would never furnish out a really corrupt world such as that of Webster, Marston, or Tourneur. Claudio is contrite enough for his offenses, including his (only momentary) wish to live by means of Isabella's unchastity. In his brief and terrified urging of his sister to submit to Angelo, Claudio tells her that

> What sin you do to save a brother's life,
> Nature dispenses with the deed so far
> That it becomes a virtue.
>
> (III. i. 134–36)

This is, within the play, not true (witness Isabella's virtuous refusal and Claudio's later repentance for his solicitation); but it is indicative. Claudio argues that nature, ordinarily violated by adultery, here must "dispense with" it; whatever nature condones "becomes a virtue."

Miss Ellis-Fermor's adjective "physical" suggests that Isabella loses a more essential chastity. But how? As to the risk of Claudio's life, why is it cruelly self-righteous of Isabella that she will not bribe the law by prostitution? Such "pitilessness" is nothing more than the demand of the most fundamental Renaissance morality. The same critic quotes Isabella's plea to Angelo for Claudio's life.

> Why, all the souls that were were forfeit once;
> And he that might the vantage best have took
> Found out the remedy.
>
> (II. ii. 73–75)

Comparing this praise of mercy with Isabella's "unmerciful" anger at her brother's willingness to buy life with her virtue, Miss Ellis-Fermor finds in Isabella a deeply divided mind.[22] The perfectly adequate answer is given by Isabella herself: "Lawful mercy / Is nothing kin to foul redemption" (II. iv. 112–13). Shakespeare brings Isabella from her convent rather a prig and educates her out of this stiff righteousness just as he brings Angelo back to grace. The play has something to do, too, with the balance between asceticism and licentiousness.

To Miss Ellis-Fermor, there is in *Measure for Measure* "the denial, not only of the nobility of man, but of the very laws which pretend to guide him." There is "a world order ineradicably corrupted," a social climate "in whose fetid air no wholesome thing can grow."[23] But actually the atmosphere of the play is clear enough; the natural order stands unshaken behind the offenses of Angelo and reasserts itself, not through theatrical coincidences and providential strokes, but by the Duke's working upon the offender's human nature, so that Angelo credibly and naturally revolts from what he has done and seizes the chance of grace which is offered him. Even in *Measure for Measure* there may be glimpsed the world of Aquinas and Hooker, the world in which Shakespearean tragedy was possible. This inherently rational order of natural law did not exist for Beaumont and Fletcher. Lacking the earlier tragedian's most basic resource—the right kind of universe—they contrived with both poetic and dramatic skill a remarkably deceptive substitute.

THE CLEAREST CASE of all is John Ford's tragedy, *'Tis Pity She's a Whore* (1632–1633). The hero, Giovanni, is tormented by an incestuous passion for his sister Anabella and turns for help to his confessor, Friar Bonaventura. The first scene opens on an interview between these two, in which Giovanni has sought to wring from the Friar some license to the claims of uncontrollable desire, some admission that "customary form" is tyrannical in forbidding what his nature demands. The Friar does not trouble to answer Giovanni's arguments; he rather warns him of the danger of reasoning on morality:

> These are no school-points; nice philosophy
> May tolerate unlikely arguments,
> But Heaven admits no jest: wits that presum'd
> On wit too much, by striving how to prove
> There was no God with foolish grounds of art,
> Discover'd first the nearest way to hell,
> And fill'd the world with devilish atheism.
> Such questions, youth, are fond: far better 'tis
> To bless the sun than reason why it shines;
> Yet He thou talk'st of is above the sun.
>
> (I. i)[24]

The light of nature and natural reason is not to be directed on him who "is above the sun." Atheism is associated with presuming too much on "wit." Reason is no guide to morality, which is God's will rather than nature's examinable demands. In no other play does the voluntarist tradition of Calvin and Bacon, heralded in these first lines, bear such striking fruit. Giovanni swears to resist his love to the limits of his power, in order "to free me from the rod / Of vengeance; else I'll swear my fate's my god" (I. i). A scene intervenes here in which Soranzo and two rivals sue to Florio for the hand of his daughter Anabella. When we see Giovanni again, he has discovered his complete helplessness:

> Lost! I am lost! the fates have doom'd my death
> The more I strive, I love; the more I love,
> The less I hope: I see my ruin certain.
> What judgment or endeavors could apply
> To my incurable and restless wounds,
> I throughly have examin'd, but in vain.
> O, that it were not in religion sin
> To make our love a god, and worship it!
> I have even wearied heaven with prayers, dried up
> The spring of my continual tears, even starved
> My veins with daily fasts: what wit or art
> Could counsel, I have practis'd; but, alas,
> I find all these but dreams, and old men's tales.
> . . . .
>   't is my fate that leads me on.
>   (I. iii)

Here is the voluntaristic moral law of Calvinism, opposed absolutely by the forces of animal nature. The dilemma traps Giovanni in a ruin which is at once a punishment for sin and a fixed destiny beyond his power to escape. The justice of the world order has receded into the inscrutable secrecy of the divine will. Here, too, is a glimpse of the mechanistic Burtonian determinism which interprets "nature" in the new post-Baconian sense.[25] Like Heywood's heroes, Giovanni embraces his own ruin, totally conscious that he does so, horrified but unable to turn aside, despite this full and clear recognition. Desperately, he reveals his love to his sister, finds it requited, and joins with her in an incestuous union. As a document in the history of literary Calvinism, the play reaches its ideological climax in the scene where this relationship is revealed to Friar Bonaventura (II. v). Giovanni offers the worn Neo-Platonic argument that Anabella's physical beauty must mirror a beautiful soul, and a virtue in her love. This is thin stuff, perhaps, but very like Ford's own thesis in *Honor Triumphant*, one of his early pamphlets glorifying Platonic love. The influence of this courtly tradition never faded from his work; it furnishes the set of cult or code values which we might expect in such a playwright, although modern critics have had some difficulty in reconciling the author of *Honor Triumphant* with the Ford who produced the sternly puritan *Christes Bloodie Sweat*. The Friar, in answer to Giovanni, urges once again the absolute separateness of morality from all that reason can perceive or nature reveal:

> O ignorance in knowledge! long ago,
> How often have I warned thee this before.
> Indeed, if we were sure there were no Deity,
> Nor Heaven nor Hell, then to be led alone
> By Nature's light—as were philosophers
> Of elder times—might instance some defence.
> But 'tis not so: then, madman, thou wilt find
> That Nature is in Heaven's positions blind.
>
> (II. v)

"Nature is in Heaven's positions blind." So does Ford's Friar, in Calvin's voice, dispose of the pretensions of Hooker, of Aquinas, of the whole medieval tradition of the morality of reason and the natural law. Were it not for revelation, what is evil might be good;

we might follow "Nature's light" as now we may not, being subject to a higher and quite conceivably opposed law. To Giovanni's argument the Friar has answered, "yes, in reason and philosophy—but not in true morality." Moral evil is no denial of man's essential nature; it is in fact the helpless acting out of his nature's dictates, not their violation, which destroys Giovanni.

Finally, Anabella's pregnancy forces her to marry Soranzo. Involved in an adulterous affair with Hippolita, he has promised to marry her should her husband Richardetto die. Richardetto goes on a journey to bring home his orphaned niece, Philotis, and Hippolita subsequently hears news of his death. Absorbed in his new love for Anabella, Soranzo repudiates his vows to Hippolita. She plots to revenge herself for his treachery, approaching his Machiavellian servant Vasques for that purpose. Actually, Richardetto has returned to Parma in disguise as a physician and lurks about, accompanied by his niece, seeking a chance to revenge himself on Soranzo and Hippolita. Richardetto uses Grimaldi, another of Anabella's suitors, as a tool against Soranzo, persuading him to assassinate his rival with a poisoned sword. The plan miscarries, and Grimaldi by accident kills Bergetto, a lolling "natural" and former suitor to Anabella. When he meets his death, Bergetto is being hurried off to the Friar's cell by the righteous-talking Richardetto, who is attempting to marry his beloved niece Philotis to this idiot nephew of the very wealthy Donado before the uncle can prevent the wedding.

At the wedding banquet of Anabella and Soranzo, Hippolita appears, and with words of forgiveness and reconciliation offers to Soranzo a cup of wine which she has arranged for Vasques to poison. Her seductions prove unequal to Vasques' loyalty, for he gives the poisoned cup to her rather than to Soranzo, and she dies cursing the newly married couple.

Soranzo discovers Anabella's advanced pregnancy but cannot force from her the father's name. Vasques, however, tricks Putana, the nasty hag who plays nurse to Anabella's Juliet, into betraying Giovanni. Giovanni is warned by a letter which his sister has smuggled out of her imprisonment, but he boldly goes to the banquet which Soranzo has prepared as a scene of public disgrace and death for the incestuous lovers. In a last private interview with his sister, Giovanni displays once more the genuineness of his love. He suffers greater grief for her rejection of it (under the Friar's influence Anabella has repented her sin) than for his own imminent death. The stature achieved in this transcendence is enlarged by Giovanni's lyric praises of his sister:

> Early and late, the tribute which my heart
> Hath paid to Anabella's sacred love
> Hath been these tears, which are her mourners now.
> Never till now did Nature do her best
> To show a matchless beauty to the world.
>
> (V. v)

and by his vindication of love against the world's artificial patterns, which crush it:

> If ever after-times should hear
> Of our fast-knit affections, though perhaps
> The laws of conscience and of civil use
> May justly blame us, yet when they but know
> Our loves, that love will wipe away that rigour.
>
> (V. v)

The play postulates nature opposed to law, love opposed to morality, virtue opposed to virtue—the code virtue of romantic love opposed to orthodox Christian virtue. The courtly-love idea of romantic passion as an irresistible force, revived in the cult of "Platonic" love which was to dominate the manners of the Caroline court, enters into the scientific-mechanistic conception of irresistible and determining animal appetite; both combine easily with the Lutheran-Calvinistic picture of concupiscence as unconquerable in depraved human nature.

Giovanni now kills Anabella to forestall Soranzo's revenge, confronts the banqueters with her heart impaled on his dagger, fights and kills Soranzo and is killed by Vasques' hired assassins. He dies exalted in his defiance, the only figure on stage who is not part of the conventional world, and the only one wonderful and terrible, rather than devious, venal, sordid, or petty.

There can be no real doubt that Ford means us to sympathize with the lovers. Their sufferings, more notably Giovanni's sufferings in his doomed and helpless effort to resist the course of nature, and their total fidelity to their love and willingness to sacrifice all to it, contribute to this end. Ford assures the effect by his treatment of the other characters, who constitute the conventional world which the lovers have abandoned in their flouting of its deepest taboo: Florio urges his daughter Anabella to accept the rich fool Bergetto. Donado attempts to deceive both Florio and Anabella into the marriage with his moronic ward. Soranzo is an adulterer who perjures himself to Hippolita, piously pleading the wickedness of keeping wicked vows. Having discovered Anabella's secret, he pretends forgiveness, plotting the most extreme Machiavellian revenges, including the traditional assurance of his victims' damnation. Hippolita is an adulterous revenge-poisoner who seeks to seduce and corrupt Vasques so that he may be a tool in his master's murder. Vasques is another poisoner, an intriguer, torturer, assassin. When instead of revealing and preventing Hippolita's revenge, he gives to her the poison meant for Soranzo, Hippolita, outdone in treachery, dies writhing in pain; the company at the wedding banquet cry out "Wonderful justice!" and her husband Richardetto echoes, "Heaven, thou art righteous." There is much verbal tribute to Providence in all of Ford's plays, and much of it sounds as odd as this. Grimaldi is a poison-sword murderer, Richardetto the suborner who uses such an instrument for his private vengeance. There is a character to represent official religion—a cardinal, a papal nuncio, uncle to Grimaldi, who flouts justice by refusing to surrender his nephew from the sanctuary of his ecclesiastical power, despite the admitted murder of Bergetto.

The only pejorative qualification of the lovers' roles is Giovanni's intoxicated gloating over his illicit delights and over his deception of the world (V. iii) and his Marlovian vaunting to the repentant Anabella:

> What danger's half so great as thy revolt?
> Thou are a faithless sister, else thou know'st
> Malice, or any treachery beside
> Would stoop to my bent brows: why, I hold fate
> Clasp'd in my fist, and could command the course
> Of time's eternal motion, had'st thou been
> One thought more steady than an ebbing sea.
>
> (V. v)

The spectator has already been shown the disaster that waits on the hero, and these high-astounding terms might seem calculated to impress us as a fatal hubris. But given the context, the main effect of the speech is to shock or thrill, and possibly to excite some further pity for the state to which Giovanni is driven by the cruel necessity of turning against the world and assuming the role of rebel and outcast. If there is intoxication in this self-image of Giovanni as regent of the fates, the feeling is that of one who has finally hurled himself along with a current which he had struggled painfully against, and which bears him now beyond the conventional and the

timid, beyond the world of ordinary men. Giovanni
turns, too, to a complete religious skepticism. This certainly is not shared by most of Ford's audience. Yet the
rebellion it expresses against an incomprehensible and
iron Providence suits well the emotion developed by the
play.

When Richardetto hears of strife between Soranzo
and Anabella, he concludes that "there is One / Above
begins to work" (IV. ii), and that he therefore need do
no more himself "to further [Soranzo's] confusion."
Since Providence will attend the matter, no additional
poison-plots are required of him. He abruptly advises
his niece, "Since things go thus," to retire to a convent,
there to "free your years / From hazard of these woes."
This is the uncle who a few scenes earlier was promising
Donado's moronic heir that if proper haste were used in
sneaking off to accomplish his marriage to the same
girl, Bergetto could "bed" her directly. Richardetto now
concludes his advice with an assurance that

> All human worldly courses are uneven;
> No life is blessed but the way to heaven.

And Philotis immediately agrees: "Welcome, chaste
vows; myself I yield to you" (IV. ii). Admittedly Ford
sometimes marches under a banner inscribed "muddle
through" and creates more than his share of inconsistencies. But it is hard not to think that here he deliberately portrays the respectable world which destroys
such lovers as Giovanni and Anabella in the name of this
same righteousness.

"There is," says Richardetto, "One / Above begins to
work." And, in fact, Soranzo, having abandoned Hippolita and married Anabella, suffers shame and misery and
comes to bloody death, as do Giovanni and Anabella.
But Soranzo's fall and death are entirely the result of
Anabella's and Giovanni's love; there is no causal

connection between this and Soranzo's relation to Hippolita. Sin and punishment are unrelated, except by Richardetto's pious assertion that God punishes sinners. Ostensibly pointing to a tragic retribution, that assertion really shows us only a fideistic piety—a "fiat" view of Providence.

Soranzo's ruin comes of the sin of Anabella and Giovanni, which is in accord with nature and "philosophy" or natural reason. It is evil solely because of divine command. It is a sin only, as Giovanni says, "in religion," and society crushes it in the name of that religion, so that its consequences are due to the taboos which forbid nature. The natural law seen in the play is the descriptive and determining law of mechanistic conception. Nature is irresistible, morality immovable; this is the Calvinistic doom of Giovanni and Anabella.

Of Ford's extant works, the earliest are nondramatic pamphlets and poems either religious or courtly in character.[26] The year 1613 saw the publication of *Christes Bloodie Sweat*, a poem of nearly two thousand lines couched, in Clifford Leech's words, in "rather savage Calvinistic terms."[27] It dwells on the efficacy of Christ's passion, condemns those who make a religion of earthly love, attacks the Roman Church and the Jesuits, speaks of predestination and the doctrine of the elect, and includes a passage on the terrors of damnation almost identical with the Friar's lecture to Anabella (III. vi).

Two earlier works, a poem and a prose pamphlet, had revealed an opposite side of Ford. *Fames Memoriall* is a poetic elegy on the Earl of Devonshire, and *Honor Triumphant* a prose "defense" of four *amour courtois* propositions: "1. Knights in Ladies service have no free will. 2. Beauty is the maintainer of valour. 3. Faire Lady was never false. 4. Perfect lovers are only wise." Here, too (and also in *Fames Memoriall*), there is an elect, an inner, special caste of the chosen, this time the perfect courtly lovers, rather than the saved. Whether they are saints of profane or holy love, Ford's subjects show this differentiation from common humanity. Leech remarks of the Calvinistic "affinity" in Ford that "it requires only a slight shifting of this viewpoint to find one's aristocracy among the damned—a shifting exemplified by Ford in *'Tis Pity She's a Whore*, as by Webster in *The White Devil.*"[28] In each of these plays the elected superior beings are those who stand up for what they (and we) are. This assertion puts them in defiance of Calvinistically conceived morality. God and nature are already at strife in Jacobean literature, and nature lends dreams as evil, if not as explicit, as those of the Victorian years.

It might be remarked that by combining the Calvinistic and courtly works, we can produce the tragic world of sundered aspirations and irreconcilable laws later seen in *'Tis Pity*. How, it may be asked, can the same man have produced, on the one hand, *Fames Memoriall*, and especially *Honor Triumphant*, with its flavor of the *demande d'amour* or tençon, and on the other, *Christes Bloodie Sweat*, *A Line of Life* (which shall help the reader, says Ford, to "unwynde himselfe from out the laborinthe and maze of this naturall and troublesome race of Fraylety"), and *The Golden Meane*? The earlier poem and pamphlet uphold a "Platonic" and courtly code, a "religion" of love opposite to the Puritan moralizing of *Christes Bloodie Sweat* but close to thematic matter in Ford's *The Broken Heart*, *Love's Sacrifice*, or *The Lover's Melancholy*. The natural world has been virtually abandoned by religion, and its values must be defined by special codes. To Shakespeare, romantic love could become by excess a folly either comic or tragic. But it is exactly the excess, the absolute, which marks the elect and serves as the standard of nobility in *The Broken Heart* or *Love's Sacrifice*, where, as Leech says of late Jacobean and Caroline drama generally, there is "an impression of a deliberate exercise in which there is only fugitive contact with the dramatist's perception of the nature of things."[29]

Leech, discussing the moral basis of Ford's tragedy, quotes a comment by Sensabaugh: " *'Tis Pity She's a Whore* . . . strikes the most decisive blow against the world's moral order . . . the play makes an open problem of incest and thus queries the Christian idea of retributive justice."[30] "Yet," says Leech, "we have seen that Ford, as we should indeed expect from his earlier writings, is sharply aware of sin and by no means an active unbeliever in the Christian cosmology." This means, for Leech, that Sensabaugh's estimate is mistaken; if there is sympathy for Giovanni and Anabella, it does not remove the odium and horror of their guilt nor indicate a diminished confidence in the morality which they offend, nor in "the Christian idea of retributive justice." In another place Leech says that "far from being antinomian" (as Sensabaugh has maintained that he is), Ford "shows at times a simple belief in Providence."[31] Both critics are right: there is no contradiction. Attribution to Providence is everywhere in Ford's plays, but a strong sense of the Calvinistic Providence has not infrequently been accompanied by rebellion and protest against its inscrutable order. In the Calvinistic Providential view, evil represents a fulfillment of God's will, rather than the free human rejection of it: freedom is denied and yet guilt is maintained. This assigns everything to Providence, but instead of a serene acquiescence in the given order of things, may produce the sinew-cracking moral strains and exacerbated feeling of *'Tis Pity She's a Whore.*

The Spanish Gipsy, first acted in 1623, is a play produced probably by collaboration between Middleton, Rowley, and Ford, although there is differing opinion as to its authorship.[32] The character Roderigo is irresist-

ibly driven to commit a rape in the helpless and protesting manner by now familiar. His father tells him that
suffering is always Heaven's punishment for sin, com-
pleting once more the implication that tragic catastrophe is both punishment and inescapable destiny:

> Fool, Twere
> Impossible that justice should rain down
> In such a frightful horror without cause.
>
> (V. i)

Roderigo's expressions of remorse are revealing:

> A thousand stings are in me: O, what vile prisons
> Make we our bodies to our immortal souls;
> Brave tenants to bad houses; 'tis a dear rent
> They pay for naughty lodging: the soul, the mistress;
> The body, the caroch that carries her;
> Sins, the swift wheels that hurry her away;
> Our will, the coachman rashly driving on,
> Till coach and carriage both are quite o'erthrown.
> . . . .
> Who would lose
> A kingdom for a cottage? an estate
> Of perpetuity for a man's life
> For annuity of that life?—Pleasure!—a spark
> To those celestial fires that burn about us;
> A painted star to that bright firmament
> Of constellations which each night are set
> Lighting our way; yet thither how few get!
>
> (III. i)

In this slightly spavined set of metaphors, the relationship of body and soul appears as that of prisoner and
prison, tenant and house, passenger and coach. "Sins"
are appropriated to body and not soul, although the
conceit which makes them the wheels of the "coach" is
one that Donne would blush to own. The Baconian-
Cartesian dualism can hardly be more faithfully re-

flected than this, although it is hard to measure the possible mixture of Platonism, with its characteristic denigration of matter as the prison of spirit and the principle of evil. The legacies of Plato, Calvin, and the early mechanists are so similar in this respect that distinction between their literary influences often cannot and need not be made. To this alienation of the spiritual from the natural is added the Puritan sense of how few are saved. ("Yet thither how few get!") Roderigo suffers torments of conscience, but they appear not as the natural inner disordering spoken of by Cicero, Aquinas, Hooker, or Primauday, but as the consciousness of a specific loss of heaven for earth—"a kingdom for a cottage."

The heroine of this part of the play's action voices her faith, later, that "Heavens great hand" has "long since decreed" all the tragic events. Again, only the play's "tragicomic" (i.e., happy) ending can relieve the feelings aroused by suffering in such a universe.

The Witch of Edmonton, by Dekker, Rowley, and Ford (1621), employs the familiar theme of the miseries of enforced marriage, as does Ford's later "Spartan" play *The Broken Heart.* Frank Thorney, the central character, is another hero-victim, unable to break through a web of evil circumstance or to resist the devil who impels him to a meaningless and unnecessary murder. What the play chiefly dramatizes is his intense suffering and his powerlessness to choose his own path:

> On every side I am distracted;
> Am waded deeper into mischief
> Than virtue can avoid; but on I must:
> Fate leads me; I will follow.
>
> (I. ii)

and his conviction that his inevitable downfall is nevertheless the punishment due his sin:

No man can hide his shame from heaven that views
  him;
In vain he flees whose destiny pursues him.

(I. ii)

Frank commits fornication, bigamy, theft, and murder,
yet retains Ford's and the audience's sympathy in his
helplessness to do otherwise. Having been forced to
conceal his marriage to Winnifride, a servant girl, he is
trapped into marrying a second time but suffers such
miseries over his life of deceit that he attempts to flee
with Winnifride. He tells Susan, his loving second
"wife," that he will be gone for some time on a trip, but
in the course of her leave-taking, she insists on accom-
panying him farther and farther on his way. Finally, in a
lonely place, Frank feels a dog (the "familiar" of the
play's witch) rub against his leg. Instantly, he reveals
the truth to Susan and murders her. Once again, the
action is so presented that the motive of the "sin" is
hardly felt to lie within the will of the sinner, which is
paralyzed by the power of evil. Like Anne Frankford,
Frank Thorney dies repentant and in hope of heaven,
religious piety providing again some reconciliation to
the otherwise intolerable suffering of a man we cannot
blame.

The title character, an old woman leagued with a
devil, is accorded what has seemed "an astonishingly
sympathetic treatment of such a suspected creature in
an age which knew many witch scares."[33] She has been
driven to witchcraft by the malice and injustice of a bad
world, which she turns against in self-defense and des-
peration. She too, dies contrite and pitiful. The tragic
emotions dwindle into sentimentality.

The Broken Heart (1631–1632) is, in a way, at an
opposite extreme from *'Tis Pity She's a Whore*: its
tragic aristocracy engage us by the nobility not of defi-

ance but of submission. The Spartan nobleman Ithocles has forced his sister Penthea to marry old Bassanes, rather than Orgilus, whom she loves, and to whom she was betrothed by her late father and by King Amyclas. Desolated by his loss, Orgilus obtains his father's consent to leave for Athens, in order to lessen Bassanes' foolish jealousy, which fixes on Orgilus as its chief suspect. Actually he remains in Sparta disguised as a poor scholar of the philosopher Tecnicus, in order to keep watch on Penthea and on his own sister Euphranea.

Confronting Penthea in a palace garden, Orgilus reveals his identity and reminds her that troth-plight and true love have made her his, despite her false marriage to Bassanes. Penthea rejects him; she will die of grief rather than violate her enforced marriage vows to Bassanes. Even should Bassanes die, she can never marry Orgilus, for "the virgin-dowry which [her] birth bestow'd / Is ravished by another."[34]

Ithocles returns from war in triumph and reveals to his sister his own despairing love for the Spartan Princess Calantha. Humbled and chastened in this affliction, he is repentant for the irreversible wrong he has done in separating Penthea from Orgilus. A fitting rubric might be found in Chaucer's *Knight's Tale*—

> The God of love, a, benedicite!
> How myghty and how greet a lord is he—[35]

or in some speech from Tristan or Troilus; Ithocles is a stricken courtly lover straight from the pages of Andreas Cappelanus.

Penthea is reconciled to her brother and pleads his love to the Princess; Calantha and Ithocles are betrothed. Penthea, unable to bear her anguish, goes mad and dies. Orgilus, revenging her death, traps Ithocles in a mechanical chair and kills him. Dancing at a wedding feast, Princess Calantha receives messages first of her father's death, then of her beloved Penthea's, then of Ithocles'. She dances stoically on, seemingly unaffected. The following scene presents her dressed in white, beside a white temple-altar on which lies Ithocles' body. After settling the succession and condemning Orgilus to death, she weds the corpse with her mother's ring and dies upon it of a broken heart, thus fulfilling the last of the riddling prophecies of the philosopher Tecnicus.

Ithocles' tyranny in forcing his sister to marry Bassanes has been the cause of tragedy—the cause of Penthea's death, of his own murder by Orgilus, and of Calantha's "broken heart." But this fact is dramatically irrelevant: Ithocles is a wholly sympathetic character. His enforcing of the marriage lies outside of the play's action; it was committed before the events of the first scene by a youth who realizes only later what he has done. From the moment we see him, Ithocles suffers as much from contrition over his past cruelty as from his love of Calantha. The sad and faithful Orgilus, too, clearly demands our sympathy, despite the misleading symbolism of his name. The martyred love-saint, Penthea, says of him

> Alas, poor genteleman,
> He look'd not like the ruins of his youth,
> But like the ruines of those ruines.
>
> (II. iii)

Not even toward Ithocles does "Orgilus" maintain real malice. His code requires him to revenge Penthea's death, but he does it with formal courtesy and generous tributes to his victim:

> Give me thy hand: be healthful in thy parting
> From lost mortality! thus, thus I free It [stabs him.]
> ·

I will be gentle even in blood; to linger
Pain, which I strive to cure, were to be cruel [stabs
    him again.]

                                                    (IV. iv)

Ithocles forgives him, and dies, and Orgilus bids his
victim "Farewell, fair spring of manhood!" (IV. iv).
Orgilus' values are much like those of Shakespeare's
Laertes, who was satisfied "in nature," but had for
"honor" to avenge his father's death. Laertes, however,
functioned as a foil to Hamlet, against whose profounder
vision his code was set, in a contrast repeatedly under-
lined.

With Penthea, "buried in a bride bed," Ford pulls all
the stops of pity. As she declines through grief and
madness to her death, she speaks lines of great pathos:

Since I was first a wife, I might have been
Mother to many pretty prattling babes;
They would have smil'd when I smil'd, and for certain
I should have cried when they cried: —truly brother,
My father would have picked me out a husband,
And then my little ones had been no bastards.

                                                    (IV. ii)

Calantha's character is entirely that of noble victim.
Even Bassanes, finally, learns through grief the wickedness of his jealousy and earns our sympathy by his
repentant sufferings. All are in effect helpless pawns of
fate or of the laws and institutions which cruelly deny
the truths of the heart. Penthea's tragedy, from which
the others spring, arises in part from the inhuman rigid-
ity of the "system," the official order. Her suffering is
inflicted by the orthodox morality of the marriage bond
and the cold virtue which binds her to it.

The absolute code ethic is completely dominant. Penthea would rather die of thwarted love for Orgilus than

be united to him, having lost her "virgin-dowry." He
yearns toward her with the fatal ardor of the hypothetical courtly lover, but she prefers a widow's death to
bringing him the favors of a "second bed." Orgilus, like
Ithocles, is wasted by passion, his "breast made tribu-
tary to the laws / Of beauty." He murders Ithocles, and
Calantha dies, in the service of extravagant and absolute
courtly canons. Dying, she voices her sense of the elect
and of this their high and special law:

> Be such mere women, who with shrieks and outcries
> Can vow a present end to all their sorrows,
> Yet live to court new pleasures, and outlive them.
>
> (V. iii)

There are no "mere women" among this aristocracy.

There is a sense that these noble creatures do well to
leave a world where "Morality / Creeps on the dung of
earth, and cannot reach / The riddles which are purposed
by the gods" (I. iii). Their greatness lies in what they
suffer with calm and dignity, not in what they do. Tecnicus advises his pupil: "Tempt not the stars; young man,
thou canst not play / With the severity of fate . . ." (I.
iii). Prophilus declares that "Fate instructs me" (I. iii).
Calantha is "crossed by fate," Ithocles, Nearchus, and
other characters express over and over, in lines too
many to quote, the sense of man's inability to prevent
the destiny which is ordained for each.

Much of the peculiar character of *The Broken Heart*
is due to the special theatrical intensity with which
Ford can endow a certain kind of isolated scene. The
private meeting where Ithocles confesses to his sister
his hopeless love for Calantha takes great emotional
vividness from their ironic personal relation. Having
denied Penthea her love, he now feels her suffering in his
own passion for Calantha. He asks forgiveness and pity,
and she grants them, her quiet tenderness suffused with

her own grief. Upon this interview bursts Bassanes, shouting obscene accusations of incest, giving poor Ithocles an unbearable instance of the torment to which he has condemned his virtuous sister. The scene in which Penthea reveals to the royal princess Ithocles' dangerous love is another theatrical *tour de force*. Calantha agrees to be executrix of the testament which Penthea purposes to make, feeling that her "glass of life . . . hath few minutes / Remaining to run down." Penthea bequeaths her youth to "virgin-wives, such as abuse not wedlock," her fame, "To Memory, and Time's old daughter, Truth," and climactically, her brother Ithocles, "By service bound and by affection vow'd, / . . . in holiest rites of love," to her dear friend Calantha (III. v).

More sensational are the scenes of Orgilus' murder of Ithocles, with its dignified exchange between revenger and victim; the dance scene in which "one news straight came huddling on another / Of Death! and death! and still [Calantha] danc'd forward"; the scene of Orgilus' suicide in execution of Calantha's judicial sentence; and finally, the scene of Calantha's death of grief over the body of Ithocles.

Ford is evidently more interested in these hypnotic theatrical moments, minutely vibrating with suppressed but exalted passion, than in his plot. Some critics hide the resulting weakness by treating *sui generis* the group of his plays to which *The Broken Heart* belongs,[36] but no critical mystique can really conceal the fact that the play is a structural monstrosity. Events are huddled together, followed or preceded by passages actionless or structurally directionless, like the episode of Orgilus' secret residence with his magister, Tecnicus, in the disguise of a scholar, an intrigue which leads nowhere, soon abandoned and forgotten. Such also are Orgilus' solemn exaction of his sister's promise not to marry without his approval, Orgilus' anger and ominous talk at discovering Euphranea's innocent meetings with Prophilus, and the sparks struck between Ithocles and Nearchus, his rival for Calantha's love.

The main plot really concludes when Penthea and Ithocles have died (IV. iv); Ford looks up, somewhat at a loss, to confront the consequences of his preoccupation with the theatrical quality of individual scenes. His solution is to proceed from here on the premise that the plot turns about the Princess Calantha, who until now was rather a minor figure, but who offers the advantage of being left alive, not having yet been spent upon a showcase death scene—the use to which the development of the Ford hero is commonly directed.

Like Beaumont and Fletcher, Ford will sacrifice almost anything in the play for theatrical effect or the heightening and vivifying of code extravagances which must fill the vacuum in tragedy—the glorifying of the absolute virtues which in a differing way make Ford's heroes as unfit for survival in their world as Webster's in theirs. Here they are the ideals of courtly love or the "Platonic" cult, or of an aristocratic honor exalted above the practical demands of the natural world, in which they can only assure the noble death of the votary whom they doom.

All critics of *The Broken Heart* have remarked that its strength lies in an ideal of resignation, not of assertion. The aspiration revealed, says Leech, is toward "the quietist ideal," which is "to accept the inevitable with calm and authority."[37] Heroic characters submit with dignity to a hostile fate, out of clear knowledge that this is the only assertion possible. Repeatedly one hears of the "immobility" of the crucial scenes in *The Broken Heart*, *Love's Sacrifice*, and *Perkin Warbeck*: they have a "Grecian Urn" quality—the motionlessness of an absolute which has been made concrete.

Heywood and others had pictured the tragic opposition between the imperative demands of human nature and the immutable decrees of Providence, creating thereby a morally unintelligible voluntarist cosmos whose laws cannot be accommodated to the demands of mind or heart. Much Jacobean tragedy had found its form in this conflict between the vital vigor and audacity of men and the iron immobility of the statutes imposed on them. Ford observed such a formula in *'Tis Pity She's a Whore*. But we see in *The Broken Heart* the other possible tragic recourse of the voluntarist worldview: the achieving of nobility and dignity by the clear-eyed courage of unflinching submission. Ford's heroes can freely choose to accept what they are not free to avoid. Death is, beyond all, their opportunity and transcendent moment.

Heroes in that tragedy which outlived the natural law are heroic, then, by reason either of rebellion against an intolerable order or of submission to one so nearly intolerable that only heroism can join clear recognition with calm acceptance. In either case, the tragic emotion exalts human values against an unacceptable order with which they conflict.

But are not the critics mistaken who see such "quietness" in *The Broken Heart*, such restraint and genuinely Stoic calm? Does not Ford's use of understatement actually make of it a shrieking hyperbole, a near-ludicrous extravagance which is a step short of the comic? The Fordian hero exchanging polite compliments with his murderer, or calmly opening his own veins in execution of judicial sentence, with only the most discreet show of feeling; the heroine dying ceremonially and publicly with perfect "Spartan" seemliness, not by poison or a knife, but by an act of the noble will which rejects life in an intolerable world: these are perfervid, faintly hysterical creations which exhibit, to borrow one of Peter de Vries' magnificent *mots,* "restraint run wild." The division of nature from goodness cannot be clearer than in the canons of "honor" which here define the good and guide the ineffably noble lords and ladies of Ford's elect.[38]

Chapter Eight

Conclusions

To RAISE THE SUBJECT of "catharsis" in connection with Renaissance tragedy is to invite a suspicion of historical naivete; at best one seems to be, in Leavis' phrase, "proposing a solemn and time-honoured academic game."[1] Yet there is a kind of tragedy which is "a special artistic and critical approach to the mystery of man's suffering on earth,"[2] and which reappears, in forms not essentially different, in several times and literatures. There is in fact a world-view which constitutes the theoretic form of this kind of tragedy, apart from the executive form by which a given age may realize it.

Allowing the idea a broader scope than its strictly Aristotelian one, we might still seek in definitions of tragic catharsis some answer to one great and perennial question of Shakespearean criticism: what in Shakespeare's tragedies accounts for the particular artistic experience generally associated with them? Why do we find so satisfying the unfolding there of misery, calamity, and death, often imagined as happening to sympathetic and good men? What explains their almost universally attested effect, not of the depression which might reasonably be expected, but of reassurance, relief, and elevation?

Aristotle, in the metaphor by which he described the affective power of Sophoclean tragedy, evidently referred to a psychic purgation; an allaying of the emotions which accompany our consciousness of evil, resulting in greater serenity or internal harmony—an affective reconciliation to the conditions of life. But "catharsis" soon enough came to mean whatever the critic wished, and it has in different centuries had contrary meanings. Renaissance commentators on the *Poetics* began the modern debate over Aristotle's assertion that tragedy "through pity and fear [effects] the proper purgation of these emotions."[3] Some of the Stoic critics of the sixteenth century held that the function of tragedy was to harden weakness by accustoming it to the painful. It was also ethically improving to see the destructive power of the passions exhibited in a sympathetic figure.[4] Eighteenth-century benevolists reversed the Stoic view; tragedy should purify by increasing the capacity for fear and pity, particularly for pity.[5] What Plato feared and Aristotle denied—that the stimulation provided by drama would strengthen rather than relieve and regulate the passions—they both affirmed and approved.

Critics and philosophers of almost every age have entered the discussion. Hobbes, Hegel, Schopenhauer, Nietzsche, and Hume all joined the argument over tragic catharsis.[6] It may be, say recent critics (grandly, if a little vaguely), no more than the fact that heroism can be displayed only in opposition to extreme adversity,[7] that "the sense of human splendor is greater even in defeat than the universe that crushes it."[8] It may be that "in a planned but terrible universe we see man justifying his existence."[9] It may be the power of great poetry to transmute other emotions. Perhaps the effective and indispensable element is a testimony to human dignity, significance, and freedom[10] which, as we were told by Joseph Wood Krutch forty-one years ago (and by many others since), may now be hard to sustain as a serious belief. The loss of power to produce this sort of tragedy, according to Krutch, is the result of a "gradual weakening of man's confidence in his ability to impose upon the phenomenon of life an interpretation acceptable to his desires." In contrast with this, "classical tragedy did consist in the successful effort to impose such a satisfactory interpretation . . . [and is] essentially an expression, not of despair, but of the triumph over despair and of confidence in the value of human life."[11] Thus, although we say that modern works which end sadly are *tragic*, "the term is a misnomer since it is obvious that the works in question have nothing in common with the classical examples of the genre and produce in the reader a sense of depression which is the exact opposite of that elation generated when the spirit of a Shakespeare rises joyously superior to the outward calamities which he recounts and celebrates the greatness of the human spirit whose travail he describes."[12]

Science, at least until very recently, has accustomed us to imagine man as a mechanism acting involuntarily,[13] despite a contrary illusion, or even as a physical epiphenomenon significant only to himself. In the deterministic and positivistic milieu, which has altered only slightly in late years, "heroes" share the ontological status of trolls and unicorns. We are little inclined to exclaim "how like a god"; we assume more easily that men are very like the "responsive" organisms seen by neo-behaviorist psychology (or even like Pavlov's "reflexive" dogs—the vanguard of science may now have left atomistic mechanism behind and abandoned deterministic explanations of even the subanimate world, but general and humane culture are influenced more by the scientific culture of the age of Newton than that of Hiesenberg). In an "absurd" world literature must make do with antiheroes. In a post-Freudian world it is not usually inclined to conceive of the roots of behavior as rational.

Part of the question of catharsis may be resigned to the psychologists, who have seen tragedy as a ritual of vicarious atonement and self-punitive satisfaction for psychic guilt.[14] The tragic function has been compared to that of soldiers' dreams and children's play in which something deeply feared is enacted so that it may be symbolically mastered.[15] Some subconscious potency may even remain in the primordial pattern of seasonal fertility rite which underlies classical tragedy. Especially interesting is Robert Sharpe's suggestion that the element of the outrageous, the obscene, or shocking, which appears in virtually all significant tragedy, is demanded by the cathartic and homeopathic function of the release of feeling.[16] None of these psychological explanations, however, does much to help us distinguish the tragedy of a Shakespeare from that of a Tourneur or a Ford.

Many of the most respected contemporary scholar-critics have, at any rate, found in the best Elizabethan tragedy both a variety of the tragic flaw and an effect which they variously call "comfort," "reconciliation," "exaltation," "relief," "vindication," and "catharsis." This is often traced to some affirmation of man's power over his destiny, some presentation of a significant human freedom with large risks and possibilities. It is, I believe, a presentation whose tracing of cause and effect in human affairs shows moral order and intelligibility behind the appearance of capricious evil. Its effect is not concentrated upon the death of the tragic hero, nor upon any single moment of the drama; it is instinct in the entire conception of the tragic world. It is thus mistaken to speak of the "reconciliation of act IV" in *King Lear* and to question whether it survives the catastrophe of act V. If there is this kind of reconciling power in the play, it is a function of the whole. It depends on our reaction to the world where good and evil are what they are in *Lear*, not upon the presence or absence of innocent suffering, which is certainly part of the world to which we are to be reconciled.

A crucial differentia of Shakespearean tragedy is its depiction of this universe of law, basically the medieval moral universe of Aquinas and Hooker. Here is a world order in which each being realizes the perfections of its kind by functioning in accord with its own essential nature; the limits and possibilities of man's nature, being imperfectly known, are investigated by the drama. Men endanger or destroy themselves in this world when they fail in the hard human responsibility of discovering or choosing or forging out of the complexities that confront them, that which is in accord with the demands of their own nature and that of society, which is a function of their nature.

"Catharsis" or reconciliation to the tragic world lies partly in our recognition of a free human responsibility for the suffering and evil which befall the tragic characters through the exactions of a natural law commensurate with human reason—a *natura naturans* which is not evil or capricious, and whose illumination is the business of tragedy. It is a response to the imaginative assurance that the conditions of life are ultimately rational and intelligible, and that the highest aspirations of man are fundamentally in accord with his own nature and the world's. It rests, therefore, upon the dramatic projection of the belief in natural law discussed in the preceding pages, which I propose as a necessary condition, not an artistic cause, of the peculiar power of the best Renaissance tragedy.

Modern readers are not likely to share this faith as a matter of literal belief. It may for some be too remote from habitual assumptions to communicate itself effectively or exercise much power. Such readers or viewers would likely prefer Webster or Tourneur, whose spirit answers more closely to that of our own time. Most, however, can enter the Shakespearean universe at least imaginatively, through the suspension of disbelief by which one participates in drama. They find there a world made for man, one in which he can consent to live even in recognition of its worst possibilities. It not only produces, but justifies, the will to live; it is a world in which man is supremely significant.

Perhaps the cosmic intelligibility of the universe which such tragedy constructs is reinforced by the aesthetic intelligibility of the literary artifact itself. Every work of literature—poem, play, novel, story—aspires to a state in which each constituent is functional in relation to a total effect. In the fully realized work, each detail contributes and can give reason for its presence and its particularity. Nothing arbitrary survives, nothing not selected or shaped, however intuitively, to have meaning by virtue of its relation to its context. In poetry especially, this organic purposiveness embraces even sound: controlled pace and rhythm, onomatopoeic suggestion, and so on. It would seem that in tragedy, aesthetic and philosophic intelligibility might conflate. Evil may be made more palatable simply by representation in a work of art structurally transparent to understanding—i.e., one in which the relation of many parts to the complex whole is evident and highly organized. The satisfying experience of full comprehension, rarely afforded by the world directly experienced, may combine with the awareness of evil through the medium of purely executive artistic form. But if the reassuring intimation of acceptable order is in this sense a purely aesthetic feat, we ought, it would seem, to find such an effect in every highly controlled representation of suffering, whatever picture of life it offers. We ought to find it in naturalistic drama where, by common agreement, it has not been found.

Theoretic and executive form must, no doubt, be mutually supportive, so that the Shakespearean tragic effect is not consistent with a nominalistic, or voluntaristic, or Calvinistic picture of the world. It cannot be produced from conceptions of natural law like those arising in the seventeenth century and dominant in the eighteenth, and it is quite incompatible with a behavioristic or mechanistic view of human nature. An indispensable element of the tragic vision is, then, this idea of a legal order founded innately in the substantial natures of things. A probing after the undiscovered human essence and a partial and experimental revelation of the law dictated for man by his rational and moral nature: this is what underlies the broad patterns of Shakespearean tragedy.

As long ago as Montaigne, observation of diversity among the world's ethical systems led to the disavowal of such a natural law: "they are pleasant, when to give some certainty to the laws, they say that there are some firm, perpetual, and immutable, which they call natural, that are imprinted in mankind by the condition of their own proper being; and of these, some reckon three, some four, some more, and some less, a sign that it is a mark as doubtful as the rest. . . . of these three or four select laws there is not so much as one that is not contradicted and disowned, not only by one nation but by many."[17] And Montaigne is one of those who retreated toward solipsism and fideism, which, in despair of reason, puts everything in the hands of faith.

Heinrich Rommen, discussing the impact of nominalism on ethics in about the period following Shakespearean tragedy, says that to the nominalist "law is will, pure will, without any foundation in reality . . . as a result, Ockham, who sees only individual phenomena, not universals, the concepts of essences, can likewise admit no teleological ordination toward God as inherent in all creation and especially in man."[18] If, as to the nominalist, there is no basis in the external world for the universal concept and term, no nature universal to and identical in all things of the same kind, there cannot be any natural law in the Scholastic or medieval sense. Both Luther and Calvin were professed Occamites, thoroughly nominalistic and voluntaristic in their thought.

There was much talk of natural law after the Renaissance, but the sense of the term in most of the seventeenth and eighteenth centuries is not that of the Middle Ages or of Shakespeare; the new conception was much like the modern one: a descriptive formulation of the involuntary physical behavior of things. It is nonteleological; its relation to morality, when not an irresistible opposition, is only that of an external and abstract pattern or model. The Jacobean period saw a great shift in feeling after which it no longer seemed that the true virtue and greatness of man was to "go with sway of all the world." Calvin's influence had effected in English thought an Augustinian separation between the orders of nature and grace; the two were seen as opposed. Platonism, Cartesian rationalism, Baconian mechanism, and Calvinism converged upon the alienation of morality from nature, of the material from spiritual, of virtue from the demands of the world.

Even Anglican minds were so deeply influenced in Jacobean times by this aspect of Calvinism that they repudiated natural reason in morality. In the seventeenth century such Anglicans as Glanville and Rust fought a rearguard action against Calvinist voluntarism in defense of free will and of the belief that "the relations governing things do necessarily and immediately flow from the things themselves."[19] But the medieval and Renaissance integrated universe had been lost beyond recovery.

The noble virtue of Webster's Duchess of Malfi and the grandeur of his Vittoria Corombona, for instance, are quite alien to the dark world in which they are set. Nature is the foil, not the standard of their greatness. In Webster's plays there is a *contemptus mundi* and a division of the "two laws," but there is at least the Stoic assurance of an invulnerable inner integrity. In plays like Tourneur's *Revenger's Tragedy*, the Jacobean split of morality and nature is even plainer; it is demonstrated by the action, and it is given explicit and repeated expression.

Ford shows us, too, the clearest possible alienation of the natural and moral orders, picturing the Calvinistic doom of characters trapped between the imposed morality of divine fiat and the irresistible forces of a mechanistic nature. Like Webster and Tourneur, he displays a Calvinistic revulsion from the corrupt world, and like Heywood he finds human carnality an irresistible principle, before whose force his tragic characters become helpless victims. His heroes achieve their stature by (1) self-immolation on the altar of an absolute morality which invites destruction by defying nature, (2) rebellion, in the name of nature, against an inhuman and incomprehensible moral law, or (3) Stoic submission to an intolerable world order which crushes them.

The reciprocal irrelevance of virtue, nature, and reason, and the resurgent Manichean feeling, the malevolent world order of late Jacobean tragedy, also help to explain why the tragic reconciliation had to turn to specious happy endings, whose effect is merely theatrical, but is for the few moments until one leaves the theater, analogous to the relief of the former tragedy, which had been achieved without such an evasion.

The typical Beaumont and Fletcher tragicomedy, or

tragedy of happy ending, deals with tragic experience by revealing at the play's end some crucial information, concealed from the audience until then, which provides a key to all conflicts. Beaumont and Fletcher do not resolve but rather dissolve or repudiate the tragic issues, when these have been wrung dry of rhetoric and sensation. Relief can come only through a transparent evasion of reality. It is as if Lear and Cordelia were returned to life and sent off to happy retirement; as if the elder Hamlet descended from a mountain retreat where he had hidden since a secret disentombment, as if Claudius repented and Hamlet married Ophelia.

It is true that the old *King Lear* (as well as the original *Timon*) had a happy ending, with Lear and Cordelia rewarded and the wicked daughters punished. The old play belongs of course to a popular drama which was evolving methods for the treatment of tragic matter. The simple device of poetic justice, although not sufficiently faithful to the real conditions of life to be capable of conveying any serious reconciliation to them, was a treatment of virtue and vice supported by the authority of many pulpits and many early doctrinal plays, and was in the popular tradition of simple moral didacticism. For the post-Elizabethan to fall back on happy endings in tragic drama is a very different thing and betrays that failure of an earlier affirmative vision which is common to the Jacobean tragedies and tragicomedies.

Shakespearean tragedy often opens from a focus upon its final personal catastrophe to regard a wider scene of order reasserted and restored by the convulsion which has engulfed the innocent with the guilty. The universe of Heywood, Webster, Chapman, Tourneur, Beaumont and Fletcher, and Ford allows no such vision. Here the axiologies by which heroes are measured may be Stoic or Platonic or Calvinist-Christian but are generally unrelated to the surrounding natural world. Heroism, in fact, is measured by its incommensurability with the world seen within the play. Chapman's Bussy, Clermont, and Cato are good examples, as are some of Webster's and Tourneur's characters; Fletcher's heroes, especially, become tragic exactly because their "nobility" is so contrary to the demands of nature that they are unfitted for survival. Amintor, of *The Maid's Tragedy,* is the perfect instance—destroyed by his virtue because it rejects the ordinary demands of life. His loyalty to his king is absolutely noble and absolutely irreconcilable with the dictates of his honor, which is also absolute. Morality having been abstracted entirely from nature and disconnected from rational judgment, *contrary* virtues now are possible.

Heywood's bourgeois heroine in *A Woman Killed with Kindness* represents another staple of Jacobean tragedy: a character whose guilt is entirely mechanical, her intellect never assenting to what passion compels her to. The result is a Shakespearean or Aristotelian plot (in which catastrophe is traceable to responsible action) yoked to the merely pathetic characterization of sentimental drama (in which our pity at the downfall of the hero must be unmarred by any emotional realization of his own hand in it); Heywood makes a constant obeisance to Christian morality, but is quite unable to integrate his conception of it with any concrete human experience, or to realize it as implicit in the inner nature of his heroine. The usual criticism that Mistress Frankford is inadequately motivated recognizes an effect, but not the ultimate cause, of Heywood's failure. The same tendency develops further in Tourneur's *The Atheist's Tragedy* and reaches its apex in Ford's *'Tis Pity She's a Whore.*

Ultimately, the fact that these Jacobean and Caroline dramatists did not continue the earlier tragic mode may be attributed, in large part, to the failure of the medieval and Elizabethan concept of natural law. It was the doctrines diffused through Luther, Calvin, Descartes, and Bacon which destroyed this belief. Calvinistic voluntarism, with its picture of an evil world order ultimately unintelligible to natural reason, and its supremely important alienation of morality from nature, was strengthened by philosophical skepticism, Cartesian dualism, and Baconian mechanism, and the historic combination of these forces put an end to the production of that sort of tragedy which we associate with Shakespeare.

Notes

INTRODUCTION

[1] Herbert Weisinger, in "The Renaissance Theory of the Reaction against the Middle Ages as a Cause of the Renaissance," *Speculum*, XX (1945), 461–67, and "Renaissance Accounts of the Revival of Learning," *Studies in Philology*, XLV (1948), 105–18, gives a sampling of humanistic opinion as to the revolutionary novelty of the period. The early humanists in fact constituted a clique "one of whose principal activities was self-praise"; it has been said that the original reputations of Agricola, Free, Tiptoft, Grocyn, Linacre, Lily, and Pace can be accounted for only as products of a narrow humanistic *Zeitgeist*. H. A. Mason, *Humanism and Poetry in the Early Tudor Period* (London, 1959), p. 28; C. S. Lewis, *English Literature in the Sixteenth Century* (Oxford, 1954), pp. 20–25; and Paul G. Kristeller, *Renaissance Thought: The Classic, Scholastic, and Humanist Strains* (New York, 1955), p. 17. In recent decades, the Renaissance myth has been largely dispelled by the "revolt of the medievalists." See W. P. D. Wightman, *Science and the Renaissance* (London, 1962), p. 6.

[2] Lewis, *English Literature in the Sixteenth Century;* Theodore Spencer, *Shakespeare and the Nature of Man* (New York, 1943); Geoffrey Bush, *Shakespeare and the Natural Condition* (Cambridge, Mass., 1956); E. M. W. Tillyard, *The Elizabethan World Picture* (London, 1943), and *The English Renaissance: Fact or Fiction?* (London, 1952); Willard Farnham, *The Medieval Heritage of Elizabethan Tragedy* (Oxford, 1956); W. C. Curry, *Shakespeare's Philosophical Patterns* (Baton Rouge, La., 1936); Samuel Bethell, *The Cultural Revolution of the Seventeenth Century* (London, 1951); A. O. Lovejoy, *The Great Chain of Being* (Cambridge, Mass., 1936); Hardin Craig, *The Enchanted Glass* (New York, 1936); Douglas Bush, *The Renaissance and English Humanism* (Toronto, 1939); F. P. Wilson, *Elizabethan and Jacobean* (Oxford, 1945); Howard Baker, *Induction to Tragedy* (New York, 1939).

[3] *Nature*, in *Recently Discovered "Lost" Tudor Plays*, ed. John S. Farmer (London, 1907), pp. 41–133.

[4] Gregory Baum, "Protestants and Natural Law," *The Commonweal*, LXXIII (Jan. 20, 1961), 427–30.

[5] Louis Bredvold, *The Intellectual Milieu of John Dryden* (Ann Arbor, Mich., 1943); Alfred Harbage, *Shakespeare and the Rival Traditions* (New York, 1952); Hiram Haydn, *The Counter-Ren-*

aissance (New York, 1950); Herschel Baker, *The Wars of Truth* (Cambridge, Mass., 1952). Baker's book is especially valuable; I have drawn upon it freely.

[6] Una Ellis-Fermor, *Jacobean Drama* (London, 1953), p. 4.

[7] The phrase is used by Chapman's "Senecal" hero Clermont (*The Revenge of Bussy D'Ambois*, III. iv. 161) in a specifically Stoic sense which perhaps postulates a cosmic view somewhat more grim than the typical Elizabethan one. *The Plays of George Chapman*, ed. Thomas Marc Parrott (New York, 1961), I, 117.

[8] Frank H. Ristine, *English Tragicomedy: Its Origin and History* (New York, 1910); Eugene M. Waith, *The Pattern of Tragicomedy in Beaumont and Fletcher* (New Haven, Conn., 1952); Marvin T. Herrick, *Tragicomedy: Its Origin and Development in Italy, France, and England* (Urbana, Ill., 1962).

[9] A distinction invaluable to the discussion of tragedy is made by these largely self-explanatory terms. Richard Sewall adopts them from R. P. Blackmur in a discussion of tragedy in Sewall's article "The Tragic Form," *Essays in Criticism*, IV (Oct. 1954), 345–58. Blackmur defines executive form as "our means of getting at . . . and then making something of . . . theoretic form," which is "what we feel the form of life itself is."

[10] See J. V. Cunningham, "Tragedy in Shakespeare," *English Literary History*, XVIII (1951), 36–46, and "Woe and Wonder: The Emotional Effect of Shakespearean Tragedy," *Tradition and Poetic Structure* (Denver, Colo., 1960), chs. iii and iv. A "tragedy" meant, to the Elizabethans, a play ending in violent deaths. But it is misleading to accept Renaissance tragic theory as more than superficially explanatory of Elizabethan tragic art. The dramatists' imaginative insights and their ethical and cosmological assumptions have small connection with the relatively naive theorizing of the period (with its insistence, for example, on didactic poetic justice) about the nature of tragedy.

[11] William Barrett, *Irrational Man* (New York, 1962), p. 51.

CHAPTER ONE

[1] See Wilson Knight, *The Wheel of Fire* (London, 1949), pp. 214ff., on this "purgatorial" element of the tragedy, and Robert Heilman, *This Great Stage* (Baton Rouge, La., 1948), pp. 31–32.

[2] Heilman, *This Great Stage*, pp. 287–91; A. C. Bradley, *Shakespearean Tragedy*, 2d ed. (New York, 1967), pp. 279, 304, 325–27; E. E. Stoll, *Art and Artifice in Shakespeare* (Cambridge, Eng., 1934), p. 165; Oscar J. Campbell, "The Salvation of Lear," *English Literary History*, XV (1945), 93, 109; J. Stampfer, "The Catharsis of *King Lear*," in *Shakespeare Survey*, XIII, ed.

A. Nicoll (Cambridge, Eng., 1960), pp. 1–10; Donald Stauffer, *Shakespeare's World of Images* (New York, 1949); H. S. Wilson, *On the Design of Shakespearean Tragedy* (Toronto, 1957). All find a note of "exaltation" in the play's end, although this depends, for several of them, on the uncertain interpretation that Lear dies thinking Cordelia is alive—a point not crucial to the kind of reconciling or cathartic power in which I am interested.

³ Fulke Greville, *Mustapha*, IV. iv. 105. *Poems and Dramas of Fulke Greville, First Lord Brooke*, ed. Geoffrey Bullough (London, n.d.), II.

⁴ *Bussy D'Ambois*, V. ii. 1–58. *The Plays of George Chapman*, ed. Thomas Marc Parrott (New York, 1961), I, 63–64.

⁵ *Tamburlaine: Part One*, II. vii. 21–22, in *The Complete Plays of Christopher Marlowe*, ed. Irving Ribner (New York, 1963).

⁶ The same is true, says Tillyard, of Pauline theology. It is rarely mentioned because it is hardly ever questioned. *The Elizabethan World Picture* (London, 1943), p. 16. Lionel Trilling comments that it was Whitehead and Lovejoy who first "taught us to look not for the expressed but for the assumed ideas of an age, . . . the assumptions which appear so obvious that people do not know that they are assuming them, because no other way of putting things has ever occurred to them." *The Liberal Imagination* (New York, 1957), p. 184.

⁷ *Troilus and Cressida*, I. iii. 75–137. All Shakespeare quotations are from *The Complete Plays and Poems of William Shakespeare*, ed. William Allen Neilson and Charles Jarvis Hill (Boston, 1942).

⁸ See Lily B. Campbell, *Shakespeare's "Histories": Mirrors of Elizabethan Policy* (San Marino, Calif., 1947); E. M. W. Tillyard, *Shakespeare's History Plays* (New York, 1946), and Irving Ribner, *The English History Play in the Age of Shakespeare* (Princeton, N.J., 1957).

⁹ *Biathanatos*, ed. J. William Hebel (New York, 1930), p. 36.

¹⁰ Gregory Baum, "Protestants and Natural Law," *The Commonweal*, LXXIII (Jan. 20, 1961), 429.

¹¹ Jacques Maritain, *The Rights of Man and Natural Law*, trans. Doris C. Anson (New York, 1943), p. 62.

¹² *The Laws of Ecclesiastical Polity*, I. x. 10. *The Works of That Learned and Judicious Divine Mr. Richard Hooker*, ed. John Keble, rev. by R. W. Church and F. Paget (Oxford, 1888). All Hooker citations are from this edition.

¹³ *Summa Theologica*, trans. The English Dominican Fathers (London, 1916–1935), I–II. xciv. 4. All Aquinas citations are from this edition.

[14] *The Complete Poems of Sir John Davies,* ed. A. B. Grosart (London, 1876), I, 20.

[15] *A Discourse of Conscience,* 2d ed. (John Legat, 1597), p. 80. Perkins was a Church of England Calvinist, a moderate Tudor Puritan who influenced both English and American religion. His frequent scholasticisms, like this one, which persist in the teeth of a belief in predestination and imputed righteousness, testify to the tenacity of the medieval disciplines.

[16] See Aquinas, *Summa Theologica,* I–II. xciii. 3, and xciv, and Hooker, *Laws,* I. viii. 4, 8.

[17] Gierke affirms that according to medieval theory, "the rules of Natural Law . . . ought to be modified and developed, amplified and restricted, regard being had to special cases. In this sense a distinction was often drawn between the immutable first principles and the mutable secondary rules, which might even be regarded as bearing an hypothetical character." Otto Gierke, *Political Theories of the Middle Age,* trans. F. W. Maitland (Cambridge, Eng., 1958), p. 76. Donne, attacking not the natural law but its abuses in rigid sectarian oversimplification ("and so every sect will a little corruptly and adulterously call their discipline Natural Law,") says that "though our substance of nature . . . may not be changed, yet *functio Naturae,* (which is the exercise and application thereof)" and deduction thence may and must. *Biathanatos,* p. 46. Both Hooker and Thomas Smith say of the state that natural law can give no specific guidance as to which "kind of regiment" is best. *Laws,* I. x. 5, 9, and *The Common Wealth of England* (London, 1601), ch. 15.

[18] T. E. Davitt, "St. Thomas Aquinas and the Natural Law," in *Origins of the Natural Law Tradition,* ed. A. L. Harding (Dallas, Tex., 1954), p. 45.

[19] *Troilus and Cressida,* I. iii. 75–137. A few scenes later, Hector appeals to the distributive justice which "Nature craves," to "this law/of nature . . . these moral laws/of Nature and of nations." When these are "corrupted through affection," he says, positive law must be invoked in their support.

[20] Charles L. Black, Jr., "The Two Cities of Law," *Saturday Evening Post,* April 2, 1966, pp. 32, 101–104.

[21] Baum, "Protestants and Natural Law," and Leo R. Ward, "The Natural Law Rebound," *The Review of Politics,* XXI (1959), 114–30. Kant, says Ward, rejected nature as a basis of law, turning to a priori rules of conduct which disregarded it. Hobbes experimented with the idea of nature; Hume attacked it; finally Sartre said man has no nature. Ethical relativism reached a high point in Ruth Benedict's influential *Patterns of Culture* (1934). In the same period, positivism told us that "law is the power to enforce law," and spoke of natural law as "this pale moonshine of metaphysics, which never had scientific reality." More re-

cently, anthropologists have again found some empirical basis for belief in a universally human nature and law. Another historian of ideas remarks that Kant segregated natural law (as belonging to merely phenomenal reality) in order to escape the implications of mechanistic science. Leonard Krieger, "Kant and the Crisis of Natural Law," *Journal of History of Ideas*, XXVI (1965), 191–210. It might be added that Walter Lippmann's "Public Philosophy" in his 1955 book of that title is the philosophy of natural law, that the Nuremberg judges generally assumed a natural-law position, and that C. S. Lewis' 1947 Riddell Lectures (published as *The Abolition of Man*) constitute a strong defense of the primary axioms of practical reason—the natural law—which Lewis here prefers to call "The Tao." Louis Bredvold, surveying the twentieth-century revival of natural law, concluded, in 1954, that "the supposedly dead theory is now vigorously alive." *"Jus Naturale Redivivum," History of Ideas Newsletter*, I (1954), 3–7. Yet at present, even within its traditional stronghold of Roman Catholic thought, the doctrine is again in retreat, before existential "situation ethics" and hostility to the "Hellenic" and to all "conceptualism." Yet there is little opposition between situation ethics and an authentic idea of natural law, which has the openness to the concrete and existent aimed at by the situationists. Recent science (*vide* the "new biology" and the radical changes in evolutionary thought) makes it plain that much of human nature is still undiscovered. The implications of this may yet be recognized if the idea of natural law can be saved from misuse. Mechanical interpretations, especially biologism in sexual ethics, have discredited it; in the reaction, the baby may once again be thrown out with the bathwater.

[22] *Pilgrim of the Absolute*, ed. Raissa Maritain, trans. John Coleman and Harry L. Binsse (New York, 1947), p. 274.

[23] Cf. Francis Fergusson, *The Idea of a Theatre* (New York, 1953), p. 53, and Alfred North Whitehead, *Science and the Modern World* (New York, 1935), pp. 14–15, on the likeness of this sort of tragedy to science. Aeschylus, Sophocles, and Euripides, says Whitehead, are "the pilgrim fathers of the scientific imagination."

[24] Northrup Frye, "A Conspectus of Dramatic Genres," *Kenyon Review*, XIII (Autumn, 1951), 543–62. In *The Anatomy of Criticism* (Princeton, N. J., 1957), Frye has distinguished five kinds of tragic fictions, according to the "height" of their persons. A tragedy may involve the persons of myth or romance, or of "high mimetic," "low mimetic," or ironic art. What he calls "high mimetic" tragedy—that in which the persons are superior in degree but not in kind to other men—is the central or at least the Shakespearean type considered here, although it is in "low

mimetic" or domestic tragedy, according to Frye, that the sense of the supremacy of natural law is always clear.

[25] Roy W. Battenhouse, *Marlowe's Tamburlaine: A Study of Renaissance Moral Philosophy* (Nashville, Tenn., 1941), sees *Tamburlaine* as a tragedy in this pattern. Marlowe's ironic view of Christianity is undeniable; he may be added to the list of those (including Lucretius, Valla, Machiavelli, Hobbes, Mandeville, and Marx) who have thought religion an opiate administered to the many by the few. But the antireligious attitude corroborated by Kyd's and Baines' letters need not imply a rejection of the natural law, which was always seen as common to Christian and pagan, and as antedating Christianity. Resignation from the Medical Association does not imply a denial of the germ theory. Marlowe's normative plays may not be *about* the nemesis of lawless and limitless aspiration: they draw their deepest vitality from the magnificence of titanic human energy. But lawlessness and excess is, in them, its own nemesis: Tamburlaine becomes a creature of fortune, and Faustus' emancipation, appealing as it is made to be, is a snare.

[26] Bradley's ontological confusion of literary characters with historical persons led, no doubt, to some egregious critical blunders. Yet his influence has now survived the countermovements and actual attacks of T. S. Eliot, G. Wilson Knight, and the New Critics; of Caroline Spurgeon and the Imagists; of E. E. Stoll and the historical critics, especially Lily B. Campbell. F. R. Leavis wrote in 1952 that "not only Bradley but, in its turn, disrespect for Bradley (one gathers) has gone out of fashion."

[27] *Laws*, I. viii. 9. My italics. Cf. Thomas Beard: "a certaine knowledge and judgement of good and evil, which being naturally engraved in the tables of man's heart, is commonly called the law of nature." *The Theatre of God's Judgements* (London, 1597), p. 9. "The divine law which we call morall is nothing else but a testimonie of the law of nature." Pierre de La Primaudaye, *The French Academie* (London, 1594), pp. 601–602. "Nature in man's heart her lawes doth pen," which "*accuse,* or else *excuse* all men,/For every thought or practise, good or ill." *Nosce Teipsum*, in *The Complete Poems of Sir John Davies*, ed. Alexander B. Grosart (London, 1876), I, 77.

[28] Called by Hooker "The greatest amongst the School-divines." *Laws*, III. ix. 2.

[29] Ibid. V. Appendix i. 1–5, 19–29. Hooker responds here to the Calvinist doctrines concerning divine prescience, predestination, and grace.

[30] A commonplace repeated endlessly in plays, poems, sermons, prose tracts, and hexameral and encyclopedic literature. There is a typical statement of it in Erasmus' *Enchiridion*, trans. Miles

Coverdale, in *Writings and Translations of Myles Coverdale*, ed. G. Pearson (Cambridge, Eng., 1844), p. 502. Hooker bitterly protests the Puritan attack on reason. *Laws*, III. viii. 3–10. Our belief in revelation, he points out, must be held in and by natural reason (although a different solution was open to those who rejected the scholastic cosmology in favor of earlier Augustinian Platonism and its doctrine of "illumination").

[31] *Laws*, III. v. 1. and x. 7—xi. 6. Old Testament law was often divided into moral, judicial, and ceremonial categories. The first was still binding, being in harmony with nature and the New Testament: the second was to be used as convenient; the third was quite obsolete. If the second commandment forbade images in Jewish temples, said Parker, "they are not lawful in the churches of the Christians. For being a moral commandment, and not ceremonial, . . . it is a perpetual commandment." *The Correspondence of Matthew Parker, D. D., Archbishop of Canterbury* (Cambridge, Eng., 1853), p. 81. Milton divides Jewish law into political and moral, "which contains in it the observation of whatsoever is substantially and perpetually true and good," and this we also have from "those unwritten laws and ideas which nature doth engrave in us," as well as from the gospel. *The Reason of Church Government Urged against Prelaty*, I. iii. *The Student's Milton*, ed. F. A. Patterson (New York, 1930), p. 510.

[32] *Laws*, I. Table of Contents.

[33] Aquinas, *Summa Theologica*, I. lxxv. 4: "it is clear that man is not a soul only, but something composed of soul and body. —Plato, through supposing that sensation was proper to the soul, could maintain man to be a soul making use of the body." Cf. Etienne Gilson, *The Spirit of Medieval Philosophy* (London, 1936), pp. 174ff. Harry K. Russel, in "Elizabethan Dramatic Poetry in the Light of Natural and Moral Philosophy," *Philological Quarterly*, XII (1933), 187–95, discusses the importance to Elizabethan drama of this belief.

[34] Cf. Aquinas, *Summa Theologica*, I. lxxv. 3. reply obj. 1. "Although man is of the same *genus* as other animals, he is of a different species." Tillyard agrees that Hamlet's praise of man is "very medieval" and that on the other hand, the spirit of the thirteenth-century *Dies Irae* would have appealed strongly to the Calvinists, who were, he says, a "small, though vigorous minority" in the Renaissance. *The English Renaissance: Fact or Fiction?* (London, 1952), p. 23. But during the Jacobean period, the aspects of Calvinism which are revelant here became in fact almost universal.

[35] See Albert Plé, "St. Thomas and the Psychology of Freud," *Crosscurrents*, IV (1954), 327–48.

[36] *The Spirit of Medieval Philosophy*, p. 251. According to St.

Thomas, says D'Arcy, "we misconceive human nature when we imagine the soul to be complete and human by itself." M. C. D'Arcy, *St. Thomas Aquinas* (London, 1953), p. 13.

[37] *The Spirit of Medieval Philosophy*, p. 420. "The tradition," says Gilson, "goes back to the remotest antiquity. . . . Tertullian left the Church as soon as he came to the conclusion that the human body is bad in itself," p. 125.

[38] Hooker, *Laws*, I. vii. 3–4, and Donne, *Biathanatos*, p. 40: "the nature of every thing is the forme by which it is constituted, and . . . to do against it, is to do against nature. Since also this forme in man is reason . . . to commit against reason is to sin against nature."

[39] "Evil," says Aquinas, "is the absence of the good, which is natural and due to a thing." *Summa Theologica*, I. xlix. 1. See also *Summa Contra Gentiles*, trans. The English Dominican Fathers (London, 1938), III, 3–36, and Hooker, *Laws*, I. viii. 1.

[40] Aquinas, *Summa Theologica*, I. cxv. 3–6, and *Truth*, trans. Robert W. Mulligan, James V. McGlynn, and Robert W. Schmidt (Chicago, 1952–1954), Q. XXII. Art. 9. Heavenly bodies and physical temperament incline the will, but it can overcome these impediments. Erasmus, in his *Enchiridion* (translated by Coverdale in 1545), takes the same orthodox position, referring to the disposing influence of planets, bodily complexions, national characteristics, and age. *Writings and Translations of Myles Coverdale*, ed. Pearson. Ficino's belief is essentially the same. See D. C. Allen, *The Star-Crossed Renaissance* (Durham, N. C., 1941), pp. 18–19. See also R. C. Bald " 'Thou, Nature, Art My Goddess': Edmund and Renaissance Free-Thought," *Joseph Quincy Adams Memorial Studies* (Washington, D. C., 1948), pp. 337–49. Mr. Bald describes Shakespeare's attitude toward astrology: "While he would have hesitated to deny that the stars could affect men's lives, there is nothing to suggest that he had so much faith in their influence as to deny the freedom of the will. Free will is the essence of tragedy."

[41] *The Mirror for Magistrates*, ed. Lily B. Campbell (Cambridge, Eng., 1938), pp. 171–72.

[42] Michael Macklem, *The Anatomy of the World* (Minneapolis, Minn., 1958), pp. 55ff.

[43] *Laws*, I. iii. 3.

[44] Gilson, *The Spirit of Medieval Philosophy*, pp. 113–15; Macklem, *The Anatomy of the World*, p. 6. The moderately Calvinistic Nowell's *Catechism* taught that original sin had affected the "whole order of nature" and that "other creatures also incurred that pain which man deserved." Alexander Nowell, *A Catechism Written in Latin by Alexander Nowell, Dean of St. Paul's: Together with the Same Catechism Translated into English by Thomas Norton*, ed. G. E. Corrie (Cambridge, Eng., 1853), p. 150.

[45] H. B. Charlton, *Shakespearean Tragedy* (Cambridge, Eng., 1948), p. 234.

[46] *Shakespeare's Tragic Heroes: Slaves of Passion* (New York, 1952).

[47] Miss Campbell refers to Thomas Wright, Timothy Bright, Thomas Newton, F. N. Coeffeteau, and other Renaissance writers on the humors and passions, remarking incidentally that Aquinas' division and classification of the passions generally persisted. *Shakespeare's Tragic Heroes*, p. 69. See also Lawrence Babb, *The Elizabethan Malady* (East Lansing, Mich., 1951), and G. F. Sensabaugh, *The Tragic Muse of John Ford* (Stanford, Calif., 1944), ch. ii.

[48] "In Shakespeare," says Charlton, "there is no hard and fast dichotomy between body and soul." *Shakespearean Tragedy*, p. 232.

[49] *The Medieval Heritage of Elizabethan Tragedy* (Oxford, 1956), pp. 290ff.

[50] "The Epistle Dedicatorie," *A Treatise of Melancholy*, ed. Hardin Craig (New York, 1940). Here Bright claims also to have "layd open howe the bodie, and corporall things affect the soule, & how the body is affected of it againe." He in fact devotes several chapters to the question.

[51] In *The Castle of Perseverance*, Stulticia is both worldly and spiritual "Folye," and the "same sentiments" may be found in Medwall's *Nature*, Rastell's *The Interlude of the Four Elements*, Skelton's *Magnygycence*, Lydgate's *Order of Fools*, Copland's *Hye Way to the Spytlel Hous*, and Brant's *Das Narrenschiff*. Paul R. Baumgartner, "From Medieval Fool to Renaissance Rogue: *Cocke Lorelles Bote* and the Literary Tradition," *Annuale Medievale*, IV (1963), 57–91. "To religious moralists such as Brant and Barclay," Miss Welsford says, "A knave was simply a fool regarded 'sub specie eternitatis.' " Enid Welsford, *The Fool: His Social and Literary History* (London, 1935), p. 237.

[52] Nature in Lydgate's poem explicitly teaches that reason and nature are ever in accord—that the dominion of reason is universal to all of nature. Ernst Sieper, ed., *Lydgate's Reson and Sensuallyte*, Early English Text Society LXXXIV (London, 1901), ll. 878–79 et passim. The same doctrine is expounded by Aquinas, *Summa Theologica*, I. lxxxi and I–II. xxiv.

[53] See John Calvin, *Institutes of the Christian Religion*, ed. John Allen, 7th American ed. (Philadelphia, 1936), II. iii. 1–5. All references to the *Institutes* are to this edition.

[54] There was another, narrower, medieval tradition of Christian Faith as a "folly," stemming from 1 Cor. 1:18–27 and 3:18–19. But it is the paradox of the cross which is "to the gentiles foolishness," and the wisdom with which St. Paul's preaching conflicts is false wisdom. The medieval Franciscan

idea of the "fool for Christ," although it uses the term somewhat paradoxically, and means by folly chiefly simplicity and the exaltation of love over learning, does show an opposition of natural and supernatural orders; and of course that strain was never absent from Christianity. Holiness could be seen as a deviation from the rational norm which rose above that norm, as sin fell below it.

[55] Barbara Swain, *Fools and Folly during the Middle Ages and the Renaissance* (New York, 1932), pp. 192–93.

[56] *The Order of Fools*, in *The Minor Poems of John Lydgate*, ed. H. N. MacCracken. Early English Text Society orig. ser. 192 (London, 1934), II, 449–55.

[57] Puritan industry, frugality, and severity may have aided historically the creation of capital, but not from any conscious belief that the spiritual and natural orders were at one. The Calvinist revolution on just this point helped to transform the drama. In any case, although worldly success was perhaps an evidence of election and godliness in "Puritan" belief, it was not so in authentic Calvinism. Puritanism is not identical with theological Calvinism; it antedates it, Tyndale and Luther having been true Puritans, and it sometimes differs with it. "Even tough Calvinism," says Knappen, "was bent backward when it met the irresistible force of the Puritan conscience," which insisted on a severe rule of moral rectitude basically incongruous with the emphasis on predestination and justification by faith. M. M. Knappen, *Tudor Puritanism: A Chapter in the History of Idealism* (Chicago, 1939), p. 341. There were Anglican, Presbyterian, and Congregationalist "Puritans": the term, first used by the separatists and then by their opponents (as an English equivalent of *Cathar*), belongs really to the partisan strife of the time, and not to theology.

[58] See Karl Rahner and Herbert Vorgrimler, *Concise Theological Dictionary*, trans. Cornelius Ernst (London, 1965), p. 490.

[59] *English Miracle Plays Moralities and Interludes*, ed. A. W. Pollard (Oxford, 1954), p. 71.

[60] II. ii. 218–22. *Gorboduc; or Ferrex and Porrex*, in *Specimens of the Pre-Shakespearean Drama*, ed. J. M. Manley (Boston, 1904), II, 224.

[61] *Medieval Heritage*, p. 219.

[62] See Aquinas, *Summa Theologica*, I–II. lxxviii–ix, and I. xlix. 1; *Truth*, XXIV, art. 2, reply; and Hooker, *Laws*, I. vii. 6.

[63] "The Monk's Tale" in *The Works of Geoffrey Chaucer*, ed. F. N. Robinson (Boston, 1957), p. 189.

[64] *Troilus and Criseyde*, IV, 940–1078.

[65] See Gilson, *The Spirit of Medieval Philosophy*, p. 359, and D. W. Robertson, Jr., "Chaucerian Tragedy," *English Literary History*, XIX (1952), 1–37. Robert O. Payne, in *The Key of Re-*

membrance: A Study of Chaucer's Poetics (New Haven, Conn., 1963), pp. 122ff., discusses the importance attached by Chaucer to the "lawe of kynde" in *The Book of the Duchess.*

[66] Dante, *The Divine Comedy: The Inferno,* Canto VII, circle iv.

[67] *Summa Theologica,* I. cxv. 3, 4, 6; cxvi. 1; and *Truth,* XXII.

[68] *Summa Theologica,* I. cxv. 4. reply obj. 3.

[69] St. Thomas recognizes the common identification of these in his treatment of the claim that "fate is nothing else than *a disposition of the stars under which each one is begotten or born,*" ibid., I. cxvi. 1. Chaucer, too, tends to identify "Fortune, executrice of wyrdes" with the "influences of thise hevenes hye." *Troilus and Criseyde,* III. 617–18. The power of the stars is connected with the humors, which have celestial correspondences and affinities. The idea is unchanged, and is succinctly stated, in Fulke Greville's *Mustapha* (1609): "For as soules, made to raigne, when they let downe their State/Into the bodies humors, straight those humours give them fate." (Chorus Quartus, ll. 49–50.) *Poems and Dramas of Fulke Greville, First Lord Brooke,* ed. Geoffrey Bullough (London, n.d.), II, 122.

[70] *Hamlet,* III. iv. 87–88.

[71] *Antony and Cleopatra,* III. xiii. 3–4.

[72] A. P. D'Entreves, *Natural Law: An Introduction to Legal Philosophy* (New York, 1951), p. 36.

[73] *The White Devil,* V. vi. 259–60. Shakespeare shows an alert sense that the customs and practices of public life, while giving lip service to the natural-law morality, often operate on Machiavellian or Hobbesian principles—on the basis of "commodity." The tension between ideal norms and social actualities appears strikingly in the person of Falconbridge, in *King John.* But even in his speeches, such "commodity" is seen as the perverter of an underlying good order which is natural; not till such characters as Bosola and Flamineo is there an open conflict of opposed laws and knowledges.

[74] Pierre de La Primaudaye, *The Second Part of the French Academie* (London, 1594), p. 327. See also *The French Academie* (London, 1594), pp. 67–68, 406–407.

[75] The original formulation of natural-law ideas had been that of Cicero and the Roman jurists, whose conceptions of natural law were oriented toward its civil and juridical implications. Faced with a need to administer law to various conquered lands, Roman legal philosophy found that "there were certain universal and eternal principles of equity and justice common to all legal systems." Robert N. Wilkin, "Cicero and the Law of Nature," *Origins of the Natural Law Tradition,* ed. A. L. Harding (Dallas, Tex., 1954). At the same time Greek Stoicism was introduced to Rome (notably by Cicero), encompassing a view of natural law alike in some ways to that which Aquinas and Hooker would

take. "True law," says Cicero, "is right reason in agreement with nature; it is of universal application, unchanging and everlasting. . . . Whoever is disobedient is fleeing from himself and denying his human nature, and by reason of this very fact he will suffer the worst penalties, even if he escapes what is commonly called punishment." *The Republic*, III. xxii, *Cicero: De Re Publica and De Legibus*, trans. C. W. Keyes (Cambridge, Mass., 1928), p. 211.

CHAPTER TWO

[1] Herschel Baker, *The Wars of Truth* (Cambridge, Mass., 1952), p. 366.

[2] Aquinas, *Summa Theologica*, I. lxxv, and Hooker, *Laws*, I. iii. 4.

[3] This conception of what is natural now occurs almost exclusively in religious discussion. What Paul Tillich calls the "formal concept" of nature—nature as distinguished from the unnatural and the supernatural, but including mind and spirit—is the medieval and early Renaissance sense of the term. What Tillich calls the "material concept" of nature—i.e., the concept excluding everything in which freedom is involved—is the modern concept which originates in the early seventeenth century. Tillich, *The Protestant Era*, trans. James Luther Adams (Chicago, 1948), p. 99.

[4] See Fredson Bowers, "Hamlet as Scourge and Minister," *PMLA*, LXX (1955), 740–49, and G. R. Elliott, *Scourge and Minister: A Study of Hamlet as Tragedy of Revengefullness and Justice* (Durham, N. C., 1951). The view that Hamlet's human nature has indeed the tragic flaw of its kind, and that evil is seen in the play as neither capricious nor inescapable by man, is verified by such particular historical explications of *Hamlet* as Bowers' reconstruction of the theme of "minister and scourge" with its issue of "public" and "private" revenge (which specifies both the Hegelian idea of the conflict of public and private motives and the Freudian idea of the conflict of id and superego).

[5] Cf. Hooker, *Laws*, I. vi. 4. "Education and instruction are the means, the one by use, the other by precept, to make our natural faculty of reason both the better and the sooner able to judge rightly between truth and error, good and evil." God gave us, said Lipsius, the necessary tools, but it is education which completes our ability to live by our (rational) nature. See Hiram Haydn, *The Counter-Renaissance* (New York, 1950), p. 470. This view follows inevitably from the Aristotelian-Thomistic tenet that a nature is defined by its end, by that toward which it moves in perfecting itself.

⁶ This was explicit in, e.g., Medwall's *Nature*. Cf. *The Winter's Tale*, IV. iv. 89–96: "Nature is made better by no mean/But Nature makes that mean; . . . the art itself is Nature."

⁷ Robert Heilman, *This Great Stage* (Baton Rouge, La., 1948), p. 119.

⁸ See John Danby, *Shakespeare's Doctrine of Nature: A Study of King Lear* (London, 1949), pp. 19–20. Danby's excellent treatment of this element in the play is quite complete. I turn to *King Lear* not because I can add much to what he has said, but because the play is almost indispensable to any review of my subject in this chapter, and such a review is desirable background against which to distinguish the revolutionary aspects of later Jacobean drama.

⁹ R. C. Bald " 'Thou Nature, Art My Goddess': Edmund and Renaissance Free-Thought," *Joseph Quincy Adams Memorial Studies* (Washington, D. C., 1948), pp. 337–49.

¹⁰ Cf. Danby, *Shakespeare's Doctrine of Nature*, Part II, ch. v.

¹¹ *Shakespeare and the Nature of Man* (New York, 1943), p. 143.

¹² *This Great Stage*, p. 119.

¹³ Henry B. Charlton, *Shakespearean Tragedy* (Cambridge, Eng., 1949), pp. 222–23.

¹⁴ Walter C. Curry, *Shakespeare's Philosophical Patterns* (Baton Rouge, La., 1937), pp. 126–27. See also Charlton, *Shakespearean Tragedy*, pp. 187–88, for a tracing of the same pattern of internal and "natural" retribution to a Stoic source.

¹⁵ *Summa Theologica*, I–II. lxxvii. 1.

¹⁶ There is a parallel to this narrative premise of *Macbeth* in Elizabeth's long refusal to name a successor, and her explanation that one would need to "honour as angels any with such piety that when they were second in the realm would not seek to be first." J. E. Neale, *Elizabeth I: A Biography* (Garden City, N. Y., 1957), p. 150.

¹⁷ *Shakespeare's Philosophical Patterns*, pp. 126–27.

¹⁸ *Shakespearean Tragedy*, pp. 20, 21, 271, 282–83.

¹⁹ See Lily B. Campbell, "Concerning Bradley's Shakespearean Tragedy," *Huntington Library Quarterly*, XIII (1949), 1–18, and "Bradley Revisited: Forty Years After," *Studies in Philology*, XLIV (1947), both of which are reprinted as appendixes in Lily B. Campbell, *Shakespeare's Tragic Heroes: Slaves of Passion* (New York, 1952).

²⁰ E. E. Stoll, *Hamlet: An Historical and Comparative Study* (Minneapolis, Minn., 1919), and *Shakespeare Studies, Historical and Comparative in Method* (New York, 1928). Roy W. Battenhouse, in "Hamlet's Apostrophe on Man, Clue to the Tragedy," *PMLA*, LXVI (1951), 1073–1113, suggested that Hamlet's tragic flaw is original sin—a conception which fits conveniently here, but seems somewhat strained.

²¹ We might note, too, that the Machiavellian and Marlovian sense of *virtu* (power) is not unrelated to the Scholastic conception of *virtue*, for a *virtue* in the Scholastic tradition was conceived as the "perfection of a power." (Aquinas, *Summa Theologica*, I–II. lvi. 1, 3; lxxi. 1.) *Virtue*, then, meant not only rectitude but also the development of powers by their exercise in accord with nature. "Health and beauty are habits of the body. . . . other habits have for subject the faculties or powers of the soul, and as these naturally tend to action, the habits related to them perfect them in their very dynamism, are operative habits; such are the intellectual and moral virtues." Jacques Maritain, *Art and Scholasticism* (New York, n.d.), pp. 8–9. Vice, says Pierre de La Primaudaye, is the sickness, and virtue the health, of the powers of the soul. *The French Academie* (London, 1594), p. 64. In medieval medicine, too, the term *virtu* means "effective power." The etymological sense of the word is retained, in differing ways, in each of its Renaissance senses.

²² "The Idea of Equality," *Proper Studies* (London, 1949).

²³ A notable exception is W. H. Auden's "Commentary on the Poetry and Tragedy of 'Romeo and Juliet,'" *Romeo and Juliet*, ed. C. J. Sisson (New York, 1958), pp. 21–39.

²⁴ See Hooker, *Laws*, I. x. 4: "to fathers within their private families Nature hath given a supreme power." "Nature and the law which preserveth nature" command obedience to parents. Primaudaye, *The French Academie*, p. 537. See also Thomas Beard, *The Theatre of God's Judgements* (London, 1597), pp. 199–236. The Elizabethan sources which might be quoted on this point are virtually endless.

²⁵ *Gorboduc; or Ferrex and Porrex*, in *Specimens of the Pre-Shakespearean Drama*, ed. J. M. Manley (Boston, 1904), II, 223–24.

²⁶ III. i.

²⁷ See Bernard Breyer, "A New Look at Julius Caesar," in *Essays in Honor of Walter Clyde Curry*, ed. Richard C. Beatty and others (Nashville, Tenn., 1954), pp. 161–80.

²⁸ Familiarity with the conventions of the Vice and the "slanderer believed" no doubt help us with the play, but not in the sense which some scholarship has implied, that the very existence of such conventions explains their use and their meaning in the work of which they become functional parts.

²⁹ II. iii. 218–20; III. iv. 5–6; II. i. 166–67.

³⁰ *Timon of Athens*, IV. i. 19–21.

³¹ Aristotle makes essentially the same point in his discussion of the tragic flaw and its consequences. It has often been objected that the Greek idea of *hamartia*, "missing the mark," is radically different from the Christian concept of sin, or disobedience to divine command. One of the values of a proper attention

to the natural-law basis of Christian morality as it is stated by Hooker is to show that the two are actually not dissimilar, and that their likeness provides a sound basis for an Aristotelian criticism of Shakespeare.

[32] See Hooker, *Laws*, I. vii. 7.

[33] This is perhaps the main reason for the critical tradition, seen at its clearest in Schücking, but still extant, that the Cleopatra of the last act is another woman from the Cleopatra of acts I–IV.

[34] Hooker, *Laws*, I. 6–8; and see Sir John Fortescue's fifteenth-century work *A Commendation of the Laws of England*, trans. Francis Grigor (London, 1917), ch. xv. Mulcaster translated Fortescue's *De Laudibus Legum Angliae* into English in 1576.

[35] E. M. W. Tillyard, *Shakespeare's History Plays* (New York, 1946), p. 320.

[36] Ibid., p. 23.

[37] See Lily B. Campbell, *Shakespeare's "Histories": Mirrors of Elizabethan Policy* (San Marino, Calif., 1947), p. 16.

[38] Jacques Maritain, *The Rights of Man and Natural Law* (London, 1944), pp. 39–40, and Hooker, *Laws*, I. x. 5–9.

[39] In *Certaine Sermons or Homilies Appointed To Be Read in Churches in the Time of the Late Queene Elizabeth of Famous Memory* (London, 1635).

[40] The importance of this is emphasized by Elyot, Raleigh, Davies, Spenser, Raymond de Sebonde, and many others. See E. M. W. Tillyard, *The Elizabethan World Picture* (London, 1943), chs. ii and iv. Aquinas says, "Now every natural governance is governance by one. In the multitude of bodily members there is one which is the principal mover, namely the heart; and among the powers of the soul one power presides as chief, namely the reason. Among bees there is one king bee, and in the whole universe there is one God. . . . it follows that it is best for a human multitude to be ruled by one person." *On Kingship*, ed. I. T. Eschmann, trans. Gerald B. Phelan (Toronto, 1949), I. ii. 9. (St. Thomas may not have written all this work; portions may represent the contribution of a pupil.)

Donne speaks of

> . . . Courts, whose Princes animate,
> Not only all their house, but all their State.
> Let no man thinke, because he is full, he hath all,
> Kings (as their patterne, God) are liberall
> Not onely in fulnesse, but capacitie.

"Eclogue," ll. 41–45, in *The Poems of John Donne*, ed. Herbert Grierson (London, 1953), I, 133, and of "My Kingdome, safliest when with one man man'd." "Elegy XIX," l. 28. *Poems*, I, 120.

See also "The First Anniversary," ll. 123–24. *Poems*, I, 235. Elyot, in the *Book Named the Governor*, ticks off all the standard analogies, from beehive to solar system. The hive image recurs in *Henry V*, I. ii. 187–204, and *Troilus and Cressida*, I. iii. 81. See Gierke, *Political Theories of the Middle Age*, trans. F. W. Maitland (Cambridge, Eng., 1927), p. 8.

[41] Hooker, *Laws*, I. viii. 3. "For that which all men have at all times learned, Nature herself must needs have taught."

[42] See, e.g., Hooker, *Laws*, I. x. 9.

[43] Edmund Forset, *A Comparative Discourse of the Bodies Natural and Politique* (1606) in James Winney, *The Frame of Order* (London, 1957), pp. 91–93.

[44] See *Julius Caesar*, II, i, 67–69; *Coriolanus*, I. i. 99–158; and Donne's "A Funerall Elegie," ll. 21–26. *Poems*, I, 246.

[45] *Of English Dogs, the Diversities, the Names, the Natures and the Properties. A Short Treatise Written in Latin by Johannes Caius* (1536) . . . *and Newly Drawn into English by Abraham Fleming*. 1576. *Social English Illustrated. An English Garner*, IX, 144.

[46] *Henry IV*, First Part, II. iv. 299.

[47] John Davies, *Nosce Teipsum*, in *The Complete Poems of Sir John Davies*, ed. Alexander B. Grosart (London, 1876), I, 22.

[48] *Bartas: His Divine Weekes and Workes* (1605), trans. Joshua Sylvester (Gainesville, Fla., 1965), pp. 193–94.

[49] See Victor Harris, "Allegory to Analogy in the Interpretation of Scriptures," *Philological Quarterly*, XLV (1966), 5–6.

[50] Stephen Manning, *Wisdom and Number: Toward a Critical Appraisal of the Middle English Religious Lyric* (Lincoln, Nebr., 1962), p. 94.

[51] *Macbeth*, II. iv. 10–18.

[52] Quoted in Winney, *The Frame of Order*, p. 13.

[53] Ibid.

[54] *The Poetical Works of Edmund Spenser*, ed. J. C. Smith and E. De Selincourt (New York, 1947), p. 407.

[55] *Laws*, I. x. 5. "Opinions about the relation between natural and positive law continued to be more fluid, and more uncertain, in the sphere of public than they were in that of private law," says Gierke. "We accordingly find a number of jurists going to the length of maintaining that the whole distinction [between uniform natural elements and variable positive elements] had no application to *public law*, and that public law, on the contrary, was entirely and totally positive." There was "a far greater latitude of discussion on questions of public law then had ever previously been possible in the sphere of civilian theory." Otto Gierke, *Natural Law and the Theory of Society 1500–1800. With a Lecture on the Ideas of Natural Law and Humanity by Ernst Troeltsch*, trans. Ernest Barker (Boston, 1957), pp. 37–39.

[56] *The Common Wealth of England* (London, 1601), ch. xv.

[57] Filmer, *Patriarcha and Other Political Works*, ed. Peter Laslett (Oxford, 1949). On Bodin, see J. W. Allen, *A History of Political Thought in the Sixteenth Century* (London, 1928), ch. viii, especially pp. 416-17.

[58] *On Kingship*, I. 49.

[59] Ibid., I. 47.

[60] Lily B. Campbell, *Shakespeare's "Histories,"* p. 176.

[61] *Laws*, VIII. ii. 9. Actually, these statements are not entirely contradictory. Gierke, citing numerous medieval texts, says that in the political theory of the Middle Ages, hereditary rule might be validly created by a grant of lordship to a family, originating the right of "hereditary birth" of which Hooker speaks, but that "the Elective principle was preferable, being in fuller accord with Divine and Natural Law." *Political Theories*, p. 42.

[62] *De Legibus*, trans. C. W. Keyes (Cambridge, Mass., 1959), p. 461.

[63] Aquinas, *On Kingship*, I. 2–7. *Summa Theologica*, I–II. lxxii. 4. Hooker, *Laws*, I. x. 1, 4, 5. See Gierke, *Political Theories*, p. 4.

[64] *Laws*, I. x. 1.

[65] Hooker, *Laws*, VIII. ii. 18, and I. x. 1. Aquinas, *On Kingship*, I. i. 10, 13; I. iii. 23, 24, 26; and I. ii. 17.

[66] Aquinas, *On Kingship*, I. ii. 17–20, and I. i. 9.

[67] Hooker, *Laws*, I. x. 4.

[68] Aquinas, *On Kingship*, I. ii. 17. See also *Summa Theologica*, I. ciii. 3.

[69] Hooker, *Laws*, VIII. ii. 9, and I. x. 8.

[70] Ibid., VIII. ii. 11–13.

[71] *On Kingship*, I. iii. 23, 24.

[72] *Political Theories*, pp. 34–35. And see Sir Thomas More, *Utopia*, Bk. I (New York, 1937), p. 39. "The comminaltie chueseth their king for their owne sake and not for his sake." Erasmus, in *The Education of a Christian Prince* and Primaudaye in *The French Academie* make exactly the same distinction between tyrant and king. The prince, says Thomas Beard, is subject to the "Lawes of man and of nature." *The Theatre of God's Judgements*, p. 12.

[73] Gierke, *Political Theories*, p. 2.

[74] Ibid., p. 75.

[75] Ibid., p. 81.

[76] *The Common Wealth*, I. xii.

[77] Ibid., I. viii.

[78] Ibid., I. x.

[79] Ibid., VIII. ix. 3.

[80] *"An Homily against Disobedience, and Wilful Rebellion: The First Part"* in *Certaine Sermons or Homilies*, p. 279.

[81] *Laws*, VIII. ix. 2.

[82] Ibid., I. x. 1.

[83] Ibid., VIII. ix. 3.

[84] See F. J. Shirley, *Richard Hooker and Contemporary Political Ideas* (London, 1949), pp. 143–53.

[85] Allen, *A History of Political Thought in the Sixteenth Century*, pp. 416–17.

[86] Ibid., p. 393. Not until later years, evidently, was it said, as by Charron, that the king is "the author and founder" of law in the state. Pierre Charron, *Of Wisdome*, trans. Samson Lennard (London, 1651), p. 24. Charron was a French priest whose *Sagesse* had some influence in England.

[87] *On Kingship*, I. iii. 26.

[88] Hooker, *Laws*, VIII. ii. 11.

[89] Tyranny, says Aquinas, is to be tolerated by private persons because of the evils attendant on deposition, which if it cannot be avoided must be undertaken by public authority in the public interest (*On Kingship*, I. iv. 47–49). Hooker is even more reluctant to admit the right of the people to resume the effective sovereignty which they have resigned forever in the original "compact" of the state. Sir Robert Filmer represents in England the Royalist extreme which held all deposition criminal and sacrilegious. See Filmer, *Patriarcha and Other Political Works*.

[90] The gardener of York Castle, like the Duke of Burgundy in *Henry V* and Friar Lawrence in *Romeo and Juliet*, comments by a vegetable analogy on the failure of "the wasteful king" to manage the "sea-walled garden" of the commonwealth by a firm and prudent discipline (III. iv. 29–66).

[91] Shakespeare gives voice in the play to other views, but this general import is clear. Richard is one of a series of kings variously unfitted for rule, in both histories and tragedies. Una Ellis-Fermor remarks a difference in the two kinds of plays: the histories ask "What does the state require of the man who rules it?" The tragedies "What does the state make of the man who rules it?" By this measure too, *Richard II* is both.

[92] *Summa Theologica*, I–II. lxxv. 1, and lxxvii. 4.

[93] Ibid., I–II. lxxvii. 4.

[94] Ibid., I–II. lxxvii. 1, 2, and lxxviii. 3.

[95] Ibid., I–II. lxxv. 2.

[96] Ibid., I–II. lxxviii. 2.

[97] Ibid., I–II. lxxviii. 1.

[98] Hooker, *Laws*, I. vii. 6.

[99] John Marston, *The Dutch Courtesan*, ed. M. L. Wine (Lincoln, Nebr., 1965), II. i. 80–81.

CHAPTER THREE

[1] W. C. Curry, *Shakespeare's Philosophical Patterns* (Baton Rouge, La., 1936), pp. 3–137.

[2] Alfred Harbage, *Shakespeare and the Rival Traditions* (New York, 1952), p. 135.

³ Paul G. Kristeller, *Renaissance Thought: The Classic, Scholastic, and Humanist Strains* (New York, 1955), pp. 33, 34.

⁴ Joseph Glanville, *Scepsis Scientifica: or, Confest Ignorance, the Way to Science; in an Essay of the Vanity of Dogmatizing, and Confident Opinion* (London, 1665), II, 6.

⁵ *Of Education,* in *The Student's Milton,* ed. F. A. Patterson (New York, 1930), p. 727.

⁶ *The Reason of Church Government,* in *The Student's Milton,* ed. F. A. Patterson (New York, 1930), p. 538.

⁷ Don Cameron Allen, *Doubt's Boundless Sea* (Baltimore, Md., 1964), p. 136.

⁸ See Ernst Cassirer, *The Platonic Renaissance in England,* trans. James P. Pettegrove (Austin, Tex., 1953), p. 17.

⁹ See Eduard L. Surtz, " 'Oxford Reformers' and Scholasticism," *Studies in Philology,* XLVII (1950), 547–56. On the scholastic disciplines of seventeenth-century Cambridge, see James B. Mullinger, *The University of Cambridge from the Royal Injunction of 1535 to the Accession of Charles the First* (Cambridge, Eng., 1884), and William T. Costello, *The Scholastic Curriculum at Early Seventeenth-Century Cambridge* (Cambridge, Mass., 1958).

¹⁰ Dorothy Bethurum, "Chaucer's Point of View as Narrator in the Love Poems," *PMLA,* LXXIV (1959), 512.

¹¹ Cf. George Saintsbury, *A History of Criticism and Literary Taste in Europe from the Earliest Texts to the Present Day* (London, 1900), p. 18.

¹² See Kristeller, *Renaissance Thought,* pp. 48–51. "Hardly a single notion which we associate with Plato," says Kristeller, "has been held by all Platonists."

¹³ C. S. Lewis, *English Literature in the Sixteenth Century* (Oxford, 1954), p. 10.

¹⁴ Ibid., pp. 51–54, and Cassirer, *The Platonic Renaissance in England,* pp. 9–10, 25ff.

¹⁵ See E. M. W. Tillyard, *The Elizabethan World Picture* (London, 1943), pp. 37–38.

¹⁶ *English Literature in the Sixteenth Century,* p. 10. But see Cassirer, *The Platonic Renaissance in England,* pp. 105, 111.

¹⁷ See John Rickaby, *General Metaphysics* (London, 1925), p. 31.

¹⁸ See, e.g., Edgar Wind, *Pagan Mysteries of the Renaissance* (London, 1958).

¹⁹ "The Scholastic Background of Marsilio Ficino," *Traditio,* II (1944), 257–318.

²⁰ Kristeller, *Renaissance Thought,* pp. 262–27.

²¹ Kristeller, "The Scholastic Background of Marsilio Ficino," p. 267.

²² Ibid., p. 260.

²³ Kristeller, *Renaissance Thought,* pp. 43–44.

²⁴ *English Literature in the Sixteenth Century*, pp. 1–65.

²⁵ *The Seventeenth Century Background* (New York, 1958), p. 18.

²⁶ While disclaiming "illusions as to the extent and quality of medieval science," Gilson points out that the medieval conception of natures and nature laid the basis for the inductive method. He protests some literary-historical treatments of medieval thought: "to go to the authors of Lapidaries and Bestiaries, as some well-known philologists have done, would be like going to an almanac-maker for the contemporary scientific astronomy." *The Spirit of Medieval Philosophy* (London, 1936), p. 365.

²⁷ M. C. D'Arcy, *St. Thomas Aquinas* (London, 1953), pp. 200–201. See also Gordon Leff, *Medieval Thought: St. Augustine to Ockham* (Baltimore, Md., 1958), p. 14.

²⁸ *The Seventeenth Century Background*, pp. 14ff.

²⁹ See Richard P. Adams, "Emerson and the Organic Metaphor," *PMLA*, LXIX (1954), 117–30.

³⁰ Pierre Teilhard de Chardin, *The Phenomenon of Man* (New York, 1959), p. 41.

³¹ Ibid., p. 110.

³² Ibid., p. 83.

³³ Ibid., p. 150.

³⁴ Marjorie Nicolson, *The Breaking of the Circle* (New York, 1960), p. 122. See also pp. 123–46.

³⁵ *Shakespeare's Philosophical Patterns*, pp. 20–21.

³⁶ Ibid., p. 22.

³⁷ *The Medieval Heritage of Elizabethan Tragedy* (Oxford, 1956), pp. 124–36.

³⁸ It is a measure of the flourishing philosophical contentions of the time that Aristotle and Thomism encountered severe rebuffs before establishing themselves as the standard of thought, partly because the Averroistic Aristotelianism of Siger of Brabant had confirmed the suspicions of the Augustinian-traditional Parisian theologians. Bans on the teaching of Aristotle were issued at Paris in 1210, 1215, and 1231. In 1277, the Parisian Bishop Etienne Tempier condemned, among a total of 219 theses, some of the chief propositions of Thomism, including individuation by matter, the influence of the body upon the soul's operations, and the control of will by intellect. Two thirteenth-century Archbishops of Canterbury condemned significant elements of Aquinas' philosophy. See Leff, *Medieval Thought*, p. 236.

³⁹ A substance is the subject, not the sum, of its properties; it is "that which stands under the manifold appearances." Aquinas, *Summa Theologica*, I. xxix. 1, 2; xxxi. 1, 2; xxiv. 3; xl. 3.

⁴⁰ *Medieval Heritage*, pp. 21–23. Farnham remarks in passing that "it is thus one distinction of St. Thomas Aquinas to have

prepared a part of the way for Shakespearean tragedy." p. 216.

[41] Maurice De Wulf, *History of Medieval Philosophy* (New York, 1920), I, and *Medieval Philosophy* (Cambridge, Mass., 1922), pp. 8–45, 66–79. Frederick Copleston, *A History of Philosophy* (London, 1953), II. Thomas Aquinas, *Concerning Being and Essence*, trans. G. G. Leckie (New York, 1937).

[42] Aquinas, *Summa Theologica*, I–II. lviii. 1.

[43] This hylomorphism is apparently first presented by Aquinas in his commentary on Aristotle's physics. On intellection, see *Summa Theologica*, I, 84–85.

[44] *Summa Theologica*, I. lxxxiv. 1.

[45] Aquinas, *Summa Theologica*, I. xxix. 1. reply obj. 5; I–II. lxxv-lxxvi, esp. lxxvi, 1; and see Gilson, *The Spirit of Medieval Philosophy*, p. 25.

[46] Aquinas, *Summa Theologica*, I. lxxxix. 1; Rickaby, *General Metaphysics*, p. 104; Leff, *Medieval Thought*, p. 222.

[47] Cf. Gibson, *The Spirit of Medieval Philosophy*, pp. 194–96. Scotus held the *haecceitas* of the individual to lie in an "ultima realitas entis" of matter, form, and their *compositum*. C. R. S. Harris, *Duns Scotus* (New York, 1959), II, 93–97.

[48] Gilson, *The Spirit of Medieval Philosophy*, pp. 199–200.

[49] Aquinas, *Summa Theologica*, I. lxxv. 4; I. l. 4; I–II. 63. 1; and *Truth* II. 6, 7.

[50] Stephen Chak Tornay, *The Nominalism of William of Ockham* (Chicago, 1936), pp. 251–55.

[51] Heinrich Rommen, *The Natural Law*, trans. Thomas R. Hanley (St. Louis, Mo., 1948), p. 60.

[52] *Summa Theologica*, I. lxxv, lxxvi; and see Hooker, *Laws*, I. iii. 4. n. 1. "The Intellectual principle is the form of man."

[53] *Summa Theologica*, I–II. xciv.

[54] Ibid., I. lxxx. 1–2; I. lxxviii. 1; I–II, xciv. 4; III. xci. 6.

[55] See Thomas E. Davitt, "St. Thomas Aquinas and the Natural Law," *Origins of the Natural Law Tradition*, ed. A. L. Harding (Dallas, Tex., 1954), p. 29. Cf. Cicero, *De Legibus*, pp. 347–49.

[56] *Summa Theologica*, I–II. xciv. 2. This question discusses man as a rational substance, touching on the several areas of human natural law.

[57] Raleigh, in his *History*, gives an Elizabethan definition of natural law which corresponds with this Thomistic one in every particular. "The law of nature in general, I take to be that disposition, instinct, and formal quality, which God in His eternal providence hath given and imprinted in the nature of every creature, animate and inanimate." *Works of Sir Walter Raleigh* (Oxford, 1829), III, 105. Hooker of course follows Aquinas closely.

[58] From the *Nichomachean Ethics* onward, Aristotelian tradition held the natural end of life to be virtue, the perfection of the

human powers in accord with reason, so that virtue is the health and vice the sickness of the soul. Cf. Primaudaye, *The French Academie* (London, 1594), p. 64.

[59] *Summa Theologica*, I–II. xciv. 4, 5, and xcvii. 4, reply obj. 3. See also xcv. 2. reply obj. 3; xciv. 4; and xciii. 3.

[60] *Summa Theologica*, I–II. xci. 2. Scholasticism, says Gilson, required man to be a "collaborator" and not merely an instrument. *The Spirit of Medieval Philosophy*, pp. 371–74, 381–82. In *Summa Theologica*, I–II. xciii. 6, Aquinas distinguishes participation in law by "inward motive principle" from participation by understanding.

[61] *Summa Theologica*, I–II. xci. 2. reply obj. 3.

[62] *Truth*, trans. Robert W. Mulligan, James V. McGlynn, and Robert W. Schmidt (Chicago, 1952–54), II, 300–11; and *Summa Theologica*, I–II. xciv. 1. reply obj. 2.

[63] *Summa Theologica*, I–II. xciv. 2.

[64] Ibid., I–II. xciv. 4, and xcv. 2. reply obj. 3.

[65] Michael Novak, review of *Philosophy in the Mass Age*, by G. P. Grant, *The Commonweal* (April 29, 1960), pp. 131–32.

[66] *The Natural Law*, p. 45.

[67] Donald H. Johnson, "The Ground for a Scientific Ethics According to St. Thomas," *The Modern Schoolman*, XL (1963), 349.

[68] *Summa Theologica*, I. lxxix. 1, and xciv. 1.

[69] Ibid., I–II. lxxi. 3.

[70] "Vertue is a proportion and uprightness of life in all points agreeable to reason." Primaudaye, *The French Academie*, p. 53. "For the Laws of well-doing are the dictates of right Reason." Hooker, *Laws*, I. vii. 4. Primaudaye answers objections to the use of reason in religious questions (based on St. Paul's warning against philosophy) with the observation that St. Paul clearly refers to erroneous philosophy, and the mark of this is its disagreement with revelation.

[71] Whitehead, *Science and the Modern World* (New York, 1935), p. 12.

[72] See Joseph Pieper, *Scholasticism* (New York, 1960), p. 45.

[73] *Laws*, viii. 4–9. Perhaps the process actually began much earlier: "Never again, after 1277, shall we see quite the same confidence in reason's ability to know that which was a matter of belief. Full tide had been reached and now it was slowly on the ebb." Leff, *Medieval Thought*, p. 231.

[74] Aquinas, *Summa Theologica*, I–II. cix. 2; and Hooker, *Laws*, V. appendix i. 2.

[75] *Summa Theologica*, II–II. ii. 3–4. "Virtue is natural to man inchoatively" (I–II. lxiii. 1) but, of the moral virtues, "man needs to be perfected by other . . . principles in relation to his supernatural end" (I–II. lxiii. 3). These are the theological virtues.

[76] "St. Augustine finds fault with [Pelagius] for ignoring the fact of sin, but not for saying that nature is a grace." Gilson, *The Spirit of Medieval Philosophy*, p. 379.

[77] *Summa Theologica*, I. xlix. 1. In *Summa Contra Gentiles* (III. vii), Aquinas says that evil is "the privation of what is connatural and due to anyone . . . now privation is not an essence, but is *the non-existence of something in a substance*. Therefore evil is not a real essence."

[78] *Summa Theologica*, I–II. lxxix. 1, 2.

[79] *Summa Contra Gentiles*, I. lxxii, lxxiii.

[80] Aquinas, *Summa Theologica*, I. lxxxii. 2. obj. 3, and reply obj. 3; I–II. lxxviii. 2; lxxviii. 1, 3. *Truth*, xxiv, art. 2, reply (p. 146). Hooker follows closely: "For evil as evil cannot be desired." *Laws*, I. vii. 6.

[81] Something can be learned about medieval cosmology from the chapter titles of the *Summa Contra Gentiles:* "That Every Agent Acts for an End"; "That Every Agent Acts for a Good"; "That Evil Is Unintentional in Things"; "That Evil Is Not an Essence"; "That the End of Everything Is a Good." There is vast distance between these propositions and the resurgent world-hatred of Calvinism.

CHAPTER FOUR

[1] See, e.g., *Institutes*, IV. xx. 16, on the moral law.

[2] E.g., Hooker, *Laws*, V. Appendix i. 39, on predestination. Aquinas' treatment of this question is actually in substantial agreement with Augustine, although the subject itself occupies a lesser place in Aquinas' theology.

[3] *Summa Contra Gentiles*, I. lxxxiv. See also Hooker, *Laws*, V. Appendix i. 22.

[4] *De Jure Belli ac Pacis*, I. i. x. Quoted in A. P. D'Entreves, *Natural Law: An Introduction to Legal Philosophy* (New York, 1951), p. 53.

[5] *Summa Contra Gentiles*, III. i. 64.

[6] *Truth*, XXIV. 2. reply.

[7] See C. R. S. Harris, *Duns Scotus* (New York, 1959), I, 177–87; Heinrich Rommen, *The Natural Law*, trans. Thomas R. Hanley (St. Louis, Mo., 1948), p. 58; Gilson, *The Spirit of Medieval Philosophy* (London, 1936), pp. 309–10.

[8] Meyrich H. Carre, *Realists and Nominalists* (London, 1946), p. 115.

[9] Stephen Chak Tornay, *Ockham: Studies and Selections* (La-Salle, Ill., 1938), pp. 126–28.

[10] Ibid., p. 180.

[11] Gilson, *The Unity of Philosophical Experience* (New York, 1950), p. 85.

[12] Leff, *Medieval Thought: St. Augustine to Ockham* (Baltimore, Md., 1958), p. 289, and Carre, *Realists and Nominalists*, p. 116.

[13] *The Natural Law*, pp. 5, 9.

[14] Tornay, *Ockham: Studies and Selections*, pp. 180–81. Robert Holcot's *Commentary on the Sentences* faces the same implications of theological voluntarism: "God can love the sinner more than [the saint]"; He can deceive; men may achieve spiritual merit by falsehood and may fail of any reward although they fulfill the divine laws. See Leff, *Medieval Thought*, p. 292, and Donne, *Biathanatos*, ed. J. William Hebel (New York, 1930), p. 36: "Many things which we call sin, and so evill have been done by the commandment of God." Aquinas considers the same problem in *Summa Theologica*, I–II. c. 8, with quite different conclusions. See also Robert Hoopes, "Voluntarism in Jeremy Taylor and the Platonic Tradition," *Huntington Library Quarterly*, XIII (1950), 341–54, on the voluntarism of Taylor and its antecedents in Luther and others.

[15] Herschel Baker, *The Wars of Truth* (Cambridge, Mass., 1952), pp. 142–43.

[16] Ibid., p. 145.

[17] *Truth*, XXIII. 6. Quoted in *The Dream of Descartes*, trans. Mabelle J. Anderson (New York, 1944), p. 147.

[18] *Summa Theologica*, I–II, xc. 1.

[19] *Laws*, I. ii. 5.

[20] John Dillenberger, *God Hidden and Revealed* (Philadelphia, 1953), p. 42.

[21] *Table Talk*, CXVIII, in Hugh T. Kerr, ed., *A Compend of Luther's Theology* (Philadelphia, 1943), p. 27.

[22] Roland Bainton, *The Reformation of the Sixteenth Century* (Boston, 1952), p. 24.

[23] *Smalcald Articles*, Part III, sec. I, in Kerr, *A Compend of Luther's Theology*, p. 84.

[24] *The Wars of Truth*, p. 25.

[25] Ibid., p. 36.

[26] *Selection of the Most Celebrated Sermons of John Calvin* (Philadelphia, 1856), p. 23.

[27] *Institutes*, II, iii. 1.

[28] Ibid., II. iii. 2, 5. See also II. ii. xix.

[29] See Alfred Harbage, *Shakespeare and the Rival Traditions* (New York, 1952), pp. 152–54.

[30] *The Jacobean Drama* (London, 1953), pp. 61–62.

[31] III. iv. 59–65. *The Plays of George Chapman*, ed. Thomas Marc Parrott (New York, 1961).

[32] *The Enchanted Glass* (New York, 1936), p. 137.

[33] *The Tragic Muse of John Ford* (Stanford, Calif., 1944), pp. 13–93.

[34] See Peter G. Phialas, *Shakespeare's Romantic Comedies* (Chapel Hill, N. C., 1966).

[35] The "moral decadence" of Jacobean drama is one of the most venerable of critical commonplaces. Fletcher, Shirley, Ford, and the rest have for centuries been said to have pandered to a jaded audience, requiring ever more powerful sensational stimulants. See, e.g., William A. Neilson's comments in the *Cambridge History of English Literature;* Ashley Thorndike, *Tragedy* (New York, 1908); and Tucker Brooke, *The Tudor Drama* (New York, 1911).

[36] Donne's "Confined Love" expresses the same ideas.

[37] Harbage, *Shakespeare and the Rival Traditions*, pp. 159–60. The passage from *The Dutch Courtesan* continues, "(*O Miseri quorum gaudia crimen habent!*)/Sure nature against virtue cross doth fall,/Or virtue's self is oft unnatural." John Marston, *The Dutch Courtesan*, ed. M. L. Wine (Lincoln, Nebr., 1965), II, i. 79–81.

[38] William Haller, *The Rise of Puritanism* (New York, 1957), pp. 19, 49–50. See also Roland Bainton, *The Reformation of the Sixteenth Century*, pp. 79–80; John T. McNeill, *The History and Character of Calvinism* (New York, 1954), p. 314; M. M. Knappen, *Tudor Puritanism: A Chapter in the History of Idealism* (Chicago, 1939), p. 349.

[39] *The Wars of Truth*, p. 191.

[40] "Calvinism," *The Hastings Encyclopedia of Religion and Ethics* (New York, 1908–1927), III, 154.

[41] And in fact, Luther and Zwingli were as firm as Calvin on predestination and other doctrines which we usually identify with Calvinism.

[42] See Jackson T. Cope, "Joseph Glanville, Anglican Apologist: Old Ideas and New Style in the Restoration," *PMLA*, LXIX (1954), 223–50, and Baker, *The Wars of Truth*, p. 37.

[43] Knappen, *Tudor Puritanism*, p. 370.

[44] McNeill, *The History and Character of Calvinism*, pp. 310, 313–14.

[45] Alexander Nowell, *A Catechism Written in Latin by Alexander Nowell, Dean of St. Paul's: Together with the Same Catechism Translated into English by Thomas Norton*, ed. G. E. Corrie (Cambridge, Eng., 1853), p. 138.

[46] See E. J. Bicknell, *A Theological Introduction to the Thirty-nine Articles of the Church of England* (London, 1955).

[47] Translator's Preface, *Institutes*, I, 8.

[48] John Marston, *The Scourge of Villanie*, ed. G. B. Harrison (New York, 1925), IV, ll. 115–29.

[49] Ibid., l. 143.

[50] Ibid., VII, ll. 66–67.

[51] Ibid., ll. 192–202.

[52] Ibid., VIII, ll. 165–72, 185–93, 201–203.

[53] *Institutes*, III. xxiii. 2.

[54] And see III. xxi. 7: "the gate of life is closed by a just and irreprehensible, but incomprehensible, judgement." Also II. xxiii. 8: "For the first man fell because the Lord had determined it was so expedient. . . . it is certain that he determined thus, only because he foresaw it would tend to the just illustration of the glory of his name." In III. xxii. 9, Calvin pours scorn on the distinction ("petty sophism") by which Aquinas had preserved the possibility of free will and control of one's own destiny.

[55] *Institutes*, III. xxiii. 2.

[56] Ibid., III. xxii. 11.

[57] Bright, *A Treatise of Melancholy*, ed. Craig, pp. 102, 187.

[58] Hooker, for instance, is very explicit that God's will ends not in will but in reason, with no diminution of divine freedom. *Laws*, I. ii. 5.

[59] See Tornay, *Ockham: Studies and Selections*, pp. 71–72.

[60] A. P. D'Entreves, *Natural Law*, p. 70. And see Richard S. Westfall, *Science and Religion in Seventeenth-Century England* (New Haven, Conn., 1958), p. 6: "Calvin's emphasis on God's irrationality found its source among the scholastic nominalists."

[61] *Institutes*, I. xvii.

[62] E.g., in II. iii. 5.

[63] *Laws*, V. Appendix i. 20–21.

[64] Otto Gierke, *Political Theories of the Middle Ages*, trans. F. W. Maitland (Cambridge, Eng., 1958), p. 99.

[65] *Institutes*, I. xvi. 2.

[66] Ibid., I. xvi. 3.

[67] Ibid., I. xvi. 4.

[68] Ibid., I. xvi. 8.

[69] See Ernst Cassirer, *The Platonic Renaissance in England*, trans. James P. Pettegrove (Austin, Tex., 1953), p. 81.

[70] *An Elegant, and Learned Discourse of the Light of Nature* (London, 1661), p. 16. The book was written earlier, and the first edition was published posthumously in 1652.

[71] M. M. Knappen, ed., *Two Elizabethan Puritan Diaries* (Chicago, 1933), pp. 60, 65, 76, 91, 93. The quotations are from the diary of Richard Rogers, written in the late 1580's.

[72] A similar punishment—a deadly "fire from heaven"—is reported in Shakespeare's *Pericles* (II. iv) to have been sent by the "most high gods" as vengeance on the incest of King Antiochus, who is here a minor character. It is unlikely, however, that Shakespeare had much to do with the first two acts of this play, which is in many ways closer to the Jacobean tragicomic mode than to the highly symbolistic Shakespearean dramatic romances which it is said to presage.

[73] Natural-law theory originated in Stoicism, but Christianity early adopted it; it was taught by St. Paul (see Rommen, *The*

Natural Law, p. 35) and reached its height in Scholasticism. When a critic notes, in relation to *Lear,* that "the essential unity and divinity of nature in its cosmic, moral and psychological aspects is . . . a familiar concept of Stoic philosophy," he seems to choose the less obvious of two Renaissance influences. If the beliefs embodied in *Lear* are Stoicism, it is of the sort virtually identical with traditional Scholasticism. Keith Rinehart, "The Moral Background of King Lear," *University of Kansas City Review,* XX (1954), 223–28.

[74] See Baker, *The Wars of Truth,* p. 38; and see A. S. P. Wodehouse, "Nature and Grace in the Faerie Queene," *English Literary History,* XVI (1949), 192–228, for an exposition of Spenser as a Christian humanist in the older tradition.

CHAPTER FIVE

[1] *Ductor Dubitantium,* II. i. 35. Quoted in Herschel Baker, *The Wars of Truth* (Cambridge, Mass., 1952), pp. 234–36.

[2] Ibid., II. i. 31, quoted in Baker, p. 237.

[3] *Patriarcha and Other Political Works,* ed. Peter Laslett (Oxford, 1949), p. 96.

[4] See Louis Bredvold, *The Intellectual Milieu of John Dryden* (Ann Arbor, Mich., 1934), p. 21.

[5] See Jackson T. Cope, "Joseph Glanville, Anglican Apologist: Old Ideas and New Style in the Restoration," *PMLA,* LXIX (1954), 229–30.

[6] *An Elegant, and Learned Discourse of the Light of Nature* (London, 1661), ch. xviii.

[7] Ibid., ch. i.

[8] Ibid., pp. 39–40.

[9] Ibid.

[10] Ibid.

[11] Ibid.

[12] Ibid.

[13] Ibid.

[14] Ibid.

[15] William Haller, *The Rise of Puritanism* (New York, 1957), pp. 75–77.

[16] *Of Wisdome,* trans. Samson Lennard (London, 1651), p. 246.

[17] Ibid., pp. 260–61.

[18] Rene Descartes, *Reply to Objections, VI. The Philosophical Works of Descartes,* trans. Elizabeth S. Haldane and G. R. T. Ross (Cambridge, Eng., 1911–1912), II, 248.

[19] Ernst Cassirer, *The Platonic Renaissance in England,* trans. James P. Pettegrove (Austin, Tex., 1953), p. 41.

[20] See Baker, *The Wars of Truth,* pp. 125, 215–16, and Cassirer, *The Platonic Renaissance in England,* passim.

[21] *The Platonic Renaissance in England,* p. 35.

[22] "An Address to the Royal Society," prefixed to *Scepsis Scientifica: or, Confest Ignorance, the Way to Science; in an Essay of the Vanity of Dogmatizing, and Confident Opinion* (London, 1665).

[23] Ibid.

[24] Richard S. Westfall, *Science and Religion in Seventeenth-Century England* (New Haven, Conn., 1958), p. 5. See also John Dillenberger, *Protestant Thought and Natural Science* (Garden City, N. Y., 1960), p. 86.

[25] *The Tragic Muse of John Ford* (Stanford, Calif., 1944), pp. 13, 15.

[26] Ibid., p. 22.

[27] *Institutes*, II. ii. 26. My italics.

[28] "An Inquisition upon Fame and Honour," Stanza 12. *Poems and Dramas of Fulke Greville, First Lord Brooke*, ed. Geoffrey Bullough (London, n.d.), I, 195.

[29] *The Cultural Revolution of the Seventeenth Century* (London, 1951), p. 58.

[30] Cf. ibid., p. 62.

[31] See Fulton H. Anderson, *The Philosophy of Francis Bacon* (Chicago, 1948), p. 3, and *Francis Bacon: His Career and Thought* (Los Angeles and Berkeley, 1962), pp. 24–25.

[32] *The Works of Francis Bacon*, ed. James Spedding, Robert Leslie Ellis, and Douglas Denon Heath (London, 1857–1861), VI, 469–70.

[33] *Advancement of Learning*, Bk. II, in ibid., III, 478–79.

[34] Ibid., pp. 478–80.

[35] *Advancement of Learning*, Bk. L. in ibid., pp. 296–97.

[36] See R. F. Jones, *Ancients and Moderns: A Study of the Background of the Battle of the Books*, "Washington University Studies," New Series, Language and Literature, No. 6 (St. Louis, Mo., 1936).

[37] Alfred North Whitehead, *Science and the Modern World* (New York, 1954), p. 80, and see Bethell, *Cultural Revolution*, p. 38.

[38] *Novum Organum*, Bk. II, xi–lii. *Works*, IV, 127–248. See esp. xviii. ff. for the "example of exclusion, or rejection of natures from the form of heat." Ibid., pp. 147ff. The frequent Baconian term "form" suggests a Scholastic conception of essence, but typically means only the mechanism of physical properties: "For he who knows the forms of yellow, weight, ductility, fixity, fluidity, solution, and so on," says Bacon, and how to "superinduce" them, can change other materials to gold. *Novum Organum*, Bk. II, v; ibid., p. 122. Bacon sometimes uses the term in other meanings as well, and without much consistency.

[39] See *Novum Organum*, Bk. II, ii: "And causes again are not improperly distributed into four kinds; the material, the formal,

the efficient and the final. But of these the final cause rather corrupts than advances the sciences." Ibid., pp. 119–20. And *Novum Organum*, Bk. I, xlviii: "Final causes . . . have relation clearly to the nature of man rather than to the nature of the universe; and from this source have strangely defiled philosophy." Ibid., p. 57. Also *Advancement of Learning*, Bk. II: "For the handling of final causes mixed with the rest in physical inquiries, hath intercepted the severe and diligent inquiry of all real and physical causes." Ibid., III, 357–58.

[40] Culverwell, for example, expresses the highest regard for "the great, and noble Verulam" in the course of his own philosophical re-creation of the Baconian dichotomized universe.

[41] Letter to Richard Bentley, Dec. 10, 1692. *The Correspondence of Richard Bentley*, ed. C. Wordsworth (London, 1842), I, 50.

[42] Ibid., p. 47.

[43] Letter to Richard Bentley, Jan. 17, 1692/3, ibid., p. 61.

[44] Ibid.

[45] Letter to Richard Bentley, Feb. 25, 1692, ibid., p. 70.

[46] *The Anatomy of the World* (Minneapolis, Minn., 1958), p. 65.

[47] The difference between this and Platonism is that the reality which this mechanism believes to underlie appearances is *physical*.

[48] *Summa Theologica*, I. xvii.

[49] *Principles of Philosophy*, LXIX–LXXI and IV. cxcviii. The *Philosophical Works of Descartes*, trans. Elizabeth S. Haldane and G. R. T. Ross (Cambridge, Eng., 1931), I, 248–50, 295–96.

[50] "Meditation VI," *Meditations on First Philosophy*, in ibid., I, 191.

[51] Ibid., p. 194.

[52] *The Passions of the Soul*, Art. XXIII, in ibid., I, 342.

[53] Charron, *Of Wisdome*, p. 49. Ralph Crum, in *Scientific Thought in Poetry* (New York, 1931), concludes that "Locke 'rudely shattered' the idea that man has a sure guide in his conscience" by denying innate ideas and making sensation the only source of knowledge. But the idea of conscience did not necessarily rest on a doctrine of innate ideas. The Scholastics had espoused a *tabula rasa* theory (and used the Latin phrase). See Aquinas, *Summa Theologica*, I. lxxix. 2. All knowledge, they said, begins in sense perception, but, as explained above, the universe thus perceived was really and objectively as it appeared to the senses; the sensible and intelligible orders cohered; nature and reason corresponded. The *tabula rasa* theory, then, does no violence to the idea of synderesis or an innate basis for conscience, except when combined with the division of mind or spirit from the body and its senses.

[54] See *The Passions of the Soul*, Arts. V, VI, in *Philosophical*

Works, I, 333, and *The Author's Reply to the Fifth Set of Objections*, in ibid., II, 208–209.

[55] *Meditations on First Philosophy*, Meditation VI ("Of the Existence of Material Things, and of the Real Distinction between the Soul and Body of Man"), in ibid., I, 190.

[56] Ibid., p. 189.

[57] *The Idea of a Theatre* (New York, 1953), p. 56.

[58] Clifford Leech, *John Webster: A Critical Study* (London, 1951), p. 56.

[59] Ibid., pp. 30, 56.

[60] Clifford Leech, *John Ford* (London, 1957), pp. 14, 22. In the same study, Leech notes that both Chapman and Ford give evidence of close familiarity with Bacon; p. 25.

[61] Ibid., p. 11.

[62] Sensabaugh sees Giovanni as Ford's sympathetic portrayal of a man powerless to control his acts, who is forced to follow his love-impulse, and "is crushed by a society that will not recognize his need and the inevitability of its assertion." *The Tragic Muse of John Ford*, pp. 171–73, 186–88.

[63] We might recall, besides Calvin, Luther's conviction that "the sexual instinct in man operates as an irresistible law of nature and tolerates no restriction in the form of vows." Hartman Grisar, *Luther*, ed. Arthur Preuss, trans. F. J. Eble (Westminster, Md., 1950), p. 510.

[64] William A. Robson, *Civilization and the Growth of Law* (New York, 1935), p. 199.

[65] Baker, *The Wars of Truth*, pp. 23–24.

[66] *Scepsis Scientifica*, pp. 15, 16.

[67] Baker, *The Wars of Truth*, p. 41.

[68] *The Everlasting Man* (New York, 1925), p. 130.

[69] From *Dialogues* (Frankfort, 1716), I, 156. Quoted in Bredvold, *The Intellectual Milieu of John Dryden*, p. 37.

[70] *The Works of Sir Walter Ralegh* (Oxford, 1829), VIII, 548–56.

[71] See Bredvold, *The Intellectual Milieu of John Dryden*, p. 87.

[72] *De Augmentis*, IX, in *Works*, X, 112.

[73] See Don Cameron Allen, *Doubt's Boundless Sea* (Baltimore, Md., 1964).

[74] *Bartas: His Devine Weekes and Works* (1605), trans. Joshua Sylvester (Gainesville, Fla., 1965), p. 550.

[75] See J. Huizinga, *The Waning of the Middle Ages: A Study of the Forms of Life, Thought, and Art in France and the Netherlands in the XIXth and XXth Centuries* (London, 1927), pp. 124–35, and Theodore Spencer, *Death and Elizabethan Tragedy* (Cambridge, Mass., 1936).

[76] Sermon XIV, Folio of 1649, in *The Sermons of John Donne*, ed. George R. Potter and Evelyn M. Simpson (Berkeley and Los Angeles, 1953–1962), III, 105.

[77] James Winney, *The Frame of Order* (London, 1957), p. 121.

[78] Baker, *The Wars of Truth*, p. 366.

CHAPTER SIX

[1] Heywood, Webster, Tourneur, Beaumont and Fletcher, and Ford are the playwrights chiefly studied in the following pages. Others such as Marston and Chapman are of equal interest, but limitation is necessary, and particular criticism must be illustrative rather than exhaustive of so general a phenomenon.

[2] Cf. Hardin Craig, "Ethics in Jacobean Drama: The Case of Chapman," *Essays in Dramatic Literature: The Parrott Presentation Volume* (Princeton, N. J., 1935), pp. 24–46, and *The Enchanted Glass: The Elizabethan Mind in Literature* (New York, 1936), p. 136.

[3] The will of man is not constrained, says Calvin, for it is moved from within, not by outside forces, so that a man's actions may be attributed to his will. Nevertheless, if he is not one of the predestined elect, there can be no possibility of his choosing good.

[4] Cf. Eugene Waith, *The Pattern of Tragicomedy in Beaumont and Fletcher* (New Haven, Conn., 1952).

[5] *Dodsley's Old English Plays*, ed. W. C. Hazlitt (London, 1874), II, 97.

[6] William Haller, *The Rise of Puritanism* (New York, 1957), p. 20.

[7] *The Countess of Pembroke's Arcadia*, III. 10. *The Complete Works of Sir Philip Sidney*, ed. Albert Feuillerat (Cambridge, Eng., 1912), I, 406.

[8] *The Complete Works in Verse and Prose of Samuel Daniel*, ed. A. B. Grosart (London, 1885–1896), I, 96.

[9] *Poems and Dramas of Fulke Greville, First Lord Brooke*, ed. Geoffrey Bullough (London, n.d.), II, 85.

[10] Ibid., I, 219–20.

[11] Some scholars would even label *Dr. Faustus* a Calvinistic play, because the hero's destiny turns upon a question of faith, there is a suggestion of predestination, evil is more prominent than goodness, and the spiritual worth of temporal activities is questioned. See David Kaula, "Time and the Timeless in *Everyman* and *Dr. Faustus*," *College English*, XXII (1960), 9–14. It must be admitted that a note of despair sounds in Marlowe's plays which is unlike anything in Shakespeare. Doctor Faustus, says Hiram Haydn, "depreciates . . . Aristotle's logic, through Ramus'; Galen's medicine, through Paracelsus'; Justinian's *Institutes* [behind which stood the natural law] through arguments like those of Agrippa; theology ('Divinitie' and 'Jerome's Bible') through Calvinism." *The Counter-Renaissance* (New York, 1950), p. 186.

[12] A. M. Clark, *Thomas Heywood, Playwright and Miscellanist* (Oxford, 1931), p. 91.

[13] Ibid., p. 6.

[14] Clark's comparison of these anonymous pamphlets with Heywood's *Life of Merlin* leaves small doubt of his authorship. Ibid., pp. 187–91.

[15] T. S. Eliot, *Elizabethan Essays* (London, 1934), p. 113.

[16] It seems that one reason why this pulpit morality is so large a part of early "domestic" tragedy is that it represents an instinctive effort to achieve the "magnitude" and seriousness otherwise achieved by the use of great or royal figures.

[17] *The Dramatic Works of Thomas Heywood*, ed. J. Pearson (London, 1874). All references are to this edition.

[18] E.g., Clark, *Thomas Heywood*, pp. 231–33.

[19] Ibid., p. 230.

[20] Calvin, *Institutes*, II. iii. 2.

[21] Ibid., II. v. 19.

[22] See Waith, *The Pattern of Tragicomedy in Beaumont and Fletcher*.

[23] See Roy W. Battenhouse, "Chapman and the Nature of Man," *English Literary History*, XII (1945), 87–107. Battenhouse finds this equally true of Chapman's characters and attributes it to his abandonment of the traditional Christian view under the influence of such writers as Plato, Plutarch, and Epictetus. In Chapman's philosophy, he says, "the body is not viewed as good, nor is the soul the 'form of the body' as for Aristotle and St. Thomas; instead, man is a Neoplatonic spirit imbedded uncomfortably in nature" (pp. 89–90). Battenhouse thinks that Cato's Stoic rejection of the natural world (in *Caesar and Pompey*) "makes of tragic catharsis a mockery" (p. 96). Surely this is true. Furthermore, Chapman's sundering of spirit from "carrion" body, and his abandonment of the natural order, although Stoic and Platonic in form, can hardly have been unconnected with Calvinist influences.

[24] See Bosola's truthful praise of Antonio to the Duchess in III. ii. 318–21. The speech is a trap, and thus makes explicit the element of almost wistful insight by which Bosola can perceive the good, though he must side with its enemies.

[25] *The White Devil*, in *The Complete Works of John Webster*, ed. F. L. Lucas (London, 1927), V. vi. 259–60.

[26] Cf. Lawrence Thompson, *Melville's Quarrel with God* (Princeton, N. J., 1952), p. 274. In *Pierre*, Melville speaks of an English ship in a Chinese port carrying Greenwich time on her chronometers. So, he says, the (Calvinist) Christian has in revealed morality and the example of Christ a "Heavenly chronometrical," a reminder of a distant heaven's different "time"; but one cannot arrange business in China according to English time,

and the Christian must manage his mundane affairs by the world's clocks, or else abandon worldly aims.

[27] Of the Vittoria of history, as seen by her contemporaries, this is equally true. Were it in her courage alone, says Lucas, "she was born for a heroine of Webster's worship." *The Complete Works of John Webster*, I, 85.

[28] "Characters of Dramatic Writers," *Works of Charles Lamb* (Boston, 1860), IV, 116.

[29] See I. i. 39–40; III. iii. 45–48, 59–64, for imagery associating the brothers with blackbirds, foxes, salamanders, porpoises; also V. ii. 348–52.

[30] Cf. the Calvinists Bacon and Greville:

> The World's a bubble; and the life of man
>   lesse then a span.
> In his conception wretched; from the wombe,
>   so to the tombe:
> Curst from the cradle . . .

"The Poems of Francis Bacon," *Miscellanies of the Fuller Worthies' Library*, Vol. I, ed. Alexander B. Grosart (London, 1870), p. 50.

> What are Mens lives, but *labyrinths of error*,
> *Shops of deceit*, and *Seas of misery?*
> Yet Death yields so small comfort, so much terror;
> *Gaine, Honour, Pleasure*, such illusions be;
> As though against life, each man whet his wit,
> Yet all Mens hearts, and sense, take part with it.

"An Inquisition upon Fame and Honour," stanza 1. *Poems and Dramas of Fulke Greville*, I, 192.

[31] *Institutes*, II. i. 7.

[32] Ibid., II. i. 8.

[33] Ibid., II. iii. 5.

[34] If St. Paul himself, in 1 Corinthians, takes a harsh view of physical love, he omits any condemnation of the body, and in Ephesians 5:25–33 gives his considered praise of sexual union.

[35] William Painter, "The Duchess of Malfy," *The Palace of Pleasure*, ed. Joseph Jacobs (London, 1890), III, 23.

[36] Ibid., p. 24. Painter takes this moralizing from Belleforest (*Histories Tragiques*, 1565), whose version was intermediary between Bandello's and his.

[37] "Fate and Chance in *The Duchess of Malfi*," *Shakespeare's Contemporaries*, ed. Max Bluestone and Norman Rabkin (Englewood Cliffs, N. J., 1961), p. 220.

[38] F. L. Lucas, *Tragedy* (London, 1957), pp. 40–41.

[39] *Gorboduc*, IV. ii. 364.

[40] The following interpretation of Ferdinand's character is based on suggestions made by R. B. Sharpe, who has treated the subject briefly in his *Irony in the Drama* (Chapel Hill, N. C., 1959).

[41] Reviews of the 1935 London production said, for example, that the play "has no logic either in its characters or its situations. Nobody can really accept the motiveless villainy of the two brothers." J. F. Grein, "The World of the Theatre," *Illustrated London News*, Feb. 2, 1935, p. 37. American critics treated the Broadway version even more harshly: "His characterization is almost comically simplified by present standards. The wicked brothers and their ally henchmen are monsters from the pit." Woolcott Gibbs, "Out of the Library," *New Yorker*, Oct. 26, 1946, p. 51.

[42] See, e.g., J. S. P. Tatlock and R. G. Martin, eds., *Representative English Plays*, 2d ed. (New York, 1938), p. 292, and Brander Matthews and Paul R. Lieder, eds., *The Chief British Dramatists* (London, 1924), p. 1072.

[43] Clifford Leech, *John Webster: A Critical Study* (London, 1951), pp. 99–105.

[44] Ellis-Fermor, *Jacobean Drama* (London, 1953), pp. 39–44, 174–77.

[45] Leech, *John Webster*, p. 68.

[46] This idea is developed in Una Ellis-Fermor's essay on Webster, *Jacobean Drama*, pp. 39–44, 170–90.

[47] Cf. Elizabeth Babb, *The Elizabethan Malady* (East Lansing, Mich., 1951), pp. 73–101.

[48] *The Anatomy of Melancholy*, ed. Floyd Dell and Paul Jordan-Smith (New York, 1927), pp. 259–82.

[49] *The Elizabethan Malady*, p. 105.

[50] "Of Ambition," *Works of Francis Bacon*, VI, 465.

[51] *The Works of Thomas Nashe*, ed. R. B. McKerrow, 5 vols. (London, 1904–1910), I. i. 309.

[52] See Babb, *The Elizabethan Malady*, pp. 39, 42–43, 57–58.

[53] Clifford Leech is able to forgive a number of other supposed inconsistencies, but judges that "Ferdinand's strange patience during the long interval between acts II and III is a more serious matter, throwing a haze of improbability over his character and this part of the action." *John Webster*, p. 68.

[54] See, e.g., M. Andreas Laurentius, *Discourse of the Preservation of Sight, of Melencholike Diseases: of Rheumes: and of Old Age*, trans. Richard Surphlet ("Shakespeare Association Facsimiles," No. 15; London, 1938), pp. 87, 129. The term "melancholy" was familiar as the name of one of the four normal humors. It also designated a diseased condition in which that humor has become abnormal in quality or quantity, and finally it indicated a black humor formed by the "burning" or perversion of any of

the natural humors. This "unnatural melancholy," or "melancholy adust" is, like natural melancholy in excess, a cause of malevolence or criminality, and notably of hatred and vengefulness. See Babb, *The Elizabethan Malady*, pp. 21–24, 56–57.

⁵⁵ William Archer characteristically thought the play "founded on a Fallacy" in that the Duchess has a son by her first marriage, who would have inherited. This son, however, has not much dramatic existence. He is created by three obscure lines (III. iii. 82–84) which could easily be omitted. Webster, in effect, cancels them by Ferdinand's later speech.

⁵⁶ For additional indication that Webster created Ferdinand "turbulent" or choleric, see I. i. 169, and III. iii. 66–67.

⁵⁷ See Lucas, *The Complete Works of John Webster*, II, 140, for documentation of the legitimacy of the marriage.

⁵⁸ Babb, *The Elizabethan Malady*, p. 16.

⁵⁹ Quoted by Babb, ibid., p. 219.

⁶⁰ Ibid., pp. 23–24. The quotation is from Luis Mercado, *Opera* (Frankfurt, 1619–1620), III, 102. Elyot pronounces in the *Book Named the Governor* that the worst of all melancholy is that produced by choler adust.

⁶¹ *Anatomy of Melancholy*, pp. 231–35.

⁶² The *NED* gives the contemporary meaning "high temper, mettle, and anger."

⁶³ This delusion that one is a were-wolf (see V. ii. 7) was attributed to the melancholy humor and considered one of the worst manias. See Burton, *Anatomy of Melancholy*, p. 558. Ferdinand's speech begins in act IV to reflect his drift toward wolfishness: "The Wolfe shall find her Grave, and scrape it up" (IV. ii. 332; also IV. i. 40, and IV. ii. 274–75).

⁶⁴ One of the few favorable comments on any modern production was made by Annabel Williams-Ellis ("A letter from England," *Saturday Review of Literature*, April 20, 1935, p. 637) who approved the use of an incest motif in the 1935 London version. But even she considered the incest theme as an ingenious and laudable effort to prop up a structure which was fundamentally unsound.

⁶⁵ Pierre Charron, *Of Wisdome*, trans. Samson Lennard (London, 1651), p. 246.

CHAPTER SEVEN

¹ *The Works of Cyril Tourneur*, ed. Allardyce Nicoll (London, 1929). All references are to this edition.

² See above, p. 137.

³ *Jacobean Drama* (London, 1953), p. 167.

⁴ Cf. Robert Ornstein, *The Moral Vision of Jacobean Tragedy* (Madison, Wis., 1960), pp. 126–27.

⁵ "By the closing of the theatres," says Ristine, "romantic

tragicomedy had well nigh elbowed other forms off the stage." Frank H. Ristine, *English Tragicomedy: Its Origin and History* (New York, 1910), p. 147.

⁶ *The Pattern of Tragicomedy in Beaumont and Fletcher* (New Haven, Conn., 1952).

⁷ Mr. Waith's discovery; ibid., pp. 86–98.

⁸ M. C. Bradbrook, *Themes and Conventions of Elizabethan Tragedy* (Cambridge, Eng., 1935), pp. 67–70.

⁹ Cf. Waith, *The Pattern of Tragicomedy*, p. 25: "the situations do not evolve by an inevitable logic," and p. 35: "the design . . . is static, determined not so much by the laws of cause and effect as by the rules of artful arrangement."

¹⁰ Ibid., p. 84.

¹¹ *Philaster*, I. i. *The Works of Francis Beaumont and John Fletcher*, ed. Arnold Glover and A. R. Waller, 10 vols. (Cambridge, Eng., 1905–1912). All references are to this edition.

¹² III. i. Demetrius, in Chapman's *Caesar and Pompey*, firmly maintains that virtue is incompatible with worldly greatness.

¹³ *Works*, II, 522.

¹⁴ Ristine, *English Tragicomedy*, p. xi.

¹⁵ Quoted in ibid., p. 37.

¹⁶ "What we consider as tragical and comical have a way of shading into one another by imperceptible advances, until the juncture is lost . . . that the pathetic is akin to the comical and laughter neighbor to tears are truisms of long-standing acceptance; while the comparison of life to a tragicomedy is almost as old as the word itself. . . . What is true of actual experience is equally true of drama." Ibid., p. ix. This idea that tragicomedy, like life, mixes joy and sadness in a "middle mood" has recurred throughout the history of criticism. It is no doubt true of much drama which can properly be called tragicomic, but to speak of the Jacobean genre represented by *Philaster* in such terms is completely misleading.

¹⁷ Ibid., p. 33, and see Waith, *The Pattern of Tragicomedy*, p. 48. Guarini, notes Waith, "leans most heavily on Aristotle's reference to tragedies with happy endings."

¹⁸ Clifford Leech, *John Ford and the Drama of His Time* (London, 1957), p. 42.

¹⁹ *Jacobean Drama* (London, 1953), p. 263.

²⁰ Ibid., p. 260.

²¹ Ibid., pp. 260–61.

²² Ibid., p. 262.

²³ Ibid., pp. 262–63.

²⁴ *The Works of John Ford*, ed. William Gifford, with additions by Alexander Dyce, 3 vols. (London, 1895). All references are to this edition.

²⁵ The case of Ford's adherence to a humors-psychology deter-

minism was made by G. F. Sensabaugh, *The Tragic Muse of John Ford* (Stanford, Calif., 1944).

[26] See Clifford Leech, *John Ford,* pp. 18–26; Joan Sargeaunt, *John Ford* (Oxford, 1935), pp. 5–16; and H. J. Oliver, *The Problem of John Ford* (Melbourne, 1955), pp. 8–12.

[27] Leech, *John Ford,* p. 23.

[28] Ibid., p. 24.

[29] Ibid., p. 46.

[30] Ibid., p. 62.

[31] Ibid., p. 14.

[32] See ibid., p. 32; Oliver, *The Problem of John Ford,* p. 34; and Ellis-Fermor, *Jacobean Drama,* p. 151.

[33] Karl J. Holzknecht, *Outlines of Tudor and Stuart Plays* (New York, 1947), pp. 383–84.

[34] Penthea regards herself as "strumpeted"; "the enterchange of holy, and chast love," prescribed by the domestic conduct books, constituted her "real marriage" to Orgilus. See Peter Ure, "Marriage and the Domestic Drama in Heywood and Ford," *English Studies,* XXXII (1951), 200–16. The author emphasizes the "orthodoxy" of Ford's attitude toward marriage. But the spirit of Ford's treatment of sexual love is ultimately one of sympathy for the offender against a morality which, although he does not deny its claims, he feels as contrary to nature.

[35] F. N. Robinson, *The Works of Geoffrey Chaucer,* 2d ed. (Boston, 1951), ll. 1785–86.

[36] E.g., Una Ellis-Fermor, in *Jacobean Tragedy,* pp. 227–46.

[37] *John Ford,* p. 90.

[38] *The Lover's Melancholy* also reveals something of the new orientation of tragedy, but there is little to say about it that has not been said of the tragicomedies of Beaumont and Fletcher, which it resembles.

CHAPTER EIGHT

[1] F. R. Leavis, *The Common Pursuit* (London, 1952), p. 126.

[2] Willard Farnham, *The Medieval Heritage of Elizabethan Tragedy* (Oxford, 1956), p. xiii.

[3] S. H. Butcher, *Aristotle's Theory of Poetry and Fine Art,* 4th ed. (New York, 1951), p. 23. But see F. L. Lucas, *Tragedy* (London, 1957), p. 43, for an alternate translation. Beyond this, Aristotle mentions the topic only in two brief passages, one in the eighth book of the *Politics,* another in the definition of pity and fear in the *Rhetoric.* See Butcher, *Aristotle's Theory of Poetry and Fine Art,* pp. 248–49, 257.

[4] See Butcher, *Aristotle's Theory of Poetry and Fine Art,* pp. 265–66, for the Aristotelian basis of this Stoic idea.

[5] See Baxter Hathaway, "John Dryden and the Function of

Tragedy," *PMLA*, LVIII (1943), 665–73. Dryden began close to the Aristotelian position and moved steadily toward a sentimental theory which made the hero a victim of external evils and more the object of pity than a fearful example of error. In the "Preface Containing the Grounds of Criticism in Tragedy," Dryden approved Rapin's interpretation of Aristotle; tragedy secured its effects by "setting before our eyes some terrible example of misfortune which happened to persons of the highest quality, for such an action demonstrates to us that no condition is privileged from the turns of fate." Thus, tragic theory comes full circle to its medieval origins.

[6] An argument which has been called "one of the disgraces of human intelligence, a grotesque monument of sterility." Lucas, *Tragedy*, pp. 35ff.

[7] See, e.g., A. C. Bradley, "Hegel's Theory of Tragedy," in *Oxford Lectures on Poetry* (London, 1959), p. 84.

[8] Lucas, *Tragedy*, p. 77.

[9] Clifford Leech, *Shakespeare's Tragedies* (London, 1950).

[10] See Edith Hamilton, *The Greek Way* (New York, 1930), pp. 138–50, and H. B. Charlton, *Shakespearean Tragedy* (Cambridge, Eng., 1948), pp. 230–43. Charlton remarks of a group of critics including Lessing, Schlegel, Hume, Burke, and Hazlett that none "denies that pleasure undoubtedly does arise from the witnessing of tragedy."

[11] *The Modern Temper* (New York, 1929), pp. 118–23.

[12] Ibid., p. 118.

[13] G. F. Sensabaugh's chapter on "Scientific Determinism" (ch. ii) in *The Tragic Muse of John Ford* (Stanford, Calif., 1944), traces in Ford's plays the patterns of Burtonian psychology. The plays, he says, are "modern" in that they display a "scientific necessity" opposed to "the highest ideals" of man; they dramatize "conflicts between necessity and ancient moral injunctions" which issue in despair.

[14] See Wayne Shumaker, *Literature and the Irrational* (New York, 1966), pp. 174–81, 189–91.

[15] See Lionel Trilling, "Freud and Literature," *The Liberal Imagination* (Garden City, N. Y., 1957), pp. 51–52.

[16] *Irony in the Drama* (Chapel Hill, N. C., 1959).

[17] *Apology for Raymond de Sebonde*, in *The Works of Michel De Montaigne*, ed. William C. Hazlett, trans. Charles Cotton (New York, 1910), V, 236–37.

[18] *The Natural Law*, trans. Thomas R. Hanley (St. Louis, Mo., 1948), p. 59.

[19] From Rust's *A Discourse of Truth*, 1679.

Index

This book has been set in
Aster, a type face designed by
Francesco Simoncini; with
Eric Gill's Perpetua for
display.

Design by Jonathan Greene

Composed, printed, & bound
by Kingsport Press, Inc.